Freemasonry in Canada

Also from Westphalia Press
westphaliapress.org

The Idea of the Digital University

Masonic Tombstones and Masonic Secrets

Treasures of London

The History of Photography

L'Enfant and the Freemasons

Baronial Bedrooms

Making Trouble for Muslims

Material History and Ritual Objects

Paddle Your Own Canoe

Opportunity and Horatio Alger

Careers in the Face of Challenge

Bookplates of the Kings

Collecting American Presidential Autographs

Freemasonry in Old Buffalo

Original Cables from the Pearl Harbor Attack

Social Satire and the Modern Novel

The Essence of Harvard

The Genius of Freemasonry

A Definitive Commentary on Bookplates

James Martineau and Rebuilding Theology

No Bird Lacks Feathers

Earthworms, Horses, and Living Things

The Man Who Killed President Garfield

Anti-Masonry and the Murder of Morgan

Understanding Art

Homeopathy

Ancient Masonic Mysteries

Collecting Old Books

Masonic Secret Signs and Passwords

The Thomas Starr King Dispute

Earl Warren's Masonic Lodge

Lariats and Lassos

Mr. Garfield of Ohio

The Wisdom of Thomas Starr King

The French Foreign Legion

War in Syria

Naturism Comes to the United States

New Sources on Women and Freemasonry

Designing, Adapting, Strategizing in Online Education

Gilded Play

Meeting Minutes of Naval Lodge No. 4 F.A.A.M

Freemasonry in Canada

by Obsborne Sheppard

Edited and introduced by
Paul Rich

WESTPHALIA PRESS
An imprint of Policy Studies Organization

Freemasonry in Canada

All Rights Reserved © 2013 by Policy Studies Organization

Westphalia Press
An imprint of Policy Studies Organization
1527 New Hampshire Ave., NW
Washington, D.C. 20036
dgutierrezs@ipsonet.org

ISBN-13: 978-1935907442
ISBN-10: 1935907441

Cover design by Taillefer Long at Illuminated Stories:
www.illuminatedstories.com

Updated material and comments on this edition
can be found at the Westphalia Press website:
www.westphaliapress.org

This edition is dedicated to Robert Cooper,
Curator of the Grand Lodge of Scotland
Library and Museum, and eminent
Masonic Scholar.

Introduction to This Edition

UNDERSTANDING CANADIAN FREEMASONRY

Every country produces its own kind of Freemasonry, and so much is that the case that it might be proper to speak about Freemasonries rather than Freemasonry. Mexican Freemasonry is light years away in some respects from the kind of Freemasonry practiced in England. Freemasonry in Scandinavia is enormously different from Freemasonry in France.

What makes Canadian Freemasonry particularly interesting is the extraordinary converging of various traditions and the cross-fertilization that it has produced in rituals and rites. Canadian Freemasonry is a mosaic, and one can see in its history a great many Masonic traditions that have come together but which still retain an identity.

The strong Irish element in Canadian Masonic history is often overlooked. Sheppard used two chapters in this volume contributed by Will Whyte and E.T.D. Chambers in his later article about origins of the Craft in Canada, asserting the importance of Irish origins and that Masonry only dated "...back to the year 1759, when the Lily flag of the Bourbon was replaced over New France by the British Union

Jack." With the advent of the British troops, English Freemasonry was transplanted to Canadian soil, or, more strictly speaking, Anglo-Saxon Freemasonry, for the Grand Lodge of Ireland was more largely represented among the regiments that took part in the capitulation of the cities of Quebec and Montreal. In these days many of the regiments in the British army carried travelling warrants authorizing them to hold lodges, and among those taking part in the siege of the first named city five regiments held Irish warrants, and one an English warrant, and at the latter city five regiments likewise held Irish warrants, one an English and one a warrant from the Grand Lodge of Scotland. Among the number, Lodge No. 227 of the Irish register in the Sixty-fourth Regiment of Foot still survives, and is now called the Lodge of Antiquity No. 1, on the registry of the Grand Lodge of the Province of Quebec."

Much of this book remains a major resource in Canadian studies, albeit somewhat neglected. It is not a great coincidence that the original publication was in Hamilton, where the Grand Lodge of Canada in the Province of Ontario and the Supreme Council of the Scottish Rite in Canada are both located. Having this title again readily available should be highly useful as Canadian Masonic scholarship progresses.

Paul Rich
Garfield House, Washington

H

HIS ROYAL HIGHNESS

PRINCE ARTHUR

DUKE OF CONNAUGHT AND STRATHEARN

Most Worshipful Grand Master of the Grand Lodge of England

Initiated March 24th, 1874 into

PRINCE OF WALES LODGE NO. 259

Grand Register of England

Installed Most Worshipful Grand Master

July 17th, 1901

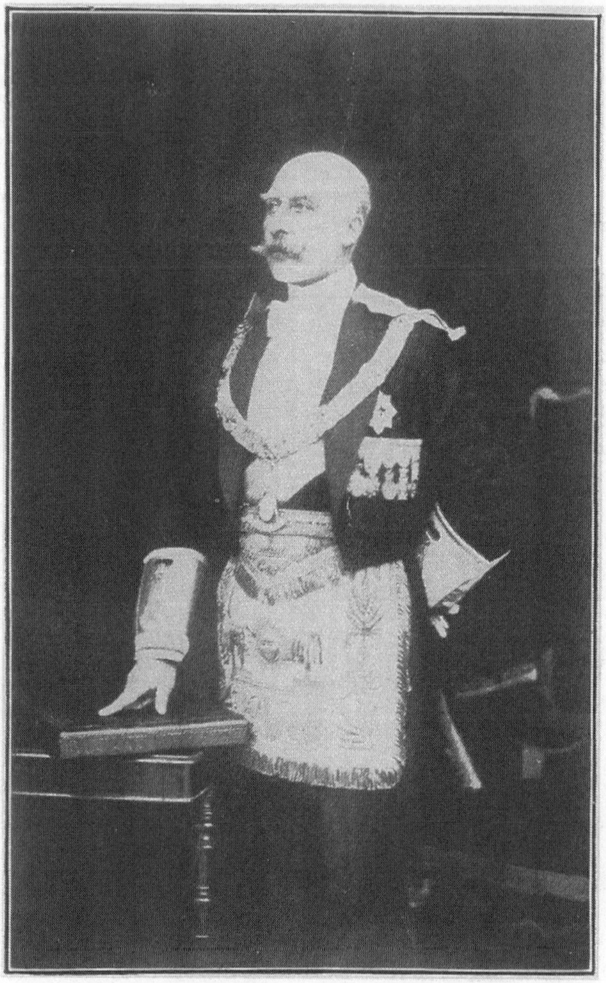

Arthur
G. M.

FREEMASONRY
IN
CANADA

WITH A CONCISE HISTORY OF OLD BRITISH LODGES,
THE INTRODUCTION OF FREEMASONRY INTO THE
UNITED STATES OF AMERICA AND OTHER
VALUABLE AND INSTRUCTIVE
INFORMATION

Compiled and Published by
OSBORNE SHEPPARD
BOX 242
HAMILTON, ONT.

THIS BOOK IS SOLD BY SUBSCRIPTION, AND TO NONE BUT MEMBERS OF THE CRAFT

CONTENTS

	Page
Old British Lodges	5
WILLIAM JAMES HUGHAN.	
The Grand Lodge of Canada in Ontario	17
GEORGE J. BENNETT.	
Early History of Freemasonry in Upper Canada	43
A. T. FREED, P.G.M.	
Freemasonry in the Province of Quebec	56
WILL H. WHYTE, Grand Sec.	
The Lodge of Antiquity, No. 1 G.R.Q.	68
J. BEAMISH SAUL.	
Early Quebec Lodges	73
E. T. D. CHAMBERS, P.G.M.	
The Grand Lodge of New Brunswick	95
THOMAS WALKER, M.D., P.G.M.	
The Grand Lodge of Nova Scotia	106
WILLIAM ROSS, P.G.M.	
Freemasonry in Cape Breton, N.S.	116
ANGUS G. McLEAN.	
The Grand Lodge of Prince Edward Island	119
Compiled from OFFICIAL RECORDS.	
The Grand Lodge of Manitoba	122
JAMES A. OVAS, P.G.M.	
The Grand Lodge of Saskatchewan	130
HARRY H. CAMPKIN, P.G.M.	
The Grand Lodge of Alberta	134
GEORGE MACDONALD, M.D., P.G.M.	
The Grand Lodge of British Columbia	138
W. A. De WOLF SMITH, Grand Sec.	
Statistics, Canadian Grand Lodges	153
Compiled from GRAND LODGE PROCEEDINGS.	
The United States of America	154
ROBERT FREKE GOULD.	
Statistics, United States Grand Lodges	164
Compiled from GRAND LODGE PROCEEDINGS.	

CONTENTS—Continued.

	Page
The Lady Mason	166
Compiled from Richard Spencer's Records.	
Origin of the Eastern Star	169
M. B. CONKLIN.	
What is Freemasonry?	172
ANONYMOUS.	
Freemasonry—the Universal Brotherhood	173
J. H. GRAHAM, P.G.M.	
Symbolism	177
Compiled from Old Masonic Monitors.	
The Ancient Landmarks of Freemasonry	213
Compiled from Old Constitutions.	
The Royal Arch	218
ALBERT G. MACKEY, M.D.	
The Banners and Their Use	220
REV. GEORGE B. MacLELLAN, B.A.	
The Banners and Their Location	227
WALTER J. FRANCIS, C.E.	
The Royal and Select Masters	232
ALBERT G. MACKEY, M.D.	
Knight Templarism in Canada	238
WILL H. WHYTE, P.S.G.M.	
The Ancient and Accepted Scottish Rite	253
WILLIAM H. BALLARD, 33°.	
The Royal Order of Scotland	267
Compiled from Old Scotch Records.	
The Mystic Shrine	274
NOBLES W. ROSS and ALEX. B. J. MOORE.	
St. Paul's Lodge, No. 374, G. L. of Eng.	283
Compiled from Official Records.	
Masonic Tradition	298
Compiled from Old Records.	

OLD BRITISH LODGES.

Compiled by OSBORNE SHEPPARD from the
writings of the late

WILLIAM JAMES HUGHAN

The Eminent English Masonic Historian.

THE name or title "Free-Mason" is met with so far back as the fourteenth century, its precise import at that period being a matter of discussion at the present time. The original statute, of A.D. 1350, reads "Mestre de franchepeer," and thus points to the conclusion that a Freemason then was one who worked in free-stone, and assuredly a superior artisan to another class, who, as less skilled masons, were employed on rough work only.

During the following century the Freemasons are frequently referred to in contracts, statutes, etc.

It will be manifest, as the evidence of the lodge-records is unfolded, that though Freemason originally signified a worker on free-stone, it became the custom to apply the term to all Craftsmen who had obtained their freedom as Masons to work in lodges with the Fraternity, after due apprenticeship and passing as Fellow Crafts. "Cowans," no matter how skilful they may have become, were not Free-masons, and the Scottish Crafts, especially, were most particular in defining the differences that existed between "freemen" and "un-freemen," in regard to all the trades then under stringent regulations.

The "Schaw Statutes," Scotland, of A.D. 1599, provided that "Na Cowains" work with the Masons; the Masters and Fellows being sworn, annually, to respect that exclusive rule. The earliest known minute of the Lodge of Edinburgh notes an apology for employing a cowan (July 31, 1599).

The venerable Melrose Lodge, in its first preserved minute, of December 28, 1674, enacted: "yt wn ever a prentice is mad frie Mason he must pay four pund Scotts"; hence we subsequently read in the records that men were "entered and received fr (free) to ye trad," and "past frie to ye trade," and similar entries.

As late as the year 1763, the "Rules and Orders of the Lodge of Free-Masons in the Town of Alnwick," provide that "if any Fellows of the Lodge shall, without the cognizance and approbation of the Master and Wardens, presume to hold private Lodges or Assemblies with an Intent to make any Person free of this honourable Lodge, they shall each forfets to the Box the sum of £3 6s. 8." This lodge, long extinct, has records preserved from the year 1701, and never joined the Grand Lodge of England.

From the year 1600 (June 8), when a non-operative or Speculative Freemason was present as a member, and attested the minutes of the meeting by his mark (as the operatives), the records are so voluminous and important of the "Lodge of Edinburgh" (Mary's Chapel), and of other old Ateliers in Scotland, that it is with extreme difficulty a selection can be made with any satisfaction, the wealth of minutes being embarrassing. The Transactions of the "Quatuor Coronati" Lodge, London,—are brimful of trustworthy accounts of the Fraternity, extending back nearly three centuries.

The Lodge of Edinburgh, No. 1, was regulated in part by the statutes of 1598, promulgated by William Schaw, "Principal Warden and Chief Master of Masons" to King James VI. of Scotland, who succeeded Sir Robert Drummond as Master of Works, in 1583, and died in 1602.

From 1600 to 1634, the records of No. 1 are silent as to the admission of speculative, but contain entries of apprentices, and admissions of Fellow Crafts.

Apprentices were members, and exercised their privileges as such, just as the Craftsmen and Members; and even attested the elections of members, being present in lodge, and thus consenting to and acknowledging the receptions of Craftsmen and Masters. This proves that the passing to superior grades could not have required any esoteric ceremonies that apprentices were ineligible to witness.

On July 3, 1634, the Right Honorable Lord Alexander was "admitit folowe off the Craft," and also Sir Alexander Strachan. On December 27, 1636, an apprentice was duly made, "with the heall consent of the heall masters, frie mesones of Endr."; there being but this one lodge in the city at that time.

Lord Alexander, Viscount Canada, "was a young man of great expectations; but he dissipated a fortune, and endured great personal hardships, in ESTABLISHING A COLONY ON THE RIVER ST. LAWRENCE. He and his brother, admitted on the same day (July 3, 1634), were sons of the first Earl of Stirling; Sir Anthony Alexander being Master of Work to King Charles I., and so noted in the minutes. Another brother, Henrie Alexander, was "admittet ane falowe" on February 16, 1638, and succeeded to the office of General Warden and Master of Work. He became third Earl of Stirling in 1640, and died ten years later.

General Hamilton was initiated on May 20, 1640, as "fellow and Mr. off the forsed Craft," and Dr. William Maxwell was received July 27, 1647. A remarkable entry of March 2, 1653, calls for mention, as it concerns the election of a "Joining member."

"The qlk day, in presence of Johne Milln deacon, Quentein Thomsone, wardeine, and remnant brethrene of maisones of the Lodge of Ednr., compeired James Neilsone, maister Sklaitter to his majestie, being entered and past in the Lodge of Linlithgow, the said James Neilsone humblie desyring to be receiued in to be a member of our Lodge off Edn., which desire the wholl companie did grant and received him as brother and fellow of our companie; in witness qrof we the wholl freemen have set our hands or marks."

Sir Patrick Hume, Bart., "was admitted in as fellow of craft (and Master) of this lodg," on December 27, 1667; and, three years later, the Right Honorable William Morray (Murray), Justice Depute of Scotland, Walter Pringle, Advocate, and Sir John Harper were admitted "Brothers and fellow crafts."

The Scottish army, having defeated the Royalists at Newburn, in 1640, advanced and took possession of Newcastle (England), where it remained for some months, during the deliberations of the Commissioners. In the army were several members of this Lodge of Edinburgh, who, on May 20, 1641, convened an emergency meeting and admitted or initiated General Quartermaster Robert Moray (Murray). On returning to the city some time afterward, the extraordinary circumstance was duly reported, and as duly entered on the records, being attested by General Hamilton aforesaid, James Hamilton, and "Johne Mylnn."

The John Mylne thus noted represented a family of Craftsmen whose connection with this lodge extended over two hundred years. The third John Mylne (of Masonic fame), came to Edinburgh in 1616, and belonged to the lodge. He was Master Mason to Charles I., and resigned that office in favor of his eldest son, John, who was "made a Fellow craft" in the lodge in October, 1633, and was with the Scottish army 1640-1641. He was Deacon of the lodge, and Warden in 1636, and frequently reëlected to the former office.

His brother Alexander was "passed fellow craft" in 1635, and his nephew, Robert, was "entered prentice" to him December 27, 1653, and passed as a Fellow Craft on September 23, 1660.

Robert's eldest son, William, was a member from December 27, 1681, "passed" in 1685, and died in 1728. His eldest son, Thomas, was admitted an apprentice December 27, 1721, and was "crafted" in 1729, being the Master of No. 1, on the formation of the Grand Lodge of Scotland, in 1736. William Mylne, second son of this brother, was "receaved and entred apprentice in the ordinary forme" on December 27, 1750, and was "passed and raised operative master," after exhibiting his due qualifications, on December 20, 1758. He died in 1790.

Thomas, his brother and eldest son to the Thomas Mylne before noted, became an "apprentice as honorary member," on January 14, 1754. He died in 1811, and was buried in St. Paul's Cathedral, having been its surveyor for some fifty years.

In 1688 a schism occurred in No. 1, by a number of members starting a separate lodge for themselves in the "Canongate and Leith," by which name it has since been known, and is now No. 5 on the Scottish Roll. The "Mother" was most indignant at such conduct, and tried every means in her power to thwart the movement, but in vain.

Another schism, but involving much more serious consequences, occurred in 1709, and was still more objectionable to No. 1, because the seceders, generally, were not Masters, but "Journeymen." This peculiarity led to the second offshoot being so named, now well known by that title, as No. 8 on the Register. Two of its members were imprisoned (who had been admitted as apprentices in 1694), and all that officialism could do to crush the recalcitrants was cruelly employed, but utterly failed. Arbitration eventually led to a suspension of hostilities, and on January 8, 1715, the "Decreet Arbitral" was made known and certified. By this award the Journeymen were empowered "to meet together by themselves as a society for giving the Mason's word"; and thus was forever broken down the monopoly of the "Incorporation of Wrights and Masons" of Edinburgh, of A.D. 1475, origin, whose Master Masons had so long claimed the exclusive right to thus admit Apprentices, pass Fellow Crafts, and elect Masters in the ancient Lodge of that city.

"Mother Lodge Kilwinning, No. 0," is universally known and respected throughout the Masonic world. Unfortunately its earliest records are lost, and have been so for many years, the oldest preserved ranging from December 20, 1642, to December 5, 1758. Its meetings were held in Kilwinning, Scotland, the jurisdiction of the lodge extending even so far as Glasgow, in the year 1599.

Schaw's Supplementary Code of 1599 (only discovered in quite recent times), refers to three "heid

Ludges" in Scotland, "the first and principal being that of Edinburgh ,the second Kilwinning, and the third Stirling; so that notwithstanding the present position of "Mother Lodge Kilwinning" as head of the Scottish Roll as No. 0, some three hundred years ago, it was the second as respects seniority, according to the decision of Schaw.

The Earl of Cassilis was Master of the Lodge of Kilwinning in 1670, though only an apprentice, and was succeeded by Sir Alexander Cunninghame. After him, the Earl of Eglintoune occupied the Chair, but was simply an apprentice, and, in 1678, Lord William Cochrane (son of the Earl of Dundonald), was a Warden. No surprise need be felt at apprentices being thus raised to the highest position in the lodge, seeing that members of the first grade had to be present at the passing or making of Craftsmen and Masters, a rule also enforced and minuted in this lodge December 20, 1643, when the brethren assembled "in the upper chamber of the dwelling house of Hugh Smithe." This most significant fact appears to be a permanent barrier against the notion that there were separate and independent Masonic degrees in the seventeenth century, as there were from A.D. 1717. Three grades or classes are clearly exhibited, but not esoteric degrees at the reception of Craftsmen, and Masters.

"Cannongate Kilwinning," No. 2, the earliest child of "The Ancient Lodge of Scotland," was originated December 20th, 1677.

"St. John's Kilwinning," now "Old Kilwinning St. John," No. 6, Inverness, was also warranted by "The Ancient Grand Lodge of Scotland," in 1678.

Brother Robert Wylie gives a list of the charters he has been able to trace in his "History of Mother Kilwinning Lodge," some thirty-five in number,—without exhausting the roll,—down to 1807 (for during a portion of its career "Mother Kilwinning" acted as a Grand Lodge, and rival to that at Edinburgh), including Tappahannock Kilwinning Lodge, Virginia (A.D. 1758), and Falmouth

Kilwinning Lodge (A.D. 1775), Virginia, America; as also, the "High Knights Templars" Lodge, Dublin, A.D. 1779.

Other Old Scotch Lodges in Scotland, all of pre-Grand Lodge origin, that ought to be noted are:—

(a) No. 3, "Scone and Perth" (its oldest preserved document being of date December 24, 1658, subscribed to by the "Maisters, Friemen and Fellow Crafts off Perth," the lodge being the "prinle (principal) within the Shyre").

(b) No. 3 bis, St. John's, Glasgow (which is noted in the Incorporation Records so early as 1613, but did not join the Grand Lodge until 1849-1850), the lodge possibly being active in 1551 when no Craftsman was allowed to work in that city unless entered as a Burgess and Freeman, and membership of the lodge was conditional on entering the Incorporation, its exclusively Operative character remaining intact until some fifty years ago.

(c) No. 9, Dunblane, is credited with having originated in 1696, according to the Scottish Register, but it certainly existed prior to that year, though that is the date of the oldest minute preserved. It was chiefly Speculative from the first. Viscount Strathalane was the Master in 1696, Alexander Drummond, Esq., was Warden; an "Eldest Fellow Craft," Clerk, Treasurer, and an "Officer" were also elected.

(d) Some lodges lower down on the Scottish Roll go much farther back than No. 9; Haddington (St. John's Kilwinning"), No. 57, dating from 1599, but the evidence for that claim is not apparent, the oldest manuscript extant being of the year 1682.

(e) One of the most noteworthy and most ancient, with no lack of documentary testimony in its favor, is the old lodge at Aberdeen, No. 34, with its "Mark Book" of A.D. 1670, and a profusion of actual minutes and records from that year.

Out of forty-nine members, whose names are enrolled in the "Mark Book," only eight are known to have been Operative Masons, the majority were Speculative Masons.

Four noblemen and several clergymen and other gentlemen were members. Harrie Elphingston, "Tutor," and a "Collector of the King's Customs," was the Master when these extraordinary records were begun, and, save as to two, all have their marks regularly registered. The "names of the successors" are also duly noted, and a list of the "Entered Prenteises," with their marks, is also inserted, dating from 1670. The Earl of Errol, one of the members, died at an advanced age, in 1674. The three classes of Apprentices, Fellow Crafts and Master Masons were recognized, the statutes of December 27, 1670, being compiled on the customary lines, only that the Code is more than usually comprehensive and interesting. Provision was made for "Gentlemen Measons," as well as "Handie Craftes prenteises" being initiated, in these old rules, and special care for the due communication of the "Mason-word." "Fees of Honour," on the assumption of office, were also payable in some of the old lodges.

(f) "Peebles Kilwinning," No. 24, seems to have started on October 18, 1716, by its own act and deed, for who was to say nay? The minute of the event begins with the declaration that, inconsequence of the great loss "the honorable company of Masons ... have hitherto sustained by the want of a lodge, and finding a sufficient number of brethren in this burgh, did this day erect a lodge among themselves." A Deacon, Warden, and other officers were then elected, and, on December 27, "after prayer," the several members present were duly examined. It was Speculative as well as Operative in its constitution.

(g) "Dumfries Kilwinning," No. 53, though only dated 1750, in the Official Register, possesses records back to 1687, and was not, even then, wholly Operative. Different fees were payable by mechanics, and by "no mechanicks," on initiation, in the seventeenth century.

A noteworthy title occurs in an "Indenture betwix Dunde and its Masoun," of the year 1536, which is the earliest known instance of a Scottish lodge being named after a Saint, viz.: "Our Lady (i.e., St. Mary's) Loge of

Dunde." The document is exceedingly curious and valuable, as illustrating the "ald vss of our luge," and another of March 11, 1659, is of still more interest, as it contains the rules then agreed to by the "Frie-Masters" (with the concurrence of the town authorities), which are mostly in accordance with the older laws of the Craft, and framed with due regard to the privileges of the sons of Freemen.

(h) Other old lodges might be enumerated in the seventeenth century, such as Atcheson-Haven, with its valuable manuscript of A.D. 1666.

(i) Banff, with many important minutes of early last century.

(j) Brechin, with rules and records from 1714. (No. 6 enacts that men not freemen, who desire to work in the lodge, shall pay a fee; No. 8 arranges for "Joining members"; No. 9, Marks to e registered; and "Frie-Masters" are noted as well as free apprentices).

(k) The Lodge of Kelso, No. 58, was resuscitated in 1878, after many years of dormancy. When it was originally formed cannot now be decided, but the earliest preserved minutes begin December 27, 1701, when "the Honorable Lodge assembled under the protection of Saint John." The Master, in 1702, was George Faa, his death as such being then noted, who was succeeded by "Sir John Pringall." This lodge, Speculative as well as Operative from the year 1701, continued its eventful career down to some fifty years since, when it fell through for some time. The members obtained a charter from the Grand Lodge of Scotland in 1754, in which year (June 18), it was discovered "That this lodge had attained only to the two degrees of Apprentice and Fellow Craft, and know nothing of the Master's part." This defect was then remedied by the formation of a Master's lodge.

Of actual lodges in South Britain, we have to come down to 1701 (save the one at Newcastle of the former century), before we meet with any minute-books. We are not, however, without information concerning English lodge meetings so far back as 1646. Elias Ashmole "was made a Freemason at Warrington, in Lancashire, with Coll. Henry Mainwaring, of Karnicham, in Cheshire," as he states in his Dairy (on October 16, 1646), which was printed and published in 1717, and again in 1774.

On March 10, 1682, Ashmole received a "Summons to app^r at a Lodge to be held the next day, at Mason's Hall, London." This noted antiquary duly attended and witnessed the admission "into the Fellowship of Free Masons" of Sir William Wilson, Knt., and five other gentlemen. He was the "Senior Fellow among them," and they all "dyned at the charge of the new-accepted Masons."

In the "Harleian MS., No. 2054," which contains another copy of the "Old Charges" (at pp. 33-34), is an extraordinary lodge entry (apparently) of 1650 circa, beginning with "William Wade w^t give for to be a free mason," and likewise, what is evidently a reproduction of the oath used at that period, to keep secret "the words and signes of a free mason."

Over a score of names are noted on one of these folios, and it seems certain that very few of them were connected with the Craft as operatives, if any.

Although Bacon (Lord Verulam), died in 1626, and Ashmole was not initiated until twenty years later, it has long been a favorite notion with many that to the "Rosicrucians" of 1614, etc., and Bacon's "New Atlantis," the Freemasons are mainly indebted for many portions of their modern rituals. There is certainly much more to be said in support of this view than in regard to any connection with the Knights Templar down to the early part of last century. The "New Atlantis" is probably the key to the modern rituals of Freemasonry.

To whom we owe modern Freemasonry of "three degrees" is a much controverted question. Bro. Hughan gives the credit to Drs. Desaguliers and Anderson.

The transactions at the inauguration of the premier Grand Lodge of the world, at London, in 1717, were not, unfortunately, duly recorded at the time, and hence the "Book of Constitutions," A.D. 1723, and the earliest minutes of the Grand Lodge of that year, with Anderson's account of the meeting in the second edition of 1738, are practically all we have to guide us.

"Four Old Lodges" for certain, and probably more, took part in the proceedings of that eventful gathering, and from that body, so formed, has sprung, directly or indirectly, every Grand Lodge of Free and Accepted Masons, working three degrees, in the universe. When these lodges originated is not known, but some of them, possibly, during the seventeenth century. There were several other old lodges working, in their own prescriptive right, in England during the second decade of last century, though they took no part in the new organization at first.

Of these, one in particular may be noted, which assembled at Alnwick from an early date, and whose preserved rules and records begin 1701-1703. Its regulations of 1701 are of considerable value, its copy of the "Old Charges" is still treasured.

The Grand Lodge was also petitioned to constitute or regularize many lodges in London and in the country, but as these all took date from their recognition, we know little of their previous career. The one at York, like its fellow at Alnwick, never joined the new body, but preferred independence, even if it involved isolation. The records of this old lodge exist from the year 1712, but a roll from 1705 was noted in the inventory of 1779. When it was inaugurated it is impossible to say, but it may be a descendant of the lodge which we know was active at York Minster in the fourteenth century.

The York brethren started a "Grand Lodge of all England," in 1725, and kept it alive for some twenty years. After a short interval it was revived, in 1761, and continued to work until 1792, when it collapsed. Prior to this date, several subordinates were chartered.

The Grand Lodge of Ireland, at Dublin, was formed 1728-1729; but there was one held previously at Cork, as the "Grand Lodge for Munster," certainly as early as 1725. The Scottish brethren did not follow the example set by England until 1736, and then managed to secure Brother William St. Clair, of Roslin, as their Grand Master, whose ancestors by deeds of A.D. 1600-1628 circa, had been patrons of the Craft but never Grand Masters, though that distinction has been long claimed as hereditary in that Masonic family.

From these three Grand Lodges in Great Britain, and Ireland, have sprung the thousands of lodges throughout the world. Through their agency, and particularly that of the "Military lodges" of last century, the Craft has been planted far and wide. Though there is evidence to prove that brethren assembled in America, and probably elsewhere, in lodges, prior to the formation of either of these Grand Lodges, or quite apart from such influence, as in Philadelphia in 1731, or earlier, and in New Hampshire, soon afterward (the latter apparently having their manuscript copy of the "Old Charges") nothing has ever been discovered, which connects such meetings with the working of the historic "three degrees" of last century origin.

Some seven years after the premier Grand Lodge was launched, authorities to constitute Lodges were issued for Bath and other towns, and a few, later, for abroad; especially through the medium of Provincial Grand Masters, first appointed in 1725 circa, as at Boston, Massachusetts, in the year 1733, to which Provincial Grand Lodge, Canadian Freemasonry owes its birth.

THE GRAND LODGE OF CANADA IN ONTARIO.

BY GEORGE J. BENNETT

Past D. D. Grand Master of the Grand Lodge of Canada in Ontario.
Grand Scribe E., Grand Chapter Royal Arch Masons of Canada.

IT is related that the founders of many of the early settlements on the coasts of, what are now familiarly known as, the Maritime Provinces and Quebec, were enterprising, adventurous and wealthy French gentlemen, Huguenots as well as Catholics. It is even stated that one of these, a certain Sieur DeMonts, was the founder of Quebec city, deponent giving only a second place to a compatriot, the fearless and gallant Champlain. The beauty and fertility of Acadia (Nova Scotia) appealed to the pioneer DeMonts who, after a coast voyage of discovery in 1604, landed on the shores of the Bay of Annapolis and there founded what was then called Port Royal, and later Annapolis Royal. The historian further states that among the artificers brought out by the explorers were a number of the craft of operative masons and that stones indented with peculiar marks have been found at various times and places.

A letter now in the possession of the New England Historic Genealogical Society, Boston, and written by Dr. Charles T. Jackson, of that city, under date 2nd June, 1856, states that, while engaged in a geological survey of Nova Scotia, in 1827, he discovered on the shore of Goat Island, in Annapolis Basin, a stone on which were rudely cut the square and compasses, and beneath them the figures 1606, all much weather worn, but quite distinct. He carried the stone to Halifax, intending to send it to the Old Colony Pilgrim Society, of Plymouth, Mass., but instead left it with the late Chief Justice Haliburton, perhaps better known abroad by his pen name "Sam Slick."

In 1829 the judge published a work entitled "Historical and Statistical Accounts of Nova Scotia," in which a description of the stone is given and the writer there avers that it presented little indications of having been intended for any pretentious structure, as it was apparently of the rough ashlar variety with no visible appearance of even an attempt at dressing. Its discovery, if it established nothing, provided material for much imaginative creation then and since.

Under British occupation Annapolis became a military post, a fort was erected and garrisoned and at the period when speculation deals with Masonry's advent in that province (1737-40) it was a place of considerable importance. To a British officer, Ensign Erasmus James Phillips, of the 40th Regiment, nephew of Gov. Phillips, is attributed the introduction of Freemasonry into Canada. This brother was appointed Fort Major at Annapolis, and in that capacity was something of an administrator. As such he had to periodically journey to headquarters at Boston, and took advantage of one of those protracted visits to seek admission into the fraternity, and as the records show received the degrees in the "First Lodge in Boston" in 1737.

There is fairly good local evidence, as well as indirect documentary proof, that he founded a lodge in Annapolis on his return and that then, or later, he was clothed with authority by the Provincial Grand Master at Boston, Henry Price, to act in a similar capacity for Nova Scotia. That this position was accepted as genuine is borne out by a letter directed to him from Halifax dated 12th June, 1750, and signed by five influential brethren, requesting his permission to establish a lodge there with Governor Cornwallis as its head. Next year a second lodge was formed at Halifax, and thereafter, down to 1791, the activity of the Craft in that city was centered in three lodges.

The authority vested in Phillips by Henry Price was confirmed by the Earl of Blessington, Grand Master of England in 1785, who signed a warrant constituting

"Erasmus James Phillips, Esq., Provincial Grand Master of Nova Scotia and the territories thereunto belonging."

The only two lodges that appear to be traceable to Phillips' authority were those claimed to have been warranted at Annapolis in 1738 and at Halifax in 1750. The Annapolis Lodge, it is said, was removed to Halifax in 1749, becoming No. 1. There is no record however of its original working or subsequently, and although the Grand Lodge of Nova Scotia possesses much ancient and valuable manuscript in connection with early Craft events in that province, the past, so far as Annapolis is concerned, is practically a blank. There will be no one to dispute Nova Scotia's just claim to the proud honor of being the first resting place of the Masonic banner in Canada, nor to deprive the memory of the soldier Mason, Bro. Erasmus James Phillips, of the distinction of being its bearer.

To quote a Massachusetts writer, "Our Fraternity may well unite with the historian in the opinion that there are few localities in America around which the memories of the shadowy past more interestingly cluster than the ancient town of Annapolis. Notwithstanding the various fortunes and misfortunes which befell that locality, the Masonic fire smouldered there with singular persistency. The soldier, the poet, the philanthropist and the historian contributed each his share to draw Acadia and Massachusetts into very close relations for the next succeeding two centuries."

If a fair knowledge of caligraphy had been incorporated with at least one of the liberal arts and sciences to which the progressive Craftsman is urged to devote his leisure, we of the present might have been brought to a better realization of the inestimable value to the Masonry of old colonial days, of the military lodges under field warrants, which were so active at that period, but alas, the secretary's achievements were not then under the supervision which has prevailed, more or less, since, and consequently much that would have been otherwise treasured by the antiquary is regretted as something that might have been, but was not.

Ireland, 1737, was the first Grand Lodge to issue these travelling warrants; England followed several years later. In the interval the number of regiments which had applied for and received those Irish authorizations had reached a comparatively formidable figure and that they were not permitted to lie idle is manifest in existing records, indicating that the activities of those soldier Masons were not confined to redcoats, but that the principles and teachings of the ancient Craft were disseminated through their missionary efforts among the best of the settlers of those primitive days.

In 1756-8 the Grand Lodge of Boston authorized warrants for lodges in the expeditions against Crown Point and other places in Canada, while Scotland, about the same period, appointed Col. Young, of the 60th Regiment, Provincial Grand Master over the "Lodges in America," holding warrants from that country.

After the siege and capitulation of Quebec, in 1759, seven lodges, holding field warrants, met and celebrated the St. John's Day festival in December, after which the Masters and Wardens discussed the formation of a Provincial Grand Lodge, which was agreed to. They elected Lieut. Guinnett, of the 47th Regiment, as P. G. M., and the following year succeeded him with Col. Simon Fraser, of the Fraser Highlanders, afterwards the 78th Regiment, who held the office a brief six months. Col. Fraser it is related, a statement since doubted, was installed by the famous Thomas Dunckerley, then a master in gunnery on H. M. S. "Vanguard" and subsequently a noted figure in English Masonic circles.

The Provincial Grand Lodge of Quebec formed, as stated, by the military lodges, developed with time, and in 1765 was presided over by the Hon. John Collins of the Executive Council, whose identity with the Craft was more pronounced than any of his predecessors, mainly owing to the zeal displayed by him in the Creation of lodges in many of the settled but distant sections of his great territory, and notably in the direction of the great lakes.

Thus the early progressive work of Masonry in Canada was, under the auspices of the Provincial Grand Lodge of Quebec, of military origin, which began with the memorable year of 1759, but of which there is little or nothing to show in the way of record. In the territory west of the Ottawa River, and which became Upper Canada in 1791 under the altered conditions, there were ten lodges, one of these working under a field warrant from England in the 8th, or King's, Regiment of Foot, two at Detroit E.R. inactive, St. James, No. 14, at Cataraqui (Kingston) and St. Johns, No. 15, Mackinac, both warranted by Quebec's Provincial Grand Lodge. St. Johns Lodge of Friendship, No. 2, origin unknown; the New Oswegatchie, No. 7, of Prov. Grand Lodge of New York, origin Brockville; St. John, No. 19, Niagara, warranted in 1787 by Quebec. Rowdon, or "The Lodge Between the Lakes," E.R. (Moderns), No. 498, at York, and a Union Lodge, Cornwall, supposed origin, Quebec.

With the political partition of, what once had been, Quebec, and which by act f Parliament became the provinces of Lower and Upper Canada, the Masonic division was likewise defined, and in 1792 Provincial Grand Masters for each were decided upon. Sir John Johnson, who, in 1788, had succeeded Sir Christopher Carleton as Provincial Grand Master, under the "Modern" regime in Quebec, was the last who held that position. The "Ancients," or Athol Grand Lodge, had three warrants in Quebec, but never had agitated for Provincial authority until this period, when learning that H.R.H. Prince Edward, afterwards Duke of Kent, father of Queen Victoria, and who, after his initiation in Switzerland, had allied himself with the first Grand Lodge of England, "Moderns," was appointed to a military command in Lower Canada, appealed to him to become their Provincial Grand Master. He graciously acquies ed, and in March, 1792, was so appointed and subsequently installed. There is no record of the "healing" of Prince Edward from "Modern" to "Ancient" allegiance, and it is presumed that his first submission to the latter body was made on the occasion of his installation.*

*See J. Ross Robertson's "History of Freemasonry in Canada."

At about the same period the appointment as Provincial Grand Master of Upper Canada was vested in R. W. Bro. William Jarvis, who had been sent out as Provincial Secretary to His Excellency Governor Simcoe. The warrant of appointment issued to Prince Edward was ample in its provisions and practically clothed its possessor with all the rights and prerogatives of a supreme power, including the issue of lodge warrants direct. On the other hand, Jarvis was restricted to the issue of dispensations subject to confirmation by the Grand Lodge at London. It is surmised that the Masonic rank and experience of the Royal brother were factors in influencing the distinction and, indeed, the Masonic activity of R. W. Bro. Jarvis in the early period of his rulership was not of a nature to excite exuberant enthusiasm.

The very imperfect records show that a Provincial Grand Lodge was summoned to meet at Newark (Niagara), then the seat of government, in 1795, the representatives of five lodges being present. A printed document of the year 1796 gives the list of lodges as twelve. Two other lodges were in existence in the province, one at Edwardsburg and the other at Niagara, both oming to the front subsequent to the Jarvis appointment and both holding their authority from Quebec. These, it is stated, however, were of posthumous rand, as each owed its origin to the former Quebec Grand Lodge, "Moderns," but had remained inactive in the interval.

Between 1793 and 1817 Jarvis had, in defiance of the terms of his authority, issued warrants for some twenty-six lodges. The administration headquarters were transferred in 1797 from Newark to York (Toronto) and the zeal of the Provincial Grand Master, who was careful to remove his warrant at the same time, perceptibly cooled. The devoted brethren at Newark with R. W. Bro. Robert Kerr, D.G.M., in command, on the contrary, kept the embers alive, and as they believed that the Grand East was rightly in their jurisdiction, they conducted and continued the business of the Grand Lodge, merely forwarding documents for necessary signature to York. Such a condition of affairs could not e expected to prevail. A spirit of enquiry and consequent unrest was aroused in the lodges by circular letter from the Grand Secretary containing a preemptory request for dues. The right to do so was challenged by the lodge at Kingston on the ground that there was no Grand East at Newark, and it may be added that Jarvis held the same view. The brethren at Newark decided to act. They notified the P.G.M. that a brother had been nominated for his office in case he failed to appear at the quarterly meeting.

The revolt took definite shape when, in April, 1803, R. W. Bro. Jarvis received a letter from the Provincial Grand Secretary at Newark (Niagara) announcing the election of George Forsyth as Grand Master and demanding the return of the jewels and other property in his possession forthwith. That the leading spirits of the Newark brethren inclined to an independent Grand Lodge was evident, but they had to reckon with the lodges which remained unshaken in their allegiance to the authority from the Duke of Athol and vested in Jarvis. The apathy displayed by the latter down to this period was inexplicable. He was induced at last to move, and called a meeting of the Provincial Grand Lodge at York for 10th February, 1804, W. Bro. Jermyn Patrick, of the lodge at Kingston, acting as Secretary. Eight lodges were represented at this meeting, each reaffirmed its loyalty to Jarvis, unanimously decided to summon the recalcitrant brethren of Newark to answer the charge of unmasonic conduct and to report the entire situation to the Grand Lodge in England.

Meantime the schismatics had proceeded on their way hopefully, if mistakenly, assuming all the prerogatives of a Grand Lodge including the issuance of warrants for new lodges, for which they remitted fees o England, unacknowledged, of course, as were their letters. The spasmodic attempt in 1804 to reinfuse life into the body headed by Jarvis proved abortive. With peculiar consistency the Provincial Grand Master had een reprimanded by England for his former neglect, and the communication apparently did not have the effect intended. Discontent was rife, and from 1804 to the death of Jarvis, in 1817, the Provincial Grand Lodge as an active body was heard of but once. It continued, in name only, down to 1822.

The irregular organization at Niagara also failed to maintain its former activity, and matters Masonic in Upper Canada were in a decidedly chaotic condition. Culpable indifference combined with blundering efforts at management contrived to bring about a deplorable state of affairs that reflected neither lustre nor credit on any one concerned in the period from 1792 to 1822, and to which the war of 1812-15 did not contribute any enlivening aid.

If, within the limits of a brief paper, it were permitted to glance at the workings of the individual lodges, it would be found that there was no lack of incident to establish the fact that the rank and file of the fraternity were in possession of the elements that tend to the conservation of the fraternity and its teachings. That the humble Craftsmen were not indifferent to existing conditions and the wretched failures of deputed authority is indicated in the records of their discussions. One of these took place at a meeting of the lodge at Bath, which originated the famous Masonic Convention at Kingston, 1817-22, a movement that materially assisted to again elevate the Craft to its appointed status in the community. The invitation to the first Convention was sent out to all the lodges, but the adherents of the irregular body at Niagara, which had by some means secured the Jarvis warrant and had entrenched itself behind its authority, declined to accept. The Convention met on August 27th, 1817, with the representatives of eleven lodges; R. W. Bro. Ziba M. Phillips was chosen President, and it was decided to memorialize England to confirm the nomination of Roderick MacKay, Esq., a local gentleman of repute, to succeed the late William Jarvis, as Provincial Grand Master. The Memorial to England was drafted with care and due courtesy and, accompanied by a draft for £30, forwarded to London, but elicited no reply for years.

In the meantime death, by accidental drowning, had removed Bro. MacKay, the nominee of the Convention. That organization was again summoned in February of 1819 and, in the absence of any communication from England, steps were taken to further organize in the interests of the existing lodges, and "Articles of Association," or a constitution, were drawn up and agreed to. Another petition to England was mailed, but with like result. At the third meeting of the Convention, a year later, it was learned indirectly that the money draft sent in 1817 had been duly received in England, but to the Convention's request an apparently deaf ear had been turned. A brother who was about to visit England offered to personally communicate with the authorities there. He did so, and a few weeks after the fifth annual meeting of the Grand Convention, February, 1822, had adjourned, a letter from the Grand Secretary of England arrived, which referred to a communication of his dated 19 November, 1819, relating to Masonic affairs and which he declared must have miscarried. He was careful to state that England's interest in Canadian matters was sincere, and conveyed a hint that "a distinguished member of our order" would probably be commissioned to enquire into the difficulties complained of.

In July, 1822, R. W. Bro. Simon McGillivray arrived from England, bearing his appointment as Provincial Grand Master for Upper Canada, and empowered, by commission, to examine into, and report upon, the condition of the fraternity in that territory. As a beginning he addressed a letter to the valued Secretary of the Convention, Bro. John Dean, with a request for information. He also interviewed R. W. Bro. Robt. Kerr, of the Niagara body, and wrote to its secretary, Bro. McBride, asking for similar information. Having acquired all the material he could, R. W. Bro. McGillivray prepared in earnest for the work of reorganization, first journeying to Niagara. His tour completed, he believed he saw his way to the formation of a Provincial Grand Lodge and took steps to that end. On the 23d Sept., 1822, the delegates assembled in York in obedience to summons, and the second Provincial Grand Lodge was constituted in form. With a justice and impartiality which characterized his acts throughout, and with a view to cementing the reconciliation, the various offices were distributed between the members of the late irregular Grand Lodge and those of the Grand Convention. In the following year Bro. McGillivray returned to England, but in 1825 again visited Canada, where finding matters were not proceeding along the lines he had mapped out, he complained of the official neglect and threatened resignation. Yet he continued to keep an interested eye on Craft matters, though handicapped by protracted but necessary absence in England and elsewhere.

About this period there was a perceptible falling away in the activities of the Provincial Grand Lodge and the individual lodges complained of the lack of a governing head. Even Bro. Beikie, the Dep. Prov. G. M., had resigned his position, ostensibly because of the Morgan panic. In the years 1834-37 Masonry was in a dormant condition in Upper Canada. A weak but ineffectual attempt at an independent body was made at London in 1836. In 1837 McGillivray was again heard from through a letter addressed to an English brother, John Auldjo, about to visit Canada, who he appointed Deputy Provincial Grand Master for the Province, and for whom he had secured a patent. Bro. Auldjo may have entered upon the mission entrusted to him, but no record survives. Then ensued a period of dormancy extending over many years. McGillivray died in London in 1840, at the age of 56, a victim of heart disease.

In 1842 R. W. Bro. Ziba M. Phillips, who, in 1817-22, displayed remarkable executive ability as president of the Kingston Masonic Convention, undertook, with something of his old zeal, an attempt at revival. He held the rank of Past Provincial Deputy Grand Master, conferred upon him many years previously in recognition of his services, by R. W. Bro. McGillivray. As of yore, appeals to England proved fruitless and remittances to headquarters remained unacknowledged. He summoned a meeting of the lodges at Kingston, where a petition to England's Grand Master was drawn up requesting that august brother to authorize the appointment of Hon. Robert Baldwin Sullivan as Prov. G. M. for Upper Canada. Leading members of the former Prov. Grand Lodge present expressed dissent at the proceedings, claiming that a resolution of that nature from an unauthorized body was *ultra vires* of the recognized regulations. They went farther, and even wrote to England in protest. No reply to the petition was vouchsafed by the mother Grand Lodge. At a second Convention, in 1843, the petition was duplicated. So too was England's eloquent silence. In 1844 the Convention confirmed all the acts of Bro. Phillips, sustained him in his position, declared for the immediate establishment of a Grand Lodge and chose their leader to preside over it as Grand Master. These efforts of Bro. Phillips to reawaken the dormant Masonic spirit were not without their effect in the west. It alarmed those who desired perpetuation in the line of descent from the provincial warrant of 1792.

Sir Allan Napier MacNab, of Hamilton, had received a patent from Scotland as Provincial Grand Master, for a territory where there were no Scotch lodges, and under peculiar circumstances. His jurisdiction covered both Upper and Lower Canada, but only in the latter province did he avail himself of the right to warrant lodges. In 1844 England appointed him Provincial Grand Master for Upper Canada, a creation that occasioned as much surprise as it did satisfaction. The Provincial Grand Lodge was summoned for the 9th August, 1845, and after the customary preliminaries, officers were appointed and installed. Although R. W. Bro. Ziba M. Phillips, had been accused, informally, of being at the head of an irregular organization, it is not recorded that he was ever arraigned therefor, probably because in a letter to the Prov. Grand Secretary the eloquent defence of his actions and position, written in reply, convinced the brethren that they were dealing with a true-hearted, unselfish Mason, earnest only for the welfare of the Craft. Apparently all was working well for the Craft under the new regime. The P.G.M. was not a regular attendant at the communications, but he had an indefatigable Deputy and Secretary, R. W. Bros. Thomas Gibbs Ridout and Francis Richardson, respectively. The old trouble however was again the canker to foster disquiet and irritation. England's cool indifference to reasonable and just demands was once more having its effect, and mutterings of an approaching storm were deep during the latter years of the existence of the third Provincial Grand Lodge.

Probably the most important and interesting epoch in the chequered history of the Craft in Canada, from the advent of R. W. Bro. Jarvis' authority as Provincial Grand Master of Upper Canada, in 1792, was the period embracing the years 1852-55, when the provincial governing body under R. W. Bro. Sir Allan N. MacNab began to chafe at the intolerable attitude of silence maintained by England's Grand Lodge to Canada's many demands and appeals in behalf of legitimate requirements. The irritation passed the grumbling stage when at the semi-annual communication, in 1852, a delegate from Belleville had the hardihood to give notice of a motion to the effect that owing to the great increase of lodges in Canada working under English and Irish authority which were annually remitting moneys which should be retained and devoted to Masonic purposes in this country, the Grand Lodge of England be petitioned to authorize the Provincial Grand Lodge to exercise sole control over Masonic affairs in its own jurisdiction and to use its influence with the sister Grand Lodge of Ireland to induce its subordinates in Canada to submit to the same local authority. At the following communication a resolution declaring for independence and to petition England to that effect was carried.

This was the germ that developed into an agitation that bore fruit later, but, alas, not through the Provincial Grand Lodge. The memorial of 1853, embodying the request expressed in the resolution, was duly, and in choice diction, drafted and forwarded to the Grand Lodge of England, where it was received and diligently pigeonholed until September, 1855, when it was exhumed and discussed by a special committee, which reported with characteristic disregard to the serious nature of the request and in a style bordering on persiflage. This, in view of modern methods, may sound harsh and perhaps uncharitable, but *litera scripta manet.*

England's action, or rather non-action, contemptuous as usual of the reasonable demands of colonial brethren, furnished the golden opportunity which unfortunately the worthy but ultra loyal element in the Provincial Grand Lodge hesitated to seize, and thus assisted to cultivate a spirit of unrest that even then threatened serious consequences.

In the meantime, the lodges holding under Ireland had mooted and actively discussed the independence question, and at a convention held at Hamilton, in May, 1855, decided to send a delegation to attend the meeting of the Provincial Grand Lodge at Niagara in the following July. The convention further adopted a resolution to the effect that an independent Grand Lodge should be at once established if the management of Masonic business was to be conducted in conformity with the dignity of the Craft and that the Grand Lodge of Ireland be communicated with, requesting its countenance and sanction to the proposition. Subsequent meetings only strengthened the determination of the Irish brethren, and as the parent body had yielded so far as to agree to the formation of a Provincial Grand Lodge it was accepted as an encouragement to proceed, and the brethren only awaited the outcome of the approaching meeting of the Provincial Grand Lodge of Canada West before resuming activities. As events proved, that august body saved all further heart burnings, but to the Irish lodges belongs the credit of the initial movement that finally led to independence.

Scant courtesy, however, was accorded their delegates when they attended the meeting and not only to the presentations of the Irish brethren, but to those also who were inclined to their way of thinking, was the deaf ear turned. Their carefully prepared resolutions were ruled out by the Deputy Grand Master presiding, who determinedly refused to submit them to the meeting and abruptly adjourned the Grand Lodge. His indiscreet action hastened the inevitable. The indignant Craftsmen at once gathered to talk the situation over, and it was resolved to hold a convention of delegates at Hamilton in the following October to consider the expediency of establishing an independent Grand Lodge of Canada, and that every lodge be notified.

On the 10th of October, 1855, the convention assembled and the gratifying announcement was made that forty-one of the lodges in Quebec and Ontario had sent duly accredited representatives. A committee was formed to prepare a series of resolutions setting forth the views of the convention. There was no evidence of inattention when those resolutions were submitted to that eager, interested gathering. The historian says:

"The resolution which placed Canadian Masons under a Sovereign body was prefaced by a preamble which briefly recited the grounds for action, viz: the diversity of interest caused by the occupation of territory by the Grand Lodges of England, Ireland and Scotland; the objections to Canadian Freemasons being made contributors to the charity funds of England from which they derived no benefit and which created a constant draw on the funds of the Canadian Craft; the inconvenience caused by delays of months, and even years, in receiving warrants and certificates, though asked and paid for; the fact that moneys sent from Canada were unacknowledged for years by England; that the communications of Canadians were treated with silent contempt by England; that the Provincial Grand Masters were merely nominees of England irresponsible to Canadians, and that under the present system the Provincial Grand Lodges were practically independent of the Canadian Craft and that these bodies had not the respect or attention of the mother Grand Lodge."

One or two pacifically disposed amendments were attempted, but received little consideration, and the resolution, as follows, was adopted *nem dis:*

"That we the representatives of regularly warranted Lodges here in Convention assembled, resolve: "That the Grand Lodge of Ancient, Free and Accepted Masons of Canada be, and is hereby, formed upon the Ancient Charges and Constitutions of Masonry."

The following day was devoted to the consideration and adoption of a draft constitution and the arranging of other necessary preliminaries, all of which received the closest care and attention, so that ancient usage and established custom might be observed and leave no loophole for a possible charge of irregularity. The election of officers was an interesting episode of the memorable session, and it was with the keenest satisfaction that the brethren received the announcement that M. W. Bro. (Judge) William Mercer Wilson, a most capable man, was the choice for first Grand Master of the new Grand Lodge.

On the 2nd November following, the convention was again summoned for the purpose of installing the Grand Master and other officers elect, the ceremony being conducted by M. W. Bro. H. T. Backus, P.G.M. of the Grand Lodge of Michigan.

With a brother of such undoubted attainments at the head of affairs it was to be expected that he not only possessed the confidence of his immediate following but was respectfully feared by not a few of those who were still opposed to the recent creation. At the first annual communication, held in the city of Hamilton on the first Wednesday of July, 1856, he presented an admirable address dealing with the leading events of the preceding nine months. England's Grand Lodge, as well as those of other countries and States had been officially notified of the establishment of the Grand Lodge of Canada. With its customary elegant leisure the former failed to even acknowledge receipt of the communication. New York, influenced by statements contained in a circular letter issued by the Provincial Grand Lodge, expressed disapproval and declined recognition, while other Grand Bodies which analyzed the situation with views unbiased, declared in favor of the regularity of Canada's position, and others again, equally satisfied but timorous, preferred to await England's action before deciding. Nothing of this daunted Grand Master Wilson. He knew that sooner or later vindication would come. To use his own words:

"We should continue all fraternal offices to those brethren whose conscientious scruples have deterred them from at once joining us in the establishment of an independent Grand Lodge, feeling assured that when the justice of our cause has become fully understood, the Grand Lodge of Canada will unite under its banner the whole Masonic Fraternity of the Province."

It was reported at that meeting that thirty lodges had affiliated in proper form and warrants issued to them, that the register showed 1,179 members in good standing, that nine dispensations for new lodges had been granted and applications for others were coming in. It was also announced that the Grand Lodge of Ireland was the first of the parent Grand Lodges to extend recognition to the Grand Lodge of Canada.

England at this juncture exhibited symptoms of shaking off its somnolency so far as Canadian affairs were concerned and gave expression to a desire to take up the matter of the complaints from its adherents across the sea. Well disposed brethren in the mother Grand Lodge had espoused the Canadian cause and vigorously condemned the official apathy which characterized the Grand Secretary's office at London in connection with the Provincial Grand Lodge of Canada West and its just demands. Little of benefit or redress was effected and the Provincial body resolved to test the merits of another memorial, which was duly drafted and despatched, and this time brought a reply dated 16th April, 1857. The memorial had been referred to a recently appointed committee termed "The Colonial Board" to deal with. As usual, these brethren, blind to the true conditions, blundered in their estimate of colonial endurance and with fatal results for the Anglo-Canadian connection. The letters from England presented to the Provincial body in June, 1857, were so indefinite, except in expressions of fraternal affection, that it was at once patent that the limit of patience had at last been reached and a series of resolutions favoring Masonic union was actually submitted and approved.

Meantime the young Grand Lodge of Canada was growing in strength and influence and receiving accessions constantly. On the other hand there was a perceptible weakening of the Provincial body and the leaders in both, anticipating the future, held frequent consultations, while the brethren appointed to discuss a possible union in committee prepared for the eventful day under a mutual understanding to present the result of their labors, when the Provincial Grand Lodge was to assemble, perhaps for the last time.

On the 9th September, 1857, the Provincial body met in special communication in Toronto. The respective committees presented their reports in the form of voluminous minutes of their proceedings, which, after discussion, were agreed to. The Provincial Grand Master then announced that by the agreement so reached the body over which he had presided had declared its independence and in the name of the Grand Master of England he called for the warrants of the various lodges issued by that authority. The parchments were on hand and duly surrendered by the delegates, whereupon it was resolved that in succession to the late Provincial Grand Lodge of Canada West a Grand Lodge be formed constituted and proclaimed under the title of the "Ancient Grand Lodge of Canada." A second resolution declared the former Provincial Grand Master to be the Grand Master of the new body and a third decided on the adoption of England's constitution *mutatis mutandis.* The prearranged programme was admirably adhered to and carried through with perfect decorum and without any unnecessary hitches. The forty-seven lodges which had surrendered their English warrants were provided with the necessary documentary authority to proceed under the new regime, in fact, every contingency was provided for as if the "Ancient Grand Lodge" was assured a future existence as prolonged as "Tennyson's "Brook." Not the least of the actions that closed a memorable three days session was a fraternally worded memorial to England in which the why and wherefore of the change effected was but lightly touched upon, but requesting recognition and expressing the hope that the herewith returned warrants might be sent back to be retained as souvenirs.

That the tidings created a sensation in England is to put it mildly. The Grand Master, the Earl of Zetland, was apparently blind to the fact that his own treatment of the Canadians had contributed to the result. In a letter in which he declared himself as unalterably opposed to any recognition of the seceders, he said with all apparent innocence:

"I cannot contemplate without the deepest concern the separation of so many lodges from the parent body, and the more so when it is attempted to be shown that the conduct of the Grand Lodge of England has driven them to that course."

This and further correspondence only served to exhibit England's dismay and irritation at the course pursued by the Canadian fraternity.

In the interval, diplomatic negotiations were progressing in Canada looking to a union of the two Grand Lodges, and history repeated itself when in Toronto, on the 14th of July, 1858, the articles of union were submitted to both bodies meeting simultaneously in distinct halls, and approved. To Grand Master Wilson, presiding over the deliberations of the third annual communication of the Grand Lodge of Canada, it was announced at the evening session that a deputation from the Ancient Grand Lodge was in waiting. The brethren were greeted, and their spokesman informed the Grand Master of the action of their Grand Lodge, to which M. W. Bro. Wilson replied that similar action had been taken in the Grand Lodge of Canada and that the latter was now prepared to receive the members of the Ancient Grand Lodge, which, on the return of the deputation, at once acquiesced in the invitation, and proceeded in a body to the hall where the Grand Lodge of Canada awaited them.

Historian John Ross Robertson graphically describes the memorable scene when Grand Master Wilson stepped down from the dais and grasping the hand of Grand Master Sir Allan MacNab bid him cordial welcome, and as the three hundred brethren of the two bodies mingled and clasped hands in a fraternal chain, the Grand Master from his place in the East and in a clear voice said: "*May the links thus united never be broken.*" Needless to add the enthusiasm that ensued was of a nature to enhance the happy consummation, and as the terms of union were ratified by the combined bodies the "Ancient Grand Lodge" was declared dissolved, and thenceforward the Craft was to be a closely united family under the paternal ægis of the Grand Lodge of Canada.

From that notable event of the 14th of July, 1858, the sun of peace and prosperity continued to shine on "The Grand Lodge of Ancient, Free and Accepted Masons of Canada," and although, in the passing of time, clouds occasionally dimmed its brightness they were of brief duration and only served as reminders of the troublous days of old when the spark of hope had well night been extinguished and when the remnant of the faithful with despairing eyes saw little in the future but disaster to reward their long suffering patience. Rejoicing in the revivifying atmosphere of home rule and with implicit confidence in their leaders, the brethren of the young Grand Lodge sought the recognition which their peers of the older creations were only too pleased to acknowledge. New York at the outset held aloof under a misapprehension of the situation. A few had taken New York's lead.

England, as was to be expected, hesitated at recognition, or, if Canada's Grand Lodge had to be acknowledged it was to be done after English fashion, in other words it vouchsafed recognition to the Grand Lodge of "Canada West," ignoring the fact that the two provinces by acts of the Imperial and Colonial Parliaments had, in 1841, become fused and the young Grand Lodge claimed jurisdiction over the united territory. In Lower Canada there were six lodges holding English warrants, while there were twelve of Canadian obedience, and the apparent object was to retain for the English lodges a maternal protection, which an admission of sovereignty in regard to the Canadian body would otherwise imperil. A tentative agreement was brought about by which England accorded recognition on the understanding that the English lodges, if they desired to maintain their allegiance, were to be permitted to do so and no further warrants were to be erected. It was a mistaken yielding on the part of Canada and occasioned no little trouble in later years.

Grand Master Wilson was continued in office until 1860. Under his beneficent sway the Grand Lodge had grown in strength and influence. He was succeeded by Thomas Douglas Harington, one of the brightest minds in a host of rare, devoted and intellectual brethren which Canada's Grand Lodge was fortunate to boast at that period. At the sixth annual convocation, held in London, Ont., in July, 1861, there were 116 lodges represented. A committee was appointed to raise an Asylum Fund, to which Grand Lodge promised to donate $20,000 if the brethren contributed a like amount. This was a similar, if more pretentious, project to which many years previously the far-seeing Provincial Grand Master Simon McGillivray had disapproved.

An incident of the year 1860 is worth relating, as it indicates the phase of opposition to which our brethren of Eastern Canada have then and since been subjected. H.R.H. Prince of Wales was then touring Canada for the first time. The government authorities at Ottawa had arranged that on the occasion of his visit to the Capital the corner stone of the Parliament Buildings would be laid, and it was understood that they were favorable to the Masonic fraternity taking part in the ceremony. The Grand Lodge was duly summoned and assembled to that end, but, in the meantime, the powerful influence of the "Roman Catholic Church" had been used to such an extent that the officers of the Masonic body were quietly told that their services could not be utilized on that occasion.

In the following year it was reported that 155 lodges were on the roll. Keen regret was expressed at the death of Thomas Gibbs Ridout, Hon. Past Grand Master. A

Board of General Purposes was organized and a permanent location for the meetings of Grand Lodge suggested. Grand Master Harington expressed himself very emphatically in the matter of the tacit support given by their Grand Lodges to subordinates of English and Irish origin, which continued to work within the jurisdiction of the Canadian Grand Lodge and dwelt upon the attitude of the English Colonial Board in its mistaken interpretation of Canada's view of the situation. His address of the next year contained similar references and deplored the anomalous condition of the Craft in Canada due to the non-recognition by England of the principle of exclusive jurisdiction.

In 1865 the Grand Lodge had completed its first ten years of existence as such and exhibited a most encouraging statement both as regards funds and membership. In the following year Grand Master Simpson was invited to instal the Grand Master of a newly-formed Grand Lodge of Nova Scotia, but declined on the ground that its preliminaries were irregular. Three years later Grand Master Stevenson reported that he had installed the Nova Scotia Grand Master.

The Grand Lodge of Quebec was formed in 1869, but was not then recognized by Canada owing to the alleged irregularity of procedure, and an edict of suspension was issued against certain brethren in connection therewith. In 1870 the claim to recognition was again rejected, but was favored, conditionally, in 1871. The conditions, however, were not acceptable to the Quebec brethren as they implied a right to the retention of lodges which might desire to hold to their former allegiance. Vermont's Grand Lodge espoused the Quebec side of the argument and threatened non-intercourse with Canada. To this Grand Master William Mercer Wilson, who had been again chosen to preside, promptly responded with an edict against Vermont. In 1874 he reported that the differences with Quebec were amicably adjusted and that fraternal relations were re-established with Vermont. A sum of $4,000 was voted to Quebec as its proportion of the accumulated funds. M. W. Bro. Wilson was re-elected Grand Master, but in the early days of January, 1875, death claimed this distinguished brother and the mourning assumed, in obedience to command, gave little indication of the genuine grief universally felt for the beloved Craftsman who had labored diligently and successfully in the interests of a united fraternity. Another serious loss was sustained in the passing of the devoted Grand Secretary R. W. Bro. T. B. Harris, who had filled the office since the formation of Grand Lodge twenty years previously.

The organization of Grand Lodges in Manitoba and Prince Edward Island marked the next year, which was also one of prosperity for Canada. A sum of three thousand dollars was paid for purposes of relief. Trouble was originated by the opposition of existing lodges in London, Ont., to the establishment of a lodge in that city recently formed and working under dispensation. Grand Lodge declined to confirm the latter and in the interests of harmony acting Grand Master J. K. Kerr offered a suggestion for consideration which the promoters of the young lodge refused. Despite the fact that their dispensation was no longer operative they continued to receive candidates, and a breach, that grew in extent daily, went beyond the possibility of closing by the secession of its members, the leaders being promptly expelled from the Craft. This was the beginning of the irregular body known as "The Grand Lodge of Ontario," which although it gained adherents, was so much out in the cold, that after a fitful tenure of many years offered unconditional submission and passed out of existence with the healing of a few of those who had labored in vain to give it a semblance of life.

The succeeding years were successful beyond the fondest hopes of even the most sanguine, but comparatively uneventful. The Grand Orient of France by removing a fundamental requirement, a belief in the Diety, was shut off from fraternal communion by Grand Lodges in general, and in 1878 Canada joined in the exclusion. In 1883

England as a disquieting element loomed up again. Grand Master Daniel Spry at the annual communication in Ottawa directed the attention of Grand Lodge to the fact that a rejected candidate of a Toronto lodge had been initiated in one of the lodges holding under England in Montreal. Complaint to England brought a characteristic reply, stating that the Grand Master could not agree with the Canadian contention touching invasion of jurisdiction and the matter took the usual protracted time for adjustment.

In 1885 the Montreal English warrants were the occasion of an edict of non-intercourse by the Grand Lodge of Quebec. Four years later M. W. Bro. R. T. Walkem, Grand Master of the Grand Lodge of Canada, undertook the role of mediator in the hope of arranging a satisfactory basis of settlement. The edict was thereupon withdrawn by Quebec and the M. W. Bro. was most fraternally received at headquarters in London. His statement of the case was accepted with every mark of courtesy and polite attention and he was assured that the matter would receive the consideration it merited. It only remains to add that the English warrants are still a working commodity in Montreal and prolific of future possibilities.

During 1888 the last of the Irish warrants, which, like those of England, were in 1858 mistakenly permitted to continue, No. 159 at Vankleek Hill, was surrendered, its membership requesting admission to the Canadian fold. The prosperity of the Grand Lodge and its usefulness were very marked at this period. Two hundred and sixty of the lodges were represented at the annual communication in Toronto and the funds reported as $70,000.

One hundred years previously R. W. Bro. William Jarvis had unfolded his warrant in historic Niagara and later held it in the little town of York. In 1892 the latter had become the great metropolitan city of Toronto with a Masonic fraternity in proportion to its remarkable expansion, and the centenary of the Craft in "Upper Canada" was fittingly celebrated by a banquet to which over four hundred leading brethren sat down, presided over by Past Grand Master M. W. Bro. J. Ross Robertson, Historian of the Grand Lodge.

The unveiling, by the same indefatigable brother, of a handsome polished granite column to the memory of "The Dead of the Craft" in Mount Pleasant Cemetery, Toronto, was the occasion of another notable Masonic demonstration in June of the following year. The plot on which the monument stands was the gift of Bro. Robertson.

Thenceforward the progress of Canada's Grand Lodge was in keeping with the country's amazing growth and prosperity and when in 1905 Grand Master Allen, presiding at the fiftieth annual convocation, congratulated Grand Lodge on its achievements of half a century, he did it no injustice when he said:

"For the Mason of to-day, who knows no other conditions than those which our predecessors aimed to create, it may be difficult to realize and appreciate fully the intangible advantages which we enjoy as the fruits of the great change effected half a century ago."

"The 1,500 Masons of the 41 lodges of our first establishment have become about 35,000, comprising 390 lodges, notwithstanding the loss of over 40 lodges ceded to Quebec and Manitoba. We have yielded up a great territory, yet our membership has increased over twenty-fold."

"Beginning with not even sufficient funds with which to purchase regalia for its Grand officers, and with an initial balance sheet showing receipts of only £93 and disbursements of but £64, Grand Lodge finds itself to-day, as the result of the sound policy of its rulers, possessed of a well-invested capital of over $110,000."

"The Grand Masters of the early years handed out, in their discretion, the few dollars then available for charitable purposes. But, with increasing resources, the institution of the 'Benevolent Fund,' and the creation of machinery for its distribution, this great department of Masonic work began to assume its proper place and proportions and to-day, in the course of steady growth, we find that about $14,000 or fifty per cent. of the moneys received by Grand Lodge from the lodges in the ordinary course during the year, has been paid out for the relief of the needy and deserving of the Craft."

To further express gratitude to the Giver of all Good "for favors already received" and to mark the particular epoch in the history of the Craft in Ontario, M. W. Bro. J. E. Harding, who presided as Grand Master in 1902-4, inaugurated a "Semi-Centennial Fund" of $100,000, to be contributed by the active members of the lodges in the jurisdiction, with a view to supplementing the good work of the Benevolent Fund and applying the income derived from it to the relief of extreme cases which the latter fund was unable to meet. The levy was at the rate of $3 per member and payable in that number of years.

Few, if any, are left who can recall the stirring events of over half a century ago, events pregnant with future benefit, but the Craft of to-day, which rejoices in an atmosphere of tranquility and comparative affluence, would be ingrate indeed were the memories of the past, to which it owes everything, permitted to fade and extinguish for lack of occasional reminder. That "The Grand Lodge of Canada in the Province of Ontario," with its 446 Lodges embracing 60,000 members, is enabled, at this period, to dispense for the relief of our less fortunate brethren, their widows and orphans, a sum of over $30,000 annually, is a tribute, not to the present generation, which but lightly feels the call, but to the brethren of the dead and gone past, who so valiantly struggled through long years of discouragement to keep the standard of the ancient Craft afloat.

The intervening years have been uniformly peaceful and the close of 1915 furnishes abundant evidence of the steadily growing vigor and influence of the fraternity. Under the rule of capable and wise brethren who realized their great responsibility the Craft in the Province of Ontario has demonstrated its ability to accomplish the great mission entrusted to it and gives promise of doing further on similar lines in the not distant future. One may well quote Historian Robertson when in looking back on the years which have sunk into a shadowy past and reviewing the achievements and failures of our pioneer fathers.

"Yet all must admit—and especially we who have a direct knowledge of their work—that in their mission they were earnest and sincere and did the right as God gave them to see the right. Their successes and reverses, their triumphs and tribulations come to the Masons of Canada as lessons eloquent of instruction."

Of the twenty-seven brethren who since 1855 have been selected to fill the chair of the Grand East, fourteen have passed to their reward, viz: M. W. Bros. Wilson, Harington, Simpson, Stevenson, Seymour, Weller, Henderson, Moffatt, Spry, Murray, Walkem, Hungerford, Wm. Gibson, and Aubrey White. The following is a list of Grand Masters in order of succession:

1856-1860—William Mercer Wilson.
1860-1864—Thomas Douglas Harington.
1864-1866—William B. Simpson.
1866-1868—William Mercer Wilson.
1868-1871—Alexander A. Stevenson.
1871-1872—James Seymour.
1872-1875—William Mercer Wilson.
1875-1877—James Kirkpatrick Kerr.
1877-1879—William H. Weller.
1879-1881—James A. Henderson.
1881-1882—James Moffatt.
1882-1884—Daniel Spry.
1884-1886—Hugh Murray.
1886-1888—Henry Robertson.
1888-1890—Richard T. Walkem.
1890-1892—John Ross Robertson.
1892-1894—John Morison Gibson.
1894-1896—William R. White.
1896-1898—William Gibson.
1898-1900—Elias Talbot Malone.
1900-1901—Richard B. Hungerford. Died 9th Sept., 1901.
1901   —John E. Harding, Acting G. M.
1902-1904—John E. Harding.
1904-1905—Benjamin Allen.
1905-1907—James H. Burritt.
1907-1909—Augustus T. Freed.
1909-1911—Daniel Fraser Macwatt.
1911-1913—Aubrey White.
1913-1915—W. D. McPherson.
1915   —Sydney A. Luke.

EARLY HISTORY OF FREEMASONRY IN UPPER CANADA

Niagara Lodge, No. 2; The Ancient St. Johns Lodge, No. 3; Sussex Lodge, No. 5; and the Barton Lodge, No. 6, and others items of interest and fact.

BY M. W. BRO. AUGUSTUS T. FREED, 33°.
Past Grand Master of the Grand Lodge of Canada in Ontario.

I HAVE had the privilege of reading the preceding excellent article written by R. W. Bro. George J. Bennett, of the early history of Masonry in Canada and of the formation of the Grand Lodge; hence I do not propose to tread the path traversed by him, but shall endeavor to supplement his narrative with some account of lodges warranted in the early days of Masonry in that part of Canada formerly called Upper Canada or Canada West, and now forming the Province of Ontario.

R. W. Bro. William Jarvis, who was appointed to the civil position of Provincial Secretary of Upper Canada in 1792, was at the same time made Provincial Grand Master of Masons; and, between the year named and 1817, he issued warrants to twenty-four lodges. Some of these continue to the present time, but most of them have "fallen on sleep."

Four of the old Jarvis lodges have, by resolutions of Grand Lodge, been permitted to wear gold lace on their aprons and to work with gold jewels, in recognition of their rank in the craft and their service to Masonry in this jurisdiction These are now known as Niagara Lodge, No. 2; The Ancient St. Johns, No. 3, of Kingston; Sussex, No. 5, Brockville; and The Barton, No. 6, of Hamilton.

Niagara Lodge, No. 2, was the first warranted by Jarvis. It has experienced many vicissitudes, and for a number of years its meetings were interrupted; but it has survived all blows of time and chance, and is now a prosperous and active body. The town of Niagara, formerly called Newark, was burned by the troops of the United States in the war of 1812, when the lodge room and all the original records were destroyed, though the warrant was saved, and hangs on the wall of the present Lodge room.

In June, 1814, while the United States troops were still in possession of Niagara, Lieut. Fitzgibbon, with a small body of British rangers, was stationed at Decew's house, a few miles south of St. Catharines, and was the cause of a good deal of annoyance to the invading force. General Dearborn therefore decided to capture him, or at least to dislodge him, and sent Col. Boerstler, commanding the Fourteenth regiment of United States regulars, with other troops, to do the work. Mrs. Laura Secord, wife of a Mason, accidentally learned of the proposed expedition, and determined to give warning to Lieut. Fitzgibbon. Accordingly, taking a pail in her hand, as if about to go out to milk her cows, she passed the sentries, and made her way for nineteen miles through woods swarming with Indians, till she reached the Decew house and warned the Lieutenant of his danger. It is not probable that the action of Mrs. Secord had any bearing upon the subsequent engagement, for the Indians, under command of Captain W. J. Kerr, were watching the movements of Colonel Boerstler; they fought the battle of Beaver Dams; and before the regulars, under Lieut. Fitzgibbon, arrived on the field the United States troops were beaten to a standstill. Lieut. Fitzgibbon succeeded in persuading Col. Boerstler that he was surrounded by a vastly superior force of Indians and British regulars, and the colonel surrendered his whole force. Bro. Secord was not a member of Niagara Lodge, but of a lodge which met at Stamford, near Niagara Falls.

In 1826 William Morgan was abducted from Batavia, New York, and taken to Fort Niagara, on the New York side, where he was temporarily placed in a magazine. Some of his abductors passed over to the Canadian side of the river, and endeavored to secure the co-operation of the Niagara brethren in disposing of the prisoner. There are several accounts, no one of them trustworthy, of subsequent events. One is that the abductors killed Morgan in the magazine of the fort, sewed the body in a sack, carried it to a boat, rowed out into the river and sunk it. The next is that, failing to get assistance from the Canadian Masons, they returned to Fort Niagara, and found that Morgan had died from dissipation, exposure and fright. A third that they took Morgan, still alive, into the boat, weighted him with irons and threw him overboard, and the fourth is that the Canadian Masons did receive him, and passed him on to Toronto, near which place he lived for a number of years. I have conversed with a number of the oldest Masons at Niagara on the subject, and they agree in the assertion that the brethren of their lodge refused to have any hand in the business, while they also think that Morgan was passed on toward Hamilton and lived for some years on the north shore of Lake Ontario.

The lodge room was destroyed by fire in 1860, and all the old documents, together with the jewels and other property of the lodge, were burned. The building now owned and occupied stands on the site of that in which the lodge first met, and in which the Provincial Grand Lodge formed by Jarvis held its meetings.

The Ancient St. Johns Lodge, of Kingston, No. 3 on the present register of the Grand Lodge of Canada, was No. 6 of the lodges warranted by William Jarvis. It worked for a short time under dispensation, and its warrant was dated November 20th, 1795. This lodge has always held a prominent place in the Masonry of Ontario; has always exercised great influence in Masonic circles; and yet there is little in its records which has more than local interest. It is remarkable rather for the number of prominent men who were initiated in it than for events of magnitude in its history. One of the charter members was Richard Cartwright, great-grandfather of Sir Richard Cartwright, who for half a century took a leading part in the political history of the country and was, from September 30th, 1904, to the time of his death a Senator of Canada. Other members of Ancient St. Johns who have made names for themselves in the history of Canada were Sir Alexander Campbell, William Henry Draper, Sir Henry Smith, and Sir John A. Macdonald, for many years Premier of Canada.

In 1834, owing to the anti-masonic excitement in the United States, the brethren deemed it prudent "to cease working until such time as the lodge might beneficially work with advantage to the craft and the world at large." The meetings were not resumed until 1843.

M. W. Bro. John Ross Robertson says that Sussex Lodge, No. 5, was originally formed in a regiment raised for the royal service by Sir John Johnson, during the Revolutionary War. Its first warrant was issued by the Grand Lodge of New York in 1783, to "a lodge in his Majesty's Loyal American Regiment." Soon after the close of the war many members of the regiment settled on the north side of the St. Lawrence, near the present town of Prescott, and they appear to have carried the lodge organization with them. There it was called the New Oswegatchie Lodge. Oswegatchie was the old name of Ogdensburg, New York. About 1790 a warrant appears to have been obtained from the Provincial Grand Lodge of Quebec. The early minutes of the lodge are full, and are of value as showing the character of the Masonry which existed in those days, but they have little interest for the general reader. At later dates the lodge worked under warrants from the Provincial Grand lodge of "Ancients" of Upper Canada, then from Provincial Grand Lodges under the United Grand Lodge of England. It was not called Sussex Lodge till 1822. It was the first named on the list of the lodges which met at Hamilton, in 1855, to form the Grand Lodge of Canada. W. B. Simpson, a Past Master of the lodge, was active in the work of organization, and was elected the first District Deputy Grand Master of the Central District. He was elected Grand Master of the Grand Lodge of Canada in 1864, and served with eminent ability for two years. Another valuable and prominent member of the lodge was R. W.

Bro. Ziba M. Phillips. He was President of a convention held at Kingston, in 1820, which promoted the revival of Masonry in Canada West in 1822, and was a power in the Craft till the time of his death.

The Barton Lodge, No. 6 on the register of the Grand Lodge of Canada, was the ninth of those warranted by William Jarvis. Its charter was dated November 20th, 1795. The document cannot now be found; but the receipt for the charter fee is preserved, dated Nov. 1795, and Lane's Masonic Record (English) says the date of the original warrant was Nov. 20th, 1795. The first members were men who were called in Canada United Empire Loyalists. They had lived in various parts of the country now forming the United States, had adhered to the royal cause in the War of the Revolution, and at the end of the struggle they were deprived of their property, and compelled to seek new homes in the then almost unbroken wilderness of Upper Canada. Those who settled on or near the spot on which Hamilton now stands put down stakes in the forest (for the land was not surveyed), and started life anew. Among these pioneers came Davenport Phelps, a missionary sent out under the auspices of Trinity Church, New York. He was also a notary public, and withal Grand Secretary of the Provincial Grand Lodge of Upper Canada, of which William Jarvis was Provincial Grand Master. Several of the settlers at "the Head of the Lake," as the country at the western extremity of Lake Ontario was then called, were Masons; and when Davenport Phelps came among them he apparently found no difficulty in gathering them together in a Masonic fold.

Of Robert Land, one of the founders of the lodge, the following story is told: He was a farmer, living in Southern New York, near the Pennsylvania line. While absent with his regiment, Indian allies of the colonials raided the settlement, burned the houses, and killed or carried off all the inhabitants, mostly women and children. Land, returning from service, found his home a heap of ashes, and was told that his wife and two children had been killed. Heartbroken, he returned to his regiment, and at the close of the war went to Canada, and was given a tract of land at the Head of the Lake. The wife and children, however, had not been killed, but were rescued by British troops and taken to New York. Thence they were sent by sea to Halifax, and there they remained for some years. In course of time information reached Mrs. Land that her husband was living at the Head of the Lake and she was sent to that place by the military authorities of Nova Scotia. As Robert Land sat in the door of his cabin one summer evening he saw a woman and two boys approaching. They proved to be his wife and sons, and the long-divided family was reunited.

The minutes of the earliest meetings of the lodge were kept on loose sheets of paper, and are lost. The first which now exist are those of a meeting held January 31st, 1796, which was attended by twelve members and four visitors. Among the members appears the name of "Bror. Capt. Brant." This was Thayendanegea, the celebrated Indian chief. He lived about ten miles from the meeting place of the lodge on a square mile of land given him by the British Government. There is no other evidence than this record to show that he was a member of the lodge.

The old minutes are very interesting, as showing the customs of the time, and illustrating the condition of the country, but they have no great interest for the general reader. We read in one place that the "Treasurer take as much money out of the chest as will purchase three gallons of whiskey against the next lodge night," and in another place that "the liquors for the use of the lodge shall be purchased with the money belonging to the lodge by the barrel or quarter cask." So we have no doubt that when the brethren were called from labor to refreshment, as they were several times in the course of the evening, the phrase used was no mere figure of speech. Again, when we read that brethren were permitted to pay their annual dues in "good merchantable wheat, delivered at Bro. Rousseaux's mill," we need no further intimation that, at the end of the eighteenth century, cash was a scarce article at the Head of the Lake.

Another entry is of wider interest, and exhibits a broader spirit. I may be pardoned for copying the minute in full. The lodge met on the 12th of December, 1800, and the Secretary—

"Read a letter from the Grand Secretary informing this Lodge of a communication received from the Grand Lodge of Pennsylvania announcing the death of the Right Worshipful Grand Master Washington, and requesting this lodge to go in mourning at their public and private meetings six months, including their first meeting; in consequence of which Bro. Aikman moved, seconded by Bro. J. Showers, that a piece of black ribbon should be purchased for that purpose. The motion being put was carried. Bro. John Lottridge agreed to furnish the lodge with ribbon."

Let it not be forgotten that a large majority of the members of The Barton Lodge at that time were men who had fought on the royalist side in the War of the Revolution, and that they had lost their property and had been exiled from the place of their birth because of the part they had taken; notwithstanding which they could rise above the passions of the conflict and resentment at what they must have believed to be injustice and spoilation, and could remember as Masons the brother who was so eminently worthy of honor.

A few years later war again broke out between Great Britain and the United States, and Upper Canada was several times invaded by the forces of the republic. Members of The Barton did their share of work in the several battles which took place along the Niagara frontier and farther west. In 1813 a strong force under Generals Winder and Chandler advanced from Niagara against the British General Vincent, who was entrenched at Burlington Heights, in the western part of what is now Hamilton. Ephraim Land, a brother of that Robert Land of whom mention has been made, fearing that the property of the lodge would be carried off or destroyed by the invaders, took the warrant, the jewels and other portable articles, and buried them in his flower garden, planting a branch of geranium over them to mark the spot. The precaution, however, was not necessary. After the battle of Stoney Creek the United States forces fell back, and Bro. Land dug up the articles so carefully interred. They were not again used for many years. When the war closed the membership of The Barton Lodge was sadly reduced. William Jarvis, the Provincial Grand Master, had for many years ceased to be active in Masonry; and he died shortly afterwards, in 1817. Besides, the warrant of the lodge had been issued under authority from the so-called Ancient, or Athol, Grand Lodge of England. That body had (in 1813) united with the original Grand Lodge to form the United Grand Lodge of England; and the brethren of The Barton were in doubt as to their Masonic standing. And so for about twenty years there was no meeting of the lodge. By the year 1835 Hamilton had grown to be a considerable village, and among its inhabitants were several unaffiliated Masons. These and a few of the survivors of the original members of The Barton met and resolved to attempt a revival of the lodge. In the end they were successful. The United Grand Lodge of England issued a new warrant, numbered 733 on the English register, and under that warrant The Barton worked until the formation of the Grand Lodge of Canada in 1855.

One of the men who took a leading part in the reorganization was William Johnson Kerr, a son-in-law of Joseph Brant, the great Mohawk chief, and a relative of Sir William Johnson, so prominent in New York during and before the War of the Revolution. Bro. Kerr was in command of the Indians who won the battle of Beaver Dams. He and his family are buried in the cemetery of the little English church at Burlington. A few years ago the members of The Barton Lodge placed a memorial stone at the head of his grave.

In November, 1895, The Barton Lodge celebrated its Centennial. A gold medal was struck to commemorate the event and Grand Lodge granted the members of The Barton Lodge permission to wear this medal as a Masonic jewel.

R. W. Bro. George J. Bennett has sufficiently told the history of the Provincial Grand Lodge of Upper Canada, and I must not duplicate the narrative. I may be permitted, however, to add a few facts. In 1844 the body was without an executive head, and a proposal was made to petition the Grand Lodge of England to appoint R. W. Bro. Thomas Gibbs Ridout, of St. Andrew's Lodge, Toronto, to the vacant position. Then, in a very dramatic manner, Sir Allan MacNab, of The Barton Lodge, appeared on the scene, and produced a patent appointing him to the place. Sir Allan was not an exemplary Mason. A resident of Hamilton, he went down to Toronto, and was initiated in St. Andrew's Lodge. The Barton Lodge protested against the invasion of its territory, and Sir Allan received his second degree in Hamilton. Soon afterward, he visited Scotland, and while there he was made Provincial Grand Master for Upper and Lower Canada. He was not even a Master Mason at the time, and there were no Scotch lodges in Upper Canada. There is no evidence that Sir Allan ever attempted to act upon his Scotch patent. After he was made Provincial Grand Master for Upper Canada by the Grand Lodge of England he took but little interest in Masonic affairs, leaving routine work to his lieutenant, Bro. Ridout, who generally presided at the meetings of the Provincial Grand Lodge. A great deal of dissatisfaction existed, not only at the carelessness and neglect shown by officials of the Grand Lodge in England, but because there was to some extent a clashing of interests between the lodges of English and Irish origin. The latter had no provincial organization, and the brethren of those lodges were also dissatisfied with the want of attention paid to their communications by the home brethren. The first open protest against this state of things came from The Barton Lodge. On the 10th of December, 1851, it was resolved, "That a committee be appointed to confer with Strict Observance Lodge concerning the propriety of addressing the various sister lodges in Canada on the subject of withdrawing from the Grand Lodge of England and establishing an independent Grand Lodge of Canada."

The brethren of the Lodge of Strict Observance declined to take part in the movement; but the matter was brought before the Provincial Grand Lodge at its next ensuing meeting in June, 1852, when notice of motion was given that at the following communication a resolution would be introduced to "petition the Grand Lodge of England to be permitted to exercise sole control over the affairs of Masonry in this province, and that the Grand Lodge of England be Masonically requested to use its influence with the Grand Lodge of Ireland to induce those lodges now working under its authority to submit to the decision of this Grand Lodge." At the next semi-annual meeting the resolution was duly moved and carried. It affirmed that feelings of respect and reverence for the Grand Lodge of England were entertained by the Canadian brethren, but added:

"That it is absolutely necessary for the welfare of Masonry that a separate Grand Lodge be established, with full power to control the working and operations of the Craft in this quarter of the globe, to secure which a committee be appointed to draft a petition to the Grand Lodge of England, based on the foregoing resolutions, praying for permission to establish a Grand Lodge in that part of the Province of Canada formerly constituting Upper Canada, with full power and authority to manage and control all matters connected with such Grand Lodge, and all lodges now working under the constitution of the Grand Lodge of England; and that the said committee be fully empowered to carry on all correspondence with the Grand Lodge of England for the purpose of securing the absolute independence of such Grand Lodge."

For the next three years letters and memorials were sent to England, pointing out the disadvantages under which Canadian Masons were suffering, but these were not even answered. The subject was before the Provincial Grand Lodge at every session, but no final action was taken.

While all this was going on the brethren of lodges chartered by the Grand Lodge of Ireland were suffering similar neglect and expressing like dissatisfaction. It must be remembered that the Irish lodges, ten in number, had no provincial or local organization, and could make representations to their mother Grand Lodge only as individual lodges or by convention specially called for the purpose. The first formal action, so far as is known, was taken by King Solomon's Lodge, Toronto, on the tenth of November, 1853, when a resolution was adopted appointing a committee to correspond with other lodges holding under the Grand Lodge of Ireland, for the purpose of establishing "a ruling power in Canada West." The committee performed the work assigned it, and, on the 8th of December, 1853, the convention was held at Hamilton. Four lodges were represented. In May, 1854, another convention was held at London, which appointed a committee to draft a constitution for the Grand Lodge of Canada West, and adjourned to meet at Hamilton in October. This meeting was again adjourned to November, at Toronto, when a proposal from the Grand Lodge of Ireland to grant a Provincial Grand Lodge to the Irish Lodges in Canada West was discussed. The Grand Lodge of Ireland was not willing to grant to the Irish Provincial Grand Lodge the powers demanded, and in May, 1855, King Solomon's Lodge instructed its representatives to unite with the English Lodges for the purpose of petitioning the Grand Lodges of England, Ireland and Scotland to grant an independent Grand Lodge for the Province of Canada West. Negotiations between the Irish lodges and the Grand Lodge of Ireland then ceased.

At the regular meeting of the Provincial Grand Lodge (English), held in May, 1855, it was resolved to summon a lodge of emergency, to be held as early in July as possible, "for the purpose of taking into consideration the motion to be proposed by the mover of this resolution," and the Grand Secretary was instructed to forward a copy of the resolution to each lodge in the jurisdiction.

The Lodge of Emergency was held at the Clifton House, Niagara Falls, on the 19th and 20th of July, and the minutes inform us that—

It was duly moved and seconded, "That a meeting of the delegates from all the lodges in the Province, under all jurisdictions, be invited to meet at an early day to take the necessary steps for communicating with the Grand Lodge of Great Britain and Ireland, for the purpose of forming an independent Grand Lodge." The motion, being put to the vote, was lost.

That, however, did not end the business. When the Grand Lodge adjourned on the 19th a number of the delegates met in convention, with several representatives of Irish lodges, and it was resolved—

That a convention of delegates be held at Hamilton on the second Wednesday in October next, for the purpose of considering the expediency of establishing an independent Grand Lodge of Canada, and to proceed with such matter as may be deemed most desirable for the benefit of Masonry in this Province.

The convention assembled in the room of The Barton Lodge, on the 10th of October. Forty-one lodges were represented, of which thirty held English warrants, nine Irish warrants, and two Scotch warrants. At that convention the Grand Lodge of Canada was formed. At an adjourned meeting, held on the 2nd of November, the Grand Lodge was formally constituted and consecrated, and its officers installed and invested, by M. W. Bro. H. T. Backus, Grand Master of Masons in the State of Michigan.

It may not be out of place to tell here why the "Grand Lodge of Canada in Ontario" retains its present title, when its jurisdiction is confined to the Province of Ontario, and when there are eight other Grand Lodges in the Dominion of Canada. In 1855, when the Grand Lodge was formed, it exercised jurisdiction over the whole of Canada as it then existed, that is, the present provinces of Ontario and Quebec. Twelve years later (in 1867), the Dominion of Canada was formed by the union of all the old provinces; and shortly afterwards the territories of the Hudson Bay Company were acquired by purchase, and the Province of British Columbia acceded to the Dominion, so that Canada extended from the Atlantic to the Pacific and from the United States border to the Arctic Ocean. About the same time the lodges in Quebec, adopting the American doctrine of territorial jurisdiction, formed the Grand Lodge of Quebec. It was not at once acknowledged by the existing Grand Lodge, but controversy extended over several years. This was ended in 1874 by recognition of the new body. Then, it may seem, it would be easy and proper to adopt the title of Grand Lodge of Ontario, and nobody would have been more happy than the brethren of Ontario to take that name. But there were lions in the path. While the controversy with Quebec was in progress some brethren, having or believing they had, a grievance, established a clandestine body, and took the territorial name. Not only so, but some colored people formed lodges, established a Grand Lodge of their own, and assumed the same title. Not only did they take the title, but they obtained an act of incorporation from the legislature, and thus fortified themselves with legal warrant. It is possible that if the legitimate Grand Lodge in this Province were to assume the same name now, its right to do so might be challenged by the colored people; and in any case it would not be pleasant for one to be asked to which Grand Lodge of Ontario he owed allegiance—the clandestine Grand Lodge, the colored Grand Lodge, or the regular and legitimate Grand Lodge. For these reasons the best course was pursued, and the body calls itself the Grand Lodge of Canada in the Province of Ontario.

FREEMASONRY IN THE PROVINCE OF QUEBEC.

BY WILL. H. WHYTE,
Grand Secretary Grand Lodge of Quebec, A. F. & A. M.

THOUGH traces of the Masonic Craft have been found, which indicate that members of the ancient fraternity had visited "Acadia," now called Nova Scotia, upwards of three hundred years ago, and although it has been affirmed by French and other writers that a Lodge of Freemasons existed in Quebec in the year 1755, yet no reliable records are known to be in existence, and Masonry in Canada, or that portion of the Dominion which formed "old Canada" before Confederation, is only reckoned back to the year 1759, when the "Lily" flag of the Bourbon was replaced over New France by the British "Union Jack." With the advent of the British troops, English Freemasonry was transplanted to Canadian soil, or, more strictly speaking, Anglo-Saxon Freemasonry, for the Grand Lodge of Ireland was more largely represented among the regiments that took part in the capitulation of the cities of Quebec and Montreal. In these days many of the regiments in the British army carried travelling warrants authorizing them to hold lodges, and among those taking part in the siege of the first-named city five regiments held Irish warrants, and one an English warrant, and at the latter city five regiments likewise held Irish warrants, one an English and one a warrant from the Grand Lodge of Scotland. Among the number, Lodge 227 of the Irish Register in the 46th Regiment of Foot still survives, and is now called the "Lodge of Antiquity," No. 1, on the registry of the Grand Lodge of the Province of Quebec.

Quebec capitulated to the army of Wolfe, September, 1759, and on the following St. John's Day, December 27th,

1759, eight Military Lodges met to celebrate the festival of their patron saint, and there and then formed themselves into a Grand Lodge, and elected Lieut. Guinnett of the 47th Regiment, a member of Lodge No. 192, under the Irish Register as Grand Master.

FIRST GRAND LODGE. "THE GRAND LODGE AT QUEBEC."

For thirty-three years this Provincial Grand Lodge had control of Masonry, as the Provincial Grand Lodge of Canada, under the Grand Lodge of "Moderns," England, the headquarters being located in the city of Quebec. Among the Grand Masters were Colonel the Hon. Simon Fraser, 78th Highlanders, 1760 (who was installed by Sir Thomas Dunkerley, then an officer on H. M. S., the "Vanguard"), Captain Milborne West, 47th Regiment, 1761; Lieut. Turner, 47th Regiment, 1763; Hon. John Collins, 1765; Col. Sir Guy Carleton (Lord Dorchester), 1786, and Sir John Johnson, Baronet, 1788. This Provincial Grand Lodge chartered many subordinate Lodges, upwards of forty having been traced, the first four being located in the city of Quebec, two, Albion No. 2 and St. John's No. 3, being still on the roll of the present Grand Lodge of Quebec, and the fifth in the city of Montreal, under the name of St. Peter's, No. 4. This Lodge was in active operation for thirty years and lapsed about 1792. In 1767 a Deputy Provincial Grand Lodge was created in Montreal, and Bro. E. Antill appointed Deputy Provincial Grand Master. On November 8, 1770, a warrant was again issued for another Lodge in Montreal, under the designation of St. Paul's, No. 10.

The Provincial Grand Lodge warranted several other Lodges in Montreal and various places, including points on Lake Champlain, Detroit, Kingston, Niagara, Cornwall, Ogdensburg and Rawdon (Ont.); the majority of these, however, disappeared at the end of the last century. In 1752 a schism occurred in Masonry in England, and a rival Grand Lodge was formed, which took to themselves the title of "Ancient" and dubbed the premier Grand Lodge the "Moderns." This new body was composed of many of the younger and more aggressive members of the craft, and proved a very formidable rival to the Premier Grand Lodge. The rivalry between the two bodies was at its height when "Prince Edward," Father of Her Most Gracious Majesty Queen Victoria, arrived at Quebec in 1791, with the 7th Royal Fusiliers, of which Regiment he was Colonel. At this time there were three lodges hailing from the "Ancients" in the City of Quebec, who were in a strong and prosperous condition.

SECOND GRAND LODGE. "THE GRAND LODGE OF LOWER CANADA."

With the advent of Prince Edward came a new era in Masonry in the Province. On March 7th, 1792, the Grand Lodge of the Ancients in England issued a patent deputing the Prince "Provincial Grand Master" of Lower Canada, and on the 22nd June, 1792, His Royal Highness was duly installed with great eclat (a religious service and procession to the Recollet Church (R.C.) forming part of the ceremony). His Royal Highness remained Grand Master of this Grand Lodge until the year 1813, when he was elected Grand Master of the Ancients in England in succession to the Duke of Athole. The Prince was created Duke of Kent in 1799, and on the amalgamation of the two Grand bodies in 1813 he nominated his brother, the Duke of Sussex, as the Grand Master of the United Grand Lodge. This Grand Lodge of Lower Canada warranted some 26 Lodges between the years 1792 and 1823, five of which are still in existence under the present Grand Lodge of Quebec. These five are: Dorchester, No. 4, at St. Johns; Select Surveyors (now Prevost), Missisquoi Bay; Nelson, at Caldwell Manor; Golden Rule, at Stanstead, and Sussex (now St. Andrew's), at Quebec. Zion, No. 1, at Detroit, still holds an original warrant, Zion, No. 10, issued by this Grand Lodge, of date September 7th, 1794. Among the Montreal warrants were Union Lodge, No. 8, chartered in 1793, which lapsed in 1826; St. Paul's, No. 12, May 1st, 1797, (which apparently was applied for and granted to the members of the former St. Paul's, No. 10), and Wellington Persevering, No. 20, formed in 1815 and dissolved 1826. These years were ones of prosperity for the brethren of the mystic tie. In 1816, Union, No. 8, made an effort to raise a fund for the purpose of building a Freemasons' Hall in the city of Montreal and founding a school for the education of children, but the effort did not materialize. The Duke of Kent having resigned, the Hon. Claude Denéchau, M.P.P., was duly elected to succeed him as Grand Master of the Provincial Grand Lodge, which important post he acceptably filled until 1822. Many pleasant and important incidents are related and on record regarding the doings of the craft during these thirty years. The celebration of St. John's Day, the 27th December, was annually held with much enthusiasm. At the request of the Royal Grand Master the lodges in Quebec met and marched in procession for some years to the Recollet (R.C.) Church, which was kindly placed at their disposal, when service was held and a sermon delivered by the Grand Chaplain, the brethren dining together in the evening. Before his departure from Canada, H.R.H. presented an antique Masonic square of gold, with an inscription that it was "a gift from H.R.H., Prince Edward, to the R. W. the Grand Lodge of Lower Canada." This, together with a large "key" of gold surmounted with a crown and monogram, the gift of H.R.H. Prince William Henry, afterwards "King William IV," are preserved with religious care by the present Grand Lodge of Quebec.

PROVINCIAL OR DISTRICT GRAND LODGES.

The War of 1812 between England and the United States had a very depressing effect on Masonry and the removal of some of the Military Lodges, as well as a number of the Brethren who had taken an active part in the Grand Lodge of Lower Canada, caused this body to become very inactive for several years.

The year 1823 marked another era in the history of the Craft in the Province of Quebec. The Lodges in Montreal, as well as some of the others in the Province, forwarded their Canadian Charters to the recently formed United Grand Lodge of England, and exchanged them for English warrants, and then petitioned England to establish two Provincial Grand Lodges under that Grand Body— one for Montreal and the Borough of William Henry (now called Sorel), and the other for the cities of Quebec and Three Rivers. This request was acceded to, and the Honorable William McGillivray was appointed Provincial Grand Master of the former, and the Honorable Claude Denechau as Provincial Grand Master of the latter.

The history of these two District Grand bodies during the thirty years that elapsed until a new Canadian Grand body was formed is not an active one, especially in the Quebec District. In the Montreal District several lodges were constituted, however.

In 1836, St. George Lodge was established, it having previously received a dispensation from the Provincial Grand Lodge in 1828. Zetland Lodge was constituted in 1844 and St. Lawrence in 1854. On September 5th, 1828, Hon. Claude Denechau, Provincial Grand Master, installed John Molson, Esq., as Provincial Grand Master of the District of Montreal and William Henry. The Brethren, accompanied by the band of the 76th Regiment, attended Divine service in Christ Church, Montreal, the sermon being delivered by the Rector, the Rev. Bro. Jno. Bethune, Grand Chaplain. In the year 1836, the Grand Master, the Hon. John Molson, died, and the Provincial Grand Lodge did not meet again for over ten years. On May 20, 1846, the Provincial Grand Lodge was again revived, an especial Grand Lodge being held in the Lodge Room in "Mack's Hotel" in the City of Montreal, to install the Hon. Peter McGill as Provincial Grand Master. In 1847, the Grand Lodge of Scotland established Elgin Lodge in Montreal, and the Lodge of "Social and Military Virtues" in the 46th Regiment (now Antiquity) was finally located in the same city. In 1849, the Hon. Peter McGill resigned office on account of ill-health and the Hon. William Badgley succeeded him. In the City of Quebec, the late Hon. Claude Denechau, deceased, was succeeded by Thos. Harington, Esq., and he in turn by James Dean, Jr., Esq., in 1857. The Provincial Grand Lodge at Quebec finally dissolved in 1870, the members joining the then new "Grand Lodge of Quebec." That of Montreal and William Henry, which had dwindled down to three Lodges after the formation of the Grand Lodge of Canada in 1855 had no active existence, and in the later years of the late Judge Badgley, who was the last Provincial Grand Master appointed by the Grand Lodge of England, it never met.

THIRD GRAND LODGE. "THE GRAND LODGE OF CANADA.

The history of Freemasonry in the Province of Quebec can be divided into periods of about thirty years each.

A third period had thus elapsed when in October, 1855, the representatives of forty-one Lodges in Canada West (now Ontario), and thirteen in Canada East (now Quebec), met in the City of Hamilton and formed the "Grand Lodge of Canada," holding jurisdiction over the two Provinces. This governing body gave quite an impetus to the fraternity, and many new Lodges were formed, some thirty in the Province of Quebec.

From 1855 to 1869 this Grand Lodge was the controlling Masonic Power in the Province of Quebec until the Confederation of the Canadian Provinces under one Government.

FOURTH GRAND LODGE. "THE GRAND LODGE OF QUEBEC."

With the birth of the Dominion of Canada, in 1867, appeared an agitation for the formation of separate Grand Lodges for each Province, the Provinces of Canada West and East being renamed Ontario and Quebec. Nothing definite was done until 1869, when a meeting was held in the city of Montreal on August 12th, and adjourned until

September 24th, when it was fully decided to call all the Lodges in the Province to a convention on October 20th for the formation of a Grand Lodge. Upon this date the present Grand Lodge of Quebec was duly formed by twenty-eight of the warranted Lodges then in the Province, M. W. Bro. John Hamilton Graham, LL.D., being elected Grand Master. The Grand Lodge of Canada strenuously opposed this movement, and a number of her Lodges held aloof, and did not at once join in. Matters Masonic were very unpleasant for several years, but in September, 1874, "Canada" finally withdrew from the Province of Quebec, her jurisdiction being now confined to the Province of Ontario only. All her 20 Lodges then in the Province of Quebec affiliated with the new Grand Lodge.

In June 1878, the Grand Lodge of Scotland instituted two new Lodges in the City of Montreal, which together with Elgin Lodge already of its obedience were formed into a "Provincial Grand Lodge." This invasion of territory was energetically opposed by the Grand Lodge of Quebec, who immediately issued an edict of non-intercourse. Three years later amicable proposals resulted in the three Scottish Lodges affiliating with the Grand Lodge of Quebec on the 27th of January, 1881, and the dissolution of the Scotch Provincial Grand Lodge.

At the formation of the Grand Lodge of Quebec, the Grand Lodge of England proffered recognition under certain restrictions which Quebec declined, but in 1906 the matter was again considered, resolutions adopted by both Grand Bodies, and an exchange of representatives made, M. W. Bro. the then Provincial Grand Master of England, the Earl Amherst, accepting Quebec's commission, and M. Wor. Bro. Sir Melbourne M. Tait, of Montreal, Chief Justice of the Province of Quebec, receiving a commission from the Grand Lodge of England.

Following closely upon this action, St. Lawrence Lodge, No. 640, of Montreal, affiliated with Quebec on the 20th of October, 1906, leaving St. Paul's, No. 374, and St. George, No. 440, still holding under England.

Since the advent of the Grand Lodge of Quebec Freemasonry has made steady strides in the Province. The first five years showed a membership of 2,700 in 40 Lodges, a number of whose warrants have since been returned, some by amalgamation and others through change of population in their localities. The advance, however, has been most marked in the past ten years. In 1901 the roll stood at 57 Lodges and a membership of 3,825. At the last session, 1915, the roll of Lodges had increased to 66 and a membership of 8,152.

The Brethren who have filled the chair of Grand Master since its formation in 1869 have been:

J. H. Graham, LL.D._____1869 to 1873, 1875, 1879 to 1881
James Dunbar, K.C. _____1874 and 1876
Sir M. M. Tait, K.B._____1877 and 1878
Edwin R. Johnson _____1883, 1884 and 1885
James Fred. Walker _____1886 and 1887
H. Luke Robinson _____   1888
I. H. Stearns _____1889 and 1890
Frank Edgar _____1891 and 1892
Col. T. P. Butler _____   1893
J. P. Noyes, K.C. _____   1894
Col. F. Massey _____1895 and 1896
E. T. D. Chambers _____1897 and 1898
B. Tooke _____1899 and 1900
Edson Fitch _____1901 and 1902
J. B. Tresidder_____1903 and 1904
D. A. Manson _____1905 and 1906
Geo. O. Stanton _____1907 and 1908
J. Alex. Cameron _____1909 and 1910
Rev. Frank Charters _____1911 and 1912
John E. Wright _____1913 and 1914
Edward A. Evans _____1915

On the roll of the Grand Lodge of Quebec there are a number of Lodges, whose history and formation, though not going back to the centenary period, have records most interesting, and have given many bright leaders to the Craft.

OLD LODGES.

Many interesting incidents could be related of some of the old Lodges now under the banner of the Grand Lodge of Quebec. No. 1 Antiquity, now 163 years old, has had an eventful history. Originating in the 46th Regiment in 1752, under the title of the "Lodge of Social and Military Virtues," it has held its meetings in many parts of Europe, Asia and North America. It was at the capitulation of Montreal in 1760. The Lodge has a Bible still in existence, upon which, tradition hath it, but not proven, Bro. General Geo. Washington took some obligation. In 1777 the chest which contained their belongings fell into the hands of the American troops in Pennsylvania. It was returned by command of the Commander-in-Chief General Washington to the 46th Regiment under a flag of truce. This old trunk again proved unfortunate by falling into the hands of the French at the defence of the Island of Dominica in 1805, but was returned by order of the Emperor, Napoleon I. In 1814 it was in Australia and the first Masonic Lodge to open and hold a meeting on that continent. In 1846 it was again in Canada, at Kingston, and finally located in Montreal in 1847. In order of its age, this Lodge, together with Albion Lodge of Quebec also instituted in 1752, St. John's, No. 3, of Quebec, formed in 1787, and originally established there; Dorchester, No. 4, at St. John's, 1792; Prevost of Dunham, 1793; Nelson, 1802; Golden Rule of Stanstead, 1803, all over the century mark, are authorized to wear gold lace on their aprons, with St. Andrew's, No. 6 of Quebec, established in 1816, fast closing in.

St. George No. 10, Montreal, dates its formation to July, 1829, and among its noted members the name of Lieut.-Col. A. A. Stevenson, Past Grand Master of the Grand Lodge of Canada in Ontario, stands out quite prominently for his strong personality as a Mason and a prominent citizen, and also for many years as an active military officer. M. Wor. Bro. Dr. Aldis Bernard, also a Grand Master of the Grand Lodge of Canada and a Mayor of the City was long an active member.

Zetland No. 12, 1844, presided over for a number of years by M. Wor. Bro. John H. Isaacson, Grand Secretary of the Grand Lodge of Quebec for 32 years, and one of its early initiates; as well as by Past Grand Master M. W. Bro. Rev. Frank Charters, D.C.L.

Elgin No. 7, 1846, formerly under the G. L. of Scotland, affiliated with the Grand Lodge of Quebec in 1881, and was given the vacant number seven on its roll. It has always been an active Lodge.

St. Lawrence No. 14, formed in 1854, was for 50 years under the jurisdiction of the Grand Lodge of England and became a Quebec Lodge on the 20th October, 1906. Its membership has been strong and vigorous.

St. Francis No. 15, of Richmond, formed in 1855, has been noted for its Masonic zeal. The late M. W. Bro. John H. Graham, the first Grand Master of the Grand Lodge, 1869, was long an active member. The third Grand Master, Most Wor. Bro. Sir Melbourne M. Tait, as well as Lieut.-Col. Thos. P. Butler, Grand Master in 1893, were both initiated therein.

Shefford No. 18, Waterloo, also formed 1855, is the Mother Lodge of M. W. Bro. John P. Noyes, Grand Master of Quebec in 1894, as also M. W. Bro. the late H. Luke Robinson, Grand Master in 1888.

Victoria No. 16, of Sherbrooke, instituted in 1856, has given many enthusiastic members to the Craft, and its confrere in the same city, "Prince of Wales Lodge No. 63," formed in 1877, is also an active Lodge.

Montreal Kilwinning No. 20, received its dispensation December, 1859, and has always been a large and energetic Lodge. It celebrated its semi-Centennial in 1910. Among its first initiates was M. Wor. Bro. Isaac H. Stearns, Grand Master, 1889, 1890. The late M. W. Bro. J. H. Isaacson assisted at its formation, and held the chair for two years.

Yamaska No. 21, of Granby, and Shawenegan, of Three Rivers, are both over fifty years old, having been instituted in 1860.

Royal Albert No. 25, of Montreal, founded 1864, has given many bright members to the Craft, among the names on the roll, the late M. W. Bro. Frank Edgar was Grand Master in 1890-1891, and M. Wor. Bro. B. Tooke in 1899-1900.

St. John's No. 27, of Mansonville, instituted in 1864, has been a steady, consistent country Lodge, and has Most Wor. Bro. David A. Manson, Grand Master of Grand Lodge in 1905-1906, on its roll.

Ascot No. 30, of Lennoxville (presided over by M. Wor. Bro. I. H. Stearns in 1860); Ashlar 31, of Coaticook; Doric 34, of Danville; Brome Lake No. 35, of Knowlton, and Sutton No. 39, of Sutton, all founded during the years 1867 and 1868.

Mount Royal No. 32, instituted in 1868, has one of the largest rolls of Past Masters. It is the Mother Lodge of Past Grand Masters Lieut.-Col. F. Massey, 1895-96; John B. Tresidder, 1903-04; and Geo. O. Stanton, 1907-08. Montarville Lodge, which amalgamated with it in 1890, brought to it a number of very active Masons, among them the late M. Wor. Bro. J. Fred Walker, Grand Master in 1886-1887.

Chateauguay No. 36, the Home Lodge of M. W. Bro. J. Alex. Cameron, Grand Master 1909-1910, has been for many years an active exponent of the Craft in the County of Huntingdon.

Mount Moriah No. 38, instituted in 1870, has had many active and zealous Masons on its roll. R. W. Bro. John McLean, a P. G. Z. of G. Chap., is its Senior Past Master.

Two Lodges composed of French Canadian Brethren, and whose work is all done in the French language, are on the roll of Grand Lodge, "Les Coeurs Unis" No. 45, founded in 1870, and "Denechau" No. 80, instituted in

1906. This latter Lodge is called after the Prov. Grand Master of Lower Canada who succeeded H. R. H. the Duke of Kent, in 1812. Both are prosperous and enthusiastic.

A number of Lodges were instituted during the years 1872-74-75, and among those who have been most active and given a number of officers to Grand Lodge are Prince Consort No. 52, St. Andrew's No. 53, Ionic No. 54, and Royal Victoria No. 57, all of Montreal. The latter is now the largest Lodge on the roll of Grand Lodge.

On the list of City Lodges is The University Lodge, founded in 1911 by the late Dr. James Chalmers Cameron. It is composed of graduates and students from McGill University, and gives promise of being not only a Lodge of much ability, but of great good and assistance to the student life of "Old McGill."

Westmount Lodge, in the suburban city of Westmount, and Waverley Lodge, instituted in the town of St. Louis, now a ward of the City of Montreal, are two Lodges that can compare most favorably with the Lodges in the greater city.

THE LODGE OF ANTIQUITY, No. 1 G.R.Q.
BY THE LATE R. W. BRO. J. BEAMISH SAUL
P. D. D. Grand Master, G. L. Quebec.

In considering the upward trend of Freemasonry in some of the famous British Regiments, the student will find much of romance, interwoven with the events of actual historic value of the prowess and kindness of heart of men long since passed away and otherwise forgotten.

In tracing the History of this Lodge, formerly "Lodge of Social and Military Virtues No. 227" in the 46th British Regiment, it is necessary to follow the movements of the Regiment in its wanderings during a period of over a century.

Raised in 1741, and being known as "Murray's Bucks," its first engagement was in Scotland, later in Ireland, the masons in the corps were granted a Travelling warrant by the Grand Lodge on March 4th, 1752. In 1757 it was found in Nova Scotia, and the next year formed part of the army which went down to defeat at Ticonderoga, July, 1758. Its Colonel being killed, the command devolved upon the Major, Eyre Massey, who had fought at Culloden, won renown at Fort Niagara in 1759, and again at Fort Levi the following year on the advance of the army under General Amherst to the surrender by the Marquis de Vaudreuil, of Montreal, the last stronghold of the French, September 8th, 1760. At this time Colonel Massey, retiring from the 46th, advanced rapidly in his profession, later gaining a peerage as Baron Clarina of County Limerick, and promoted Field Marshal. In 1761-2 the regiment is fighting at Martinique and Cuba, and later, 1764-5 in Canada, around Niagara and Detroit in the fierce warfare of Pontiac and his Indian confederates.

In 1776 it is again in America, operating with much success in the Revolutionary War, at Brooklyn, New York, White Plains, Fort Washington, and following the

Americans through New Jersey, wintered at Amboy. In the Spring of 1777, under Colonel Bird, it destroyed the enemy's supplies at Peekskill on the Hudson, then with General Howe in the defeat of Washington's army at the Brandywine River, September 11th, and Germantown, where Colonel Bird fell October 4th. Next the regiment is in Philadelphia with the army of occupation, and later in the fight at Monmouth, N.J., June, 1778, on the passage of the Army to New York, and in September with Major-General Charles (afterwards Earl) Grey in the attack on New Bedford, Mass., then again with Grey in the surprise and slaughter at night of Colonel Baylor's Horse at Tappan, N.J., on the west side of the Hudson, September 28th, and while scouting and reconnoitering in that section, is recalled to New York, going aboard the fleet with the army under Major-General Grant, which sailed for the West Indies November 2nd, 1778.

In 1805 it was found guarding the Island of Dominica, when the French fleet appears and landing four thousand men sets fire to the town, and after in vain demanding the surrender of the chief officer, departs, taking on board regimental property, including the Masonic chest. After correspondence, the Masonic property was restored some two years later by order of the French Government, with complimentary apologies. The loss of the warrant is recorded by Grand Lodge, 1805, with revival in July the same year. Owing to the brave defense of the Island, the Royal authority was issued permitting the 46th to bear the word "Dominica" on its colors and appointments.

It has travelled to Australia, and spent many years in Southern India. Being much reduced in numbers, it returned to England in 1833, Captain Lacy, one of the Masons of the regiment, bringing back the chest containing the Bible, warrant and what remained of the jewels of the Lodge which had fallen into decay owing to the heavy toll of its members by disease, death and exchanges. A new warrant was granted, and Lieutenant-Colonel Lacy, with other brethren, were installed as first officers of the revived Lodge in 1834. The regiment continued on its travels, arriving in Montreal in 1845, when the Lodge, having already become dormant owing to changes in the regiment, what remained of the regalia, jewels, books, etc., were transferred by Bro. Captain W. Child, its custodian, to Sergeant-Major W. Shepherd, W. Robinson and R. Balfour, to form a permanent semi-military Lodge in Montreal. The warrant having been returned to Grand Lodge, a new one at the same number was issued July 1st, 1847, when the above named brethren were installed in St. George's Lodge, Montreal, and its career began with varying success.

In 1855 it joined in the formation of the Grand Lodge of Canada, the name being changed in 1857 to the Lodge of Antiquity authorized to wear gold instead of silver and enrolled at the head of the list. After the formation of the Grand Lodge of Quebec, it became affiliated as number one, and the brethren were later commissioned to wear a centenary jewel.

The famous Bible of the regiment, which, from the family history written on its pages during a series of years to 1769, proved to be the property of Benj. West, of Bedford, Mass., was taken away by men of the 46th when that village was sacked September 5th, 1778, during the expedition under Grey, and the following month, when the regiment was foraging and reconnoitering, also under Grey, already alluded to, on the west side of the Hudson, the Masonic chest, with the Bible and regalia, together with other regimental baggage, was seized by a body of American troops operating near the British base.

General Washington at the time (October, 1778) had his headquarters at Fredericksburg, a village a few miles distant on the east side of the Hudson, and was regularly informed of all movements in that section. When the above mentioned capture became known to him he ordered the return, under a flag of truce, of the Masonic property, at the same time sending a message that the Americans were not warring against institutions of benevolence.

In confirmation of these particular events we have the very clear statement found in the oration (preserved in the archives of G. L. of Mass.), delivered at the service held in Boston in memory of the General two months after his decease. Whatever Masonic degree was conferred upon Washington in connection with this Bible, which was a strong tradition handed down to Brothers Lacy, Child and Maxwell, of the old regiment, and which we do not attempt to cast aside, still following the march of events the honor could only have been conferred before the book came into possession of the regiment. Washington was made, passed, and raised at Fredericksburg, Va., 1752-3. Of this fact the records speak for themselves.

In 1782 territorial distinctions having been adopted for the Infantry, the 46th was named the "South Devonshire." In 1903, the Grand Master of New South Wales addressing Grand Lodge, said: "The earliest record of duly recognized Masonic work was in the year 1816, when the Lodge of Social and Military Virtues held meetings at Sydney, and that Lodge No. 227 was its sponsor for 'Australian Social 260,' granted by Ireland in 1820."

Immediately after the defeat at the Brandywine, the Light battalion won the distinction of the "Red Feathers" September 20th, 1777, by a night attack with the bayonet on a detachment of fifteen hundred men hidden in a forest under General Wayne, who had been ordered by Washington to attack any troops who might be found away from the main body. Major-General Grey was sent with a force of light infantry of the 46th and those of five regiments as a counter-blast, and he having detached the flints from the guns, approached Wayne's sleeping camp in silence in two divisions, and by the light of the camp fires made such havoc with the bayonet that those who escaped vowed vengeance, sending word that should they meet again no quarter would be given. The "Light Bobs" replied that to prevent others from suffering, they had stained their "Feathers Red," and throughout the war the light battalion was so distinguished, and later by Royal warrant, the 46th were permitted to wear a "Red Ball Tuft" in memory of bravery on that occasion. The following month, at the battle of Germantown, the men, under Wayne, seeing the light infantry, cried out, "Have at the bloodhounds, revenge Wayne's affair at Paoli."

Notwithstanding the excitement of war and hurried marches, the brethren met, and many fraternal visits were exchanged and kindness shown, even to prisoners between the contending forces. The late Bro. Charles E. Myers, in his records and writings of the G. L. of Pennsylvania, says: "In the Lodge during the turmoil of war, the Royalists and Federalists were wont to meet upon the Square, both sides meeting upon the Level."

The Marquis Duquesne, Governor General of New France, under whose regime Fort Duquesne (Pittsburg captured by the British November, 1758) was built, was a member of the Masonic Order.

The Lodge has in its archives a few of the old jewels, some of tin, very crude in workmanship, also the jewels of a past master and warden, together with a silver trowel, engraved with the donor's name and date, 1819, which are much esteemed. The Bible is still with the regiment, and in its new Lodge "Dominica" is preserved with care, while the Lodge of Antiquity has a fac-simile copy, with about thirty of the pages containing the written data of the West family, which have been photozincographed, with which is bound a paper written by Lieut.-Colonel Lacy, in which he endeavored to trace the history of the Bible, read by him before the Royal Gloucester Lodge, in Southampton, in 1870.

The Lodge holds an Annual Military Night on the 17th of March, in honor of its Irish origin, when our military brethren, both members and visitors, appear in the uniform of the corps to which they are or were attached, and the banquet hall fittingly decorated with banners, shields and arms, is alive with music, song and story, recalling to mind feats of daring and the fraternal actions of our military brethren of the past.

EARLY QUEBEC LODGES.

BY M. W. BRO. E. T. D. CHAMBERS,
P. G. M., Grand Lodge of Quebec.

ALBION LODGE No. 2.

The earliest written records of Albion Lodge known to be extant are to be found in a Minute Book still in its possession, the first entries in which were made at Woolwich, England, on the 9th of January, 1789. The temporary residence of the Lodge at Woolwich was due to the fact that it was attached for some time to the Fourth Battalion of the Royal Artillery. Less than two years after the dates of the early entries in the Minute Book in question the Lodge had held its first meeting in Quebec. This was on the 4th of November, 1790. It was not then known as Albion Lodge, however, its official designation at that time having been simply "No 9 E. R. (Ancients)". Not until 1814 was the Lodge known as Albion.

Under a charter for a Lodge in the Fourth Battalion of the Royal Artillery, then stationed in New York, to be known as No. 213 E. R. (Ancients), the Lodge first met in that city on the 3rd of July, 1781, and took part in the following year in the formation of the Provincial Grand Lodge for New York of the Ancients. The independence of the United States having been recognized by England in 1783, the Fourth Battalion of the Royal Artillery was removed from New York to Newfoundland, and thence to England. It must not, however, be supposed that what is now Albion Lodge had no earlier existence than that accorded by charter in New York to old 213. Long prior to the issue of the charter, "No. 9 E. R. (Ancients)" had been engaged in Masonic work. It was chartered as No. 11 on the 12th of June, 1752. To the English warrant of that date can Albion Lodge legitimately trace its lineage, though it passed into possession, in 1787, of what had hitherto been known as No. 213. The latter had practically worked without interruption, save such as was necessitated by the removal of the Battalion to which it was attached from place to place, while No. 9 had remained dormant since about 1760. For the privilege of working in future under the Warrant of No. 9, or Albion as it is now called, "No. 213," in accordance with the then prevailing practice under the Grand Lodge of England, paid five guineas to the Grand Charity. It was only under the English Union enumeration of 1814 that No. 9 of the Ancients became Albion Lodge No. 17 on the New Registry of the United Grand Lodge of England, and not till the 27th of January, 1829, that Albion became, by renewal warrant, a civilian Lodge. It continued its allegiance to the Grand Lodge of England until the formation of the Grand Lodge of Quebec, with which it affiliated by unanimous vote on the 27th of December, 1869.

Its old records furnish many interesting details of the late eighteenth and early nineteenth century history of Freemasonry.

For some time there was a Mark Mason Lodge in connection with old No. 9, and half a dozen large pages of the early Minute Book already described are filled with the marks of the different members of the Lodge and with the description of the same.

At a meeting held at the Royal Mortar at Woolwich on the 13th of November, 1789, a complaint was made that a certain Bro. had deserted the Regiment, and as there appeared to be no doubt as to the fact, he was at once excluded by unanimous consent and ordered to be reported to the Grand Lodge.

On the 27th of December, 1790, the first St. John's day spent by the Lodge in Quebec, the Brethren dined together and also sent a delegation to No. 214 (Now St. John's, No. 3), who returned the same compliment.

At first the Lodge met at the home of Bro. Ward; afterwards at Mr. Daly's, St. John street; then at the Cork Arms; later, in their Lodge room over the Artillery mess, and at a still later date, in the Dauphin barracks.

The quaintly worded minutes of St. John's day, 1791, record that:

"At one o'clock the Wor: Master call'd to order and open'd a Master's Lodge, when having sumptuously dined together, Bro. Burrell had the honour confer'd upon him of passing the chair and setting the Lodge to work in due form. Then the elected officers were regularly install'd with an Anthem and Homaged by the Brethren according to the Ancient custom. A deputation was sent to visit the Brethren of Lodges Nos. 40 and 214, to congratulate with them on the Joy of the Day, the Compliment being gratefully returned by the above Brethren."

The minutes of the 22nd of June, 1792, describe the installation of His Royal Highness, Prince Edward, as Grand Master of Ancient Masons in the Province of Lower Canada, and we are told that R. W. Bro. Alexander Wilson gave the necessary obligation to His Royal Highness. The Brethren then proceeded to the Recollet Church, which stood near the present site of the English Cathedral, where "a truly Masonic sermon was preached by the Rev. Bro. Keith, Grand Chaplain. After Divine service we accompanied the Grand Lodge to where we joined them. Took a respectful leave and returned to our respective Lodges. After dining sumptuously and a repast at half-past four o'clock, the Brethren of No. 9 went by desire of the Right Worshipful Grand Master and joined the Grand Lodge. The usual compliments were passed and returned, the Grand Lodge being closed. We returned to our Lodge room again, where we took regular refreshments till 10 o'clock."

Under date of the 17th of December, 1792, it is recorded that the Wor: Master proceeded to raise certain Brethren to the Degree of a Mark Mason.

A curious misunderstanding occurred in February, 1793, between the Lodge and His Royal Highness, the Duke of Kent, Grand Master, which is instructive as illustrating two important facts: First, that the Lodge was unwilling to admit material into the Lodge as ordinary members, of which it could not approve, even though recommended by the highest authority; and, second, that it was never the intention of the Duke of Kent to recommend such a line of action. The following extracts from Minutes in connection therewith speak for themselves.

"The persons recommended by His Royal Highness, Prince Edward, Grand Master of Ancient Masons for the province of Lower Canada, last regular lodge night, in obedience to our bylaws lay over on our books one month, and came forward by ballot this night: Drum Major Smith, rejected; Biggs, not finally decided; Barefield, rejected; McGinnis to be entered the ensuing Lodge night or before if it meets with the approbation of the body; Fraser found to be under mature age, did not come forward to a ballot."

The following letter was subsequently forwarded to Prince Edward: "We had the honour to explain our reasons for not initiating into the mysteries of Freemasonry part of the Candidates recommended to us by Your Royal Highness. Since which time we have been credibly informed they were all meant to perform as musicians at our grand ceremonies, which, of course, puts them in the same state with those made in December last, who were admitted without a ballot."

"With the utmost humility and respect we beg leave to express our regret in not understanding the intention of Your Royal Highness in this particular."

"We hope Your Royal Highness will not be offended at our close adherence to the laws we have bound ourselves to. At the same time we beg leave to answer you it is both our inclinations and wish to comply with your commands in receiving not only those who met with the approbation of our Body, but also all those that may receive Your Royal Highness' recommendation."

Appearing in the Minute Book after the above letter is the following entry:

"His Royal Highness, Prince Edward, Right Worshipful Grand Master, in open Grand Lodge, was pleased to signify to the Worshipful Master of Lodge No. 9, pro tempore, his entire approbation of the above letter, and at the same time signifies his wish that the same might be communicated to Lodge No. 9 on their first night of meeting."

In April, 1855, Albion Lodge donated the sum of ten pounds sterling for the benefit of widows and orphans of Brethren who fell in the Crimean War, and in 1862 the Grand Lodge of England, to which the lodge at that time owed obedience, issued a Centenary Jewel warrant to the Lodge, authorizing the members to wear a special centenary jewel, in celebration of the fact that the Lodge had experienced an existence of over a century.

On the 9th of January, 1880, Albion received a large accession of membership by the amalgamation with it of two Quebec Lodges, Harrington, No. 17, Q.R., formerly Independent Lodge, No. 237, I.R., and St. George's Lodge, No. 23, Q.R., formerly Quebec Garrison Lodge, No. 160, C.R.

Though ranking as No. 2 on the Grand Registry of Quebec, Albion wants but a few weeks of being the oldest Lodge in the jurisdiction. It has just cause to be proud, not only of its early association with the Craft in the Old Land as well as in the New, in New York and Newfoundland as well, but also of its loyalty and devotion to the Mother Grand Lodge of England, remaining of obedience to her until such time as Canadian Freemasonry shared in the constitutional self-government so graciously accorded to the Dominion in a political sense by the Mother Land, and now and for many years past contributing to the peace and harmony of the Masonic world, by its union with and obedience to the Grand Lodge of Quebec, and thus adopting the course so well known to be in harmony with the wishes and desires of the dear old Mother Grand Lodge herself.

Like the other Lodges of the Quebec and Three Rivers District, Albion has had its dark as well as it bright days.

The withdrawal of the British troops caused it quite a loss of membership, for it was always a favorite Lodge with the military.

To the Grand Lodge of Quebec it has furnished a number of its most useful and most devoted officers.

Some of the weaker Lodges of the District practically owe their very existence today to the sacrificing labors on their behalf of members of old Albion, who gave freely and ungrudgingly of their time and talents to the work and sustenance of these weaker sisters.

In recent years, prosperity has smiled upon the good old Lodge, the ability and zeal of its officers have been the pride of the District, and the veterans whose interest in its affairs is unflagging have good cause to be congratulated not only upon the present condition of No. 2, but also upon its prospects of continued pre-eminence in work, in peace and in harmony.

ST. JOHN'S LODGE No. 3.

The original Minutes of the establishment of St. John's Number 3 are still in possession of the Lodge, and as fresh and distinct as they were on the day they were written, over a century and a quarter ago. They bear no signature, but are doubtless in the handwriting of Brother Thompson, the first secretary.

Their introductory portion reads as follows:—

"Lodge of Emergency, Quebec, 30th May, 1788. Present B: Wm. Beatty, W.M., etc., etc.

"The W. Master intimated to the Brethren the cause of their being called together was at the request of Brother Archibald Ferguson, who then informed the Body the reason for his doing so, and opened the business of the day by laying before the Brethren the Warrant from the Ancient Grand Lodge of England, and the instruction that accompanied it; the W. Master then proceeded to close the Lodge under the sanction of the Dispensation, when the Body, agreeable to the instructions given, formed a Grand Lodge by virtue thereof.''

Brother Archibald Ferguson acted as Grand Master. "Grand Lodge being opened, the Grand Master ordered the Warrant to be read and all the intelligence the Grand Lodge had favored him with, and the instruments for the solemn constituting and installing the officers mentioned in the Warrant. The G. M. ordered the Master who acted under the Dispensation to perform the ceremony of installing the Master to act under the Warrant, when the D. G. M. (Brother Charles Chambers) took the chair the Worshipful Brother Archibald Ferguson was installed Master in the Grand Lodge in the name of Grand Master Antrim, Chas. Chambers, Senior Warden, and Samuel Casey, Junior Warden. This finished the business of the Grand Lodge, the G. L. proceeded to close with the usual solemnity and opened a Lodge in the third degree of Masonry, when all the necessary business was performed, the remaining part of the day was spent in harmony, to the general satisfaction of the whole, with every testimony of sincere and warm regard to the welfare and general good of the Antient Craft, and the greatest prosperity to the Antient Grand Lodge of England, and all those under her sanction, of which we have the honor to be a part."

The date of issue of the Warrant was the 22nd of October, 1787, as appears by the records of the Grand Lodge, in which the Lodge was recorded as No. 241. This number it retained until the union of the two formerly existing Fraternities of Masons on the 27th December, 1813, when it became No. 302. By the closing up and consequent alteration of numbers in the year 1832, it became No. 214. In the English enumeration of 1863, its last-mentioned number was changed to 182, and under this number it continued its allegiance to the Grand Lodge of England, until the formation of the independent Lodge of Quebec, with which it then threw in its lot.

After 65 years of honorable existence—or slightly more than midway between its organization and the date of the present sketch, it was found that the original

Warrant, bearing the honored name of "Antrim" as Grand Master, had "by time or accident" become defaced, and on due representation of the fact having been made to the Grand Lodge of England, and a Warrant of Confirmation applied for, Grand Master the Earl of Zetland was pleased to order the issue of the Warrant of Confirmation, under which the Lodge now meets and works. It is interesting to note that the then W. Master of St. John's, who with his officers applied for the Warrant of Confirmation was Brother Thomas Douglas Harington, afterwards Grand Master himself of the Grand Lodge of Canada, and who for many years during his residence in Quebec as Receiver-General, took a prominent part in the affairs of St. John's Lodge and indeed in those of Freemasonry in the ancient capital in general. The Senior Warden who joined in the petition was Dr. James A. Sewell, a son of Chief Justice Sewell, the great friend in Canada of the late Duke of Kent, and a man who played a prominent part in Canadian history.

One of the most interesting incidents in the history of St. John's Lodge was the part taken by it in the installation, as Provincial Grand Master, of His Royal Highness Prince Edward, Duke of Kent, who was at that time (June 22nd, 1792), in command of the 7th Royal Regiment of Fusiliers at Quebec. The old minute book already referred to, and which is at present open before the writer at the date just above mentioned, says of the installation ceremony: "The Body proceeded to Frank's Tavern or Freemason's Hall, in order to install His Royal Highness, Prince Edward, as Provincial Grand Master of Lower Canada, which ceremony being performed, a grand procession was formed in order to hear Divine Service at the Recollet Church. After Divine Service was over, returned in form to Frank's, and the Right Worshipful Grand Master closed and adjourned the Lodge till a quarter past four o'clock. At that time the R. W. G. M. opened an Entered Apprentices' Lodge. After drinking several Masonic Toasts, and our thanks returned in ample form, the R. W. G. M. was pleased to close the Grand Lodge and everybody returned to their proper Lodges. After spending the evening in social harmony attended by the Masonic Band, the W. M. No. 241 was pleased to close with the usual solemnities, and the Brethren departed in peace and harmony. Expenses £9 6s 1½d. Money collected."

St. John's Lodge carried no drones on its books in its early years. The W. M. on one occasion brought to the notice of the brethren the case of a member who had already missed two meetings in succession and failed to appear also on the following meeting. It was decided to serve the Brother in question with a special summons, and in case of non-attendance he was to be expelled.

On the 11th November, 1789, it was voted to send home the Grand Lodge report and dues, the latter amounting to ten shillings sterling, by the hands of Captain Watt of the Brig Hope. A year later the Lodge was notified that the Hope had been wrecked on the coast of Holland and that every soul perished.

In August 1792, two candidates were recommended by The Duke of Kent for membership in the Lodge and were duly initiated.

Brother Pennoyer, on one occasion, observed a person entering while the Lodge was at refreshments and taking his seat as a Brother. He moved "That he be examined regarding his pretentions... and on being examined was found not worthy of sitting in this Body, having pretended to be a member of No. 40 Nova Scotia. His name is James McDonnell, but as he could give no further satisfaction he was desired not to attempt the like in future."

Brother Alex. Galloway of the Royal Artillery, a member of Lodge 241, died on the 18th March, 1793, leaving a widow and two children in poor circumstances, "and without the means of interring him in a decent manner." When the case was brought to the notice of the Prince, he gave orders to the different Lodges to assemble for the funeral, declaring that he would be there himself and that there would be a band of music. He also urged that subscriptions should be taken up for the distressed family. After the funeral a vote of thanks was passed by Lodge 241 to "our royal and R. W. Grand Master for his personal attention and his distinguished affability in promoting the good of Masonry by ordering such a splendid interment to our late Brother Galloway."

The Lodge records furnish further proof of the deep interest taken in the Craft by His Royal Highness during his stay in Quebec. A report of a Committee of members of the Lodge written in 1806, states for instance that "a social intercourse of visitation" was recommended to them by His Royal Highness the Duke of Kent.

The Masonic charity of the brethren of old 241 even extended to their country's prisoners of war, and during the war of 1812-14 between the United States and Canada, they voted the sum of two pounds for the relief of a Brother who was an American prisoner of war in the Quebec jail, and whose needs had been represented to them.

Persistent drunkenness was punished by the Lodge in those days by expulsion, while profanity, like non-attendance at Lodge meetings, called for the payment of fines.

On several occasions the Lodge attended the Duke of Kent, at his request, during his Grand Mastership, and the minutes of the celebration of St. John's Day, 1792, show that the brethren went with the Grand Master to church to hear Divine service, which was performed by Brother Wetherall, Grand Chaplain, and then at 7 o'clock met him again for the installation of officers, after which "His Royal Highness," says the minutes, "was pleased to enjoy in company several Masonic songs and toasts selected for the occasion," the day having been spent "with that harmony and conviviality so conspicuous among the ancient Craft."

Many of the leading citizens of Quebec during the last century and a quarter were members of St. John's Lodge, as it is now called, and many other leading Masons of the same period, besides the Duke of Kent, have closely identified themselves with the members and the meetings of this time-honored Lodge.

Two prominent members of St. John's Lodge, namely H. P. Leggatt, Past Master, and George Veasey, Treasurer, were among those who signed the call for the convention which met in Montreal on the 20th of November, 1869, to establish the Grand Lodge of Quebec. It was another distinguished Past Master of the Lodge, in the person of Brother James Dunbar, who presided at the convention in question, and who became the second Grand Master of the newly formed jurisdiction.

During a portion of the last decades of the nineteenth century a period of depression, almost amounting, for a time, to stagnation, was experienced by St. John's Lodge, but such a revival of prosperity has marked its more modern history, such ability and zeal have distinguished its management and work, and such a series of brilliant successes has attended the administration of its affairs by those who have presided over its destinies for several years past, that it may be truthfully said that its high rank as No. 3 upon the Grand Registry of Quebec is justified, not only by the age of its Character, but also by the efficiency of its work and its devotion and zeal to the principles and teachings of the Craft.

ST. ANDREW'S LODGE No. 6.

St. Andrew's Lodge No. 2, Quebec, which was attached to the famous 78th Regiment of Highlanders in 1760, then in garrison in the Ancient Capital, is supposed by M. W. Brother Graham to have had a continued existence, some years later, with change of allegiance, as "St. Andrew's Scotch Lodge," No. 349, R.S., working under a Warrant granted by the Grand Lodge of Scotland, and dated the 2nd of August, 1819. The above supposition led Brother Graham to remark that "further researches 'may show' that St. Andrew's Lodge No. 6, Q.R., is of actual descent from the St. Andrew's Lodge No. 2, Quebec, 1760, attached to the famous 78th." Unfortunately for what would undoubtedly have been a source of much pride of pedigree to the members of No. 6, G.R.Q., there is nothing to establish any such connection. It is only necessary to compare the date of St. Andrew's of 1819 with that of the origin of the present St. Andrew's No. 6, in order to prove its absolute impossibility. The present St. Andrew's received its Warrant on the 29th April, 1816, from the Grand Lodge of Lower Canada, under the Jurisdiction of the Antient Grand Lodge, or Antient York Masons of England. This Warrant was for the holding of Lodge No. 22, afterwards known as Sussex Lodge. So that St. Andrew's No. 6, was really in existence, under another name, three years before St. Andrew's Scotch Lodge of 1819 origin.

Sussex Lodge, as the present St. Andrew's was at first called, received a Warrant of Confirmation in June, 1825, on due petition therefor, from the United Grand Lodge of England, through the Provincial Grand Lodge of Quebec and Three Rivers, under which it worked as 1801 and afterwards as No. 531, when on the 9th of May, 1849, the Lodge delivered up its Warrant from the United Grand Lodge of England to Sir Allan MacNab, Provincial Grand Master in Canada for the Grand Lodge of Scotland, and received in lieu thereof, a dispensation from the Grand Lodge of Scotland for Lodge St. Andrew, subsequently No. 356. The same W. M. Brother William Clark, who had ruled the Lodge as Sussex No. 531, G.R.E., and who presided as W. M. of such Lodge on the 10th April, 1849, opened his Lodge the following month as St. Andrew's, No. 356, G.R.S., and read the dispensation from Sir Allan MacNab, which was his Warrant for so doing. The minutes of the Lodge fail to show either when or why application was made by the members of the Sussex Lodge for a Scotch Warrant under the name of St. Andrew's, but it may have been brought about by a difficulty which seems to have existed about credit for dues. The following not over clearly expressed entry appears in the minutes of the meeting of the 11th July, 1848. "The quarterly return from the Grand Lodge of England having been received, up to the 1st March, 1848, after having perused the same, 'Sussex' still remains blank in regards their monies, in acknowledgment to their having sent home, on former occasions."

Sussex Lodge was so called after H. R. H. the Duke of Sussex, Grand Master from 1813 to 1842, of the United Grand Lodge of England, and it is understood that the beautiful old chairs used by the principal officers of the Lodge with backs formed of Masonic devices, were presented to it by His Royal Highness.

Another much prized relic of the Lodge's early days is an old snuff mull which was lost for a number of years and finally recovered in June, 1848, through the good offices of Albion Lodge. This action was so much appreciated that a resolution was moved and seconded by all the officers and brethren present to the effect "that the unqualified thanks of Sussex Lodge be given to Albion Lodge for the prompt and Masonic manner in which they responded to the request of Sussex Lodge regarding a snuff mull, and that a copy of the above resolve be transmitted to the Wor. Master of Albion Lodge, assuring him that the Sussex Lodge highly value this proof of the fraternal spirit of Albion Lodge."

There was some delay in receiving the Charter of St. Andrew's Lodge from Scotland, and there are letters in existence showing that direct charges of neglect of Masonic duty were in consequence laid against Sir Allan MacNab, the representative in Canada of that Grand Lodge.

By the removal of the 54th Regiment from Quebec to Kingston, in 1853, the Lodge was deprived of thirteen of its best members, and a resolution was passed expressive of regret at the parting. The thirteen brethren in question were also entertained at a farewell dinner.

The Degree of Past Master was quite commonly conferred in this Lodge upon brethren who had but just before taken the Master Mason's Degree, and frequent mention of the fact is made on the minutes.

Some of the entries in the various minute books of the Lodge are worthy of special mention. Thus in describing the calling off of the Lodge from labor to refreshment on St. John's day, 1849, the Secretary records as follows: The Junior Warden having erected his column, the Brethren refreshed themselves according to their several inclinations until 6 p.m., when they sat down to an excellent dinner, when, after having honored the day in the usual manner, also sending and receiving deputations of congratulations to and from the city Lodges of Albion and St. John's, the W. M. was pleased to close his Lodge in good time and with solemn prayer. The Brethren then departed to their respective homes well satisfied with Masonry, themselves and their entertainment.

In October, 1869, St. Andrew's Lodge co-operated in the formation of the Grand Lodge of Quebec, becoming No. 5 Q.R., in 1870, and No. 6, in 1876. Two of the Past Masters of the Lodge signed the call for the Convention at which the Grand Lodge was established, and one of them, R. W. Brother John Soles Bowen was elected the first Deputy Grand Master of the newly-formed Grand Lodge.

St. Andrew's has furnished two Grand Masters to the Grand Lodge of Quebec, the first Brother from the Quebec District to hold that office having been M. W. Brother James Dunbar, who presided over the convention at which the Grand Lodge was formed, and who was an honorary member of St. Andrew's Lodge. The Lodge has always been noted for the efficiency and zeal of its officers and members, and has furnished to the Grand Lodge some of its most active and most devoted members.

DORCHESTER LODGE No. 4.

Dorchester Lodge, No. 4, located at St. Johns on the Richelieu River, about 24 miles south of Montreal, is one of the historical Lodges of the Province of Quebec, and dates its institution to the year 1792. The conflagration of 1876, which destroyed the greater part of the business portion of the Town of St. Johns, swept away all the minute books and many rare records, documents and Masonic relics belonging to this old, historic and centenary Lodge, which for over one hundred years, with varying success, had strived and struggled on the banks of the "Richelieu," and was named in honor of Sir Guy Carleton, "Lord Dorchester," Governor of the Province from 1786 to 1796, and who was acting Grand Master of the Provincial Grand Lodge in 1785-1787.

The appellation of "Dorchester" likewise designated the Town of St. Johns at this time, in Bouchette's "Canadian Topography," 1815, it is referred to as the Town of Dorchester and Fort of St. Johns in the "Barony of Longueuil," in the Counties of Huntingdon and Kent. The town was also known as St. Johns-Dorchester, but in later years the latter part of the designation was dropped.

1790.—The earliest information is to be found in the minutes of No. 241, A.Y.M., in the city of Quebec, now called St. Johns Lodge, No. 3, Q.R., for at a meeting of the said No. 241 held at the Merchant's Coffee House at Quebec, November 3rd, 1790, a letter was read from Sergeant-Major Reid, of the 65th Regiment, and Master of Lodge No. 631, Irish Register, stating that a number of the inhabitants of St. Johns in this Province wished to get an "Ancient Warrant" from the Grand Lodge. It was resolved to forward the information and that No. 241 would recommend them.

1792.—The next record is of date March 14, 1792, and is also from the minutes of Lodge No. 241, wherein it is stated that "a letter was read from Mr. William Thompson endorsing another from Brother Thomas Franks, of St. Johns Fort, asking advice and assistance how he and other brethren could obtain a warrant. A brother, Patrick Conroy, being present, named the following brethren as officers, viz: Simon Zilotas Watson, Master; Thomas Franks, Senior, and James Bell, Junior Wardens.

It was agreed to lay the letter before Lodge No. 9 (now Albion No. 2) and Lodge No. 40 (then Merchants) and with their concurrence to petition H. R. H. Prince Edward after his installation as Grand Master, to grant the first warrant under his sanction to the brethren of St. Johns.

The petition was duly granted, but the desire of the brethren of St. Johns to receive the first warrant from Prince Edward was not realized, for the first charter was issued to the "Glengarry Lodge No. 1," 2nd Batt. Royal Canadians, the next to the "Royal Rose" Lodge, in the 7th foot at Richelieu (now Sorel), the third warrant, however, going to St. Johns under the nomenclature of "Dorchester" No. 3.

H. R. H. Prince Edward (created in 1799 Duke of Kent) father of Her late Most Gracious Majesty Queen Victoria, arrived at Quebec in March 1792 in command of the 7th Royal Regiment of Fusiliers. He immediately formed the Lodges then existing into the Provincial Grand Lodge of Lower Canada (Ancients) and was installed as Grand Master on the 22nd day of June, 1792.

The old warrant of Dorchester Lodge is still in existence and is at present in the custody of the Grand Lodge of England. It bears the signatures of "Edward," Grand Master; Alexander Willson, Deputy Grand Master; Jonas Watson, Senior Grand Warden; Thomas Ainslie, Junior Grand Warden; and James Davidson, Grand Secretary.

1793.—A record of this date states that Dorchester No. 3 purchased three Lodge chairs from Lodge No. 7 in the Six Regiment of Foot, which at this time was temporarily stationed at Fort St. John, but was ordered off to Europe, Great Britain having declared war against France.

Tradition connected these chairs with H. R. H. Prince Edward during his residence in Quebec, and they were much prized. Unfortunately they were destroyed in the disastrous fire previously mentioned.

1795.—R. W. Bro. Thos. B. Harris, Grand Secretary of the Grand Lodge of Canada, in 1859 endorsed the following on the Warrant of Dorchester Lodge:

"It appears from a minute book now in possession of this Lodge that No. 3, A.Y.M., was regularly working in St. Johns, Dorchester, as early as the 2nd of July, A. L. 5795, and continued to meet up to the year A. L. 5818, when its officers were regularly installed. From which date no minutes transpire until revived under Dispensation on the 4th day of April, A. L. 5843."

1815.—In connection with the above record a Lodge certificate still in existence bears the following: "And God said, 'Let there be Light'." We, the Master and Wardens of Dorchester Lodge, No. 3, A. Y. M., held in the Town of Dorchester, in the Province of Lower Canada (now Quebec), under the patronage of His Royal Highness, the Duke of Kent, do hereby certify that the bearer, and beloved Brother, James Badger, who has signed his name in the margin, has been regularly entered, passed and raised to the sublime degree of a Master Mason in our said Lodge. His upright conduct during his residence among us induces us to recommend him in the strongest terms to all the Fraternity wheresoever convened or congregated round the Globe.

"Given under our hands and the seal of our Lodge at Dorchester, this 10th day of April, 1815, and in the year of Masonry, 5815, (Signed) Louis Marchand, Master; Thomas Goulden, Senior Warden; James Drennon, Junior Warden; Morey Bingham, Secretary."

1816.—The Parish Record Book of St. James Episcopal Church, St. Johns, contains the following entry:

"The corner-stone of St. James Church was laid in Dorchester, in the Province of Lower Canada, the 22nd day of July, A.D. 1816, and the 56th year of the reign of His Majesty George the 3rd, of the United Kingdom of Great Britain and Ireland, King, Defender of the Faith, by the Reverend Micajah Townsend, Minister of Caldwell and Christie Manor in the name of the Holy and undivided Trinity, and the event celebrated with Masonic honors by the members of Dorchester Lodge, No. 3, A. Y. M., acting under the Warrant of His Royal Highness the Duke of Kent, G.M."

1823.—The Province of Lower Canada (Quebec) was now divided into two separate Masonic districts under England, and called the District of Quebec and Three Rivers; and the District of Montreal and William Henry. In a Provincial list, of date 1824, Dorchester Lodge is numbered No. 1, and in 1848, No. 4.

1842.—In 1842 R. W. Bro. Ben. Burland was transferred from the "Customs" in Montreal to the Port of St. Johns, when he gathered the old members of "Dorchester," No. 3 together, and revived the Lodge, which had been for some time dormant, and sent a petition to the Grand Lodge of England, which now held jurisdiction in the Province, for a Charter. The Grand Lodge issued a Dispensation dated April 4th, 1843.

1846.—Of date August 1, 1846, Dorchester Lodge obtained a warrant numbered 775, E. R. The warrant had the signatures of "Zetland," the Grand Master, Worsley, D.G.M., and William H. White, Grand Secretary.

In this year the Lodges in Montreal together with Dorchester Lodge called a meeting and reorganized the District or Provincial Grand Lodge for the District of Montreal and William Henry, which had been for some years dormant.

1855.—The Grand Lodge of Canada, with jurisdiction over the Provinces of Upper and Lower Canada (now Ontario and Quebec) was formed on the 10th day of October, 1855, and Dorchester Lodge was represented and took part in the formation.

1859.—On petition Dorchester Lodge obtained a renewal Charter or Warrant of Confirmation from the Grand Lodge of Canada, dated August 1st, 1859.

1869.—The Majority of the Lodges in the Province of Quebec met and organized the Grand Lodge of Quebec. The members of Dorchester Lodge, however, declined to affiliate with it ,whereupon a number seceded and obtained a Warrant from the G. L. of Quebec on the 26th of September, 1872, under the name of "Burland."

1873.—For a number of years Dorchester Lodge was attached to the Bedford District under Canada, and at the Annual Communication this year, R. W. Bro. Geo. H. Wilkinson was elected as D.D.G.M. of the District.

1874.—On the 23rd of September, 1874, Dorchester Lodge, No. 4, Canada, affiliated with the Grand Lodge of Quebec, and ultimately became No. 4, under that G.R.

1876.—What is still called the great fire of St. Johns took place this year. The Masonic Hall was completely destroyed, and the Lodge lost all its old and valuable possessions and documents, many of them priceless.

1877.—Burland Lodge united with Dorchester Lodge on the 4th day of December.

1884.—At the Annual Communication of the Grand Lodge of Quebec in January, 1884, Dorchester Lodge was transferred to the Montreal District where it had been attached to the Provincial Grand Lodge thirty years previously.

1892.—July 20, 1892. The Centenary Anniversary of Dorchester Lodge was held this date. The Grand Master and many of his Grand Officers paid the Lodge a visit and participated in a most enjoyable excursion up the historic Richelieu River, or "River of the Iroquois," as it was called by the French settlers of New France, and the Lodge has since worn gold fringe on their aprons and collars as a centennial lodge.

A number of the past masters of this lodge have held rank in Grand Lodge. R. W. Bros. G. H. Wilkinson and George T. Morehouse, D.D.G.Ms; R. W. Bros. I. B. Futroye and E. R. Smith, Grand Registrars; Rev. Bros. Canon Renaud and the Rev. W. Windsor, Grand Chaplains; V.W. Bros. J. I. Phillips and W. J. Wright, Grand Directors of Ceremonies.

GOLDEN RULE LODGE, No. 5, Q.R.

Golden Rule Lodge, A. F. & A. M., located at the border town of Stanstead close to the line between the Province of Quebec and the State of Vermont, is one of the Centennial Lodges of Quebec. The Lodge possesses its original charter ordered issued by the Grand Lodge of Vermont, October, 1803. It was then named "Lively Stone" Lodge, and located on the boundary between the present villages of Rock Island, Quebec, and Derby Line, Vermont. Their first hall was destroyed by fire, the second was situated on the boundary line with entrances from the Canadian and Vermont sides.

The War of 1812 between England and the United States cause a re-adjustment of this friendly intercourse, and it was decided by the Canadian Brethren, who were in the majority, that it would be better to open in the village of Stanstead, a few miles from the border on Canadian territory, in order to allay the suspicions of the civil authorities, and application was made to the Grand Lodge at Quebec. A warrant was granted under the name of "Golden Rule" Lodge No. 19, December 27th, 1813, and signed by the Hon. Claude Denechau, Grand Master. Twenty-two names were on the petition, two of them being also the charter members of the original "Lively Stone" Lodge, and they were duly instituted January 18th, 1814.

The Grand Lodge at Quebec becoming somewhat dormant, 1820 to 1823, a number of the Lodges exchanged their Canadian Warrants with the newly amalgamated "United Grand Lodge of England" for English charters, and Golden Rule Lodge among the number, obtaining Warrant No. 517, E.R., of date April 26th, 1824, signed by the "Duke of Sussex," Grand Master. The majority of the Quebec Lodges thus coming under control of the Grand Lodge of England, the province was divided into two Provincial or District Grand Lodges and designated "Quebec and Three Rivers" and "Montreal and William Henry."

Golden Rule came under the rule of the latter Provincial Grand Lodge, and its charter was endorsed by the Hon. Peter McGill, the Provincial Grand Master, at Montreal, March 24th, 1847.

In 1856 the Brethren in the Provinces of Canada East and Canada West (now Quebec and Ontario) formed a Grand Lodge for both the Canadas, and Golden Rule Lodge threw in its lot with the new Grand Body and received Warrant No. 8 from the Grand Lodge of Canada, and signed by Wm. Mercer Wilson, Grand Master, of date April 30th, 1856.

In 1857 it received permission to hold a Lodge once in every year on the top of "Owl's Head" Mountain, 2,400 feet high, on the shores of Lake Memphremagog, which can be seen from their present Lodge room. Many notable Lodge meetings have since then been held in accordance with this authority.

On the 20th October, 1869, Golden Rule co-operated in the formation of the Grand Lodge of Quebec, and has been an ardent supporter of that Grand Body since that date. Under their Warrant Golden Rule Lodge claimed authority, as a number of others in the early days did, to work other than the Craft degrees, and their records show that the Mark Degree was conferred in 1817, 1818 and 1819, and that on the 22nd April, 1821, they organized a Chapter of Royal Arch Masons under the name of St. John's Chapter.

On the 21st May, 1861, the Grand Lodge of Vermont generously handed to Golden Rule Lodge the original charter of "Lively Stone Lodge," by which they were designated and held Lodge at Derby Line, Vermont, previous to 1812. In April, 1903, Gold Rule Lodge submitted proofs of their existence for 100 years and received authority as a Centennial Lodge to wear gold lace on their Regalia and celebrate their Centenary. This was accordingly held on June 24th, 1903. The Grand Master of the Grand Lodge, M. Wor. Bro. J. B. Tresidder and most of his Grand Lodge officers attending. The Master of the year was R. W. Bro. A. N. Thompson, and all the chairs were filled by Past Masters R. W. Bros. H. E. Channell, W. M. Pike, R. C. Parsons and E. W. Morrill. Chairmen of the various committees arranged a most entertaining programme. The three neighboring villages of Rock Island, Derby Line and Stanstead being "en fete" and gaily decorated for the occasion, a large concourse of Brethren from both the Province of Quebec and the State of Vermont joined in the festivities. The Grand Master of the Grand Lodge of Vermont, M. W. Bro. O. W. Daly, with many of his Grand Officers, joining with the Grand Master of Quebec and his suite. The Lodge has had a most interesting history, and by authority given them by the Grand Lodge of Vermont, has concurrent jurisdiction across the border in the Vermont village of Derby Line.

THE GRAND LODGE OF NEW BRUNSWICK.

BY THOMAS WALKER, M.D., 33°

P. G. M., Grand Lodge of New Brunswick.

THE history of Freemasonry in New Brunswick may be said to have commenced the 7th November, 1783, when Jared Betts wrote from St. Ann's, N.S., now Fredericton, the capital of New Brunswick, to Joseph Peters, Secretary of the Masters Lodge No. 211, Halifax, to know if he could proceed under a warrant which he held granted by Dermott who is described as the Grand Master of Ireland. The authority to this warrant was denied and a dispensation was actually issued from the two warranted lodges, Nos. 155 and 211, then existing at Halifax. On August 22nd, 1792, a warrant was granted by the Provincial Grand Lodge at Halifax, to Ephraim Betts and others, at St. Ann's, for Solomons Lodge, No. 22—now No. 6, Registry of New Brunswick. New Brunswick was made a separate province in 1784, and the first Lodge instituted there September 7th, 1784, was Hiram Lodge. The second Lodge instituted was St. George Lodge, Maugerville, in 1788. The third Lodge, New Brunswick, was instituted at Fredericton in 1789.

In 1795 Hiram Lodge "rebelled" against the authority of the Provincial Grand Lodge, at Halifax, by which it had been warranted as No. 17. On September 7th, 1796, its warrant was withdrawn by the Provincial Grand Lodge, and all its members, twenty-two in number, were "expelled for apostacy," etc. There were so far as can be ascertained 5 lodges in New Brunswick contemporary with Hiram Lodge, viz., New Brunswick No. 541 at Fredericton; St. George No. 19 at Maugerville, 1788; Zion No. 29 at Kingston, Kings Co., N.B., 1792; Solomon's No. 22 at Fredericton, 1792; Hiram York No. 23, at Fredericton, 1793. The first of these lodges was chartered by the Grand Lodge of England, and the others by the Provincial Grand Lodge of Nova Scotia; all of these ceased to exist many years ago. Of the lodges existing at present in New Brunswick, St. Johns Lodge No. 2 is the oldest, and was constituted April 5th, 1802, under a warrant issued by the Provincial Grand Lodge of Nova Scotia. The ceremony was performed by the R. W. Brother William Campbell, Deputy Provincial Grand Master at St. John.

While it is undoubtedly a fact that steps were taken towards the formation of a Grand Lodge as early as the year 1829, and the Rev. Benjamin Gerrish Gray, D.D., Rector of Trinity Church, actually elected as Grand Master, no further proceedings were taken, and the Grand Lodge so attempted to be formed, apparently died a natural death.

In the year 1867, however, after the confederation of the various Provinces of Canada, there was a meeting of the Masters and Past Masters of Lodges held in the City of St. John on 16th August, 1867, looking to the formation of a Grand Lodge. There were present representatives from Albion Lodge, St. John's Lodge, Carleton Union Lodge of Portland, New Brunswick Lodge, Hibernia Lodge and Leinster Lodge. It was resolved at this meeting to address a circular to all the lodges in New Brunswick under the jurisdiction of England, Ireland and Scotland stating that this meeting deemed it desirable that a convention be held to consider the present position of Masonic affairs in the Province, and to take such action thereon as may be deemed necessary. The lodges so addressed to be requested to authorize their Masters, Past Masters and Wardens to meet in such convention. Pursuant to this resolution a meeting was held in the City of St. John on the 9th and 10th of October, 1867. There were present representatives from Albion Lodge, St. John's Lodge, Solomons Lodge, Carleton Union Lodge, Midian Lodge, Union Lodge of Portland, Woodstock Lodge, St. George Lodge, Alley Lodge, Howard Lodge,

Northumberland Lodge, Miramichi Lodge, Zetland Lodge, New Brunswick Lodge, Hibernia Lodge, Sussex Lodge, Leinster Lodge, St. Andrew's Lodge, and Lodge St. Andrew. Worshipful Bro. B. Lester Peters, P.M., of Albion Lodge, was called to the chair and W. Bro. Wedderburn, P.M., of St. John's Lodge, was requested to act as Secretary. At this meeting it was resolved to form a Grand Lodge of New Brunswick. The delegates from St. Andrew's Lodge asked and obtained permission to retire from the convention, and the delegates from Howard and Zetland Lodges stated that though personally in favor of the resolution they had no authority to record a vote for their respective lodges. The remainder of the lodges unanimously voted in favor of forming a Grand Lodge of New Brunswick. R. W. Bro. Robert T. Clinch was unanimously, and by acclamation, elected M. W. Grand Master. Brother Clinch, however, while appreciating the compliment paid him, declined to accept the office on account of the official position he held as District Grand Master under the M. W. Grand Master of the Grand Lodge of England, and which he had not resigned. In consequence thereof, Worshipful Brother B. Lester Peters was unanimously elected in his place as the first M. W. Grand Master of the Grand Lodge of New Brunswick, together with the following: William Wedderburn, Deputy Grand Master; Hon. William Flewelling, Senior Grand Warden; David Brown, Junior Grand Warden; Rev. William Donald, D.D., Grand Chaplain; and William H. A. Keans, Grand Treasurer; William F. Bunting, Grand Secretary.

On January 22nd, 1868, the Grand Master elect and the other grand officers were duly installed "in the presence of a large and influential gathering of the Craft," of the Registries of England, Ireland and Scotland, "from all parts of the Province," by Worshipful Brother John Willis, Past Master of Hibernia Lodge, and the Senior Past Master of the jurisdiction. The Grand Lodge was thereupon "consecrated and dedicated."

A resolution was adopted proffering equal privileges to all outstanding lodges in the Province, which should adhere to the Grand Lodge of New Brunswick, on or before the 31st day of March following; and that any lodge not of allegiance to Grand Lodge, on or before the 31st of May succeeding, should be dealt with by the Grand Master as he may in his wisdom and discretion determine, until the next communication of Grand Lodge. Ultimately all the lodges in New Brunswick came under the authority of the Grand Lodge and received new warrants.

The V. W. Grand Secretary reported that, immediately after appointment to the responsible office he had the honor to fill, he, with the concurrence of the M. W. Grand Master, addressed a printed note to the Grand Secretaries of the respective Grand Lodges of Canada, the United States and elsewhere, asking to be furnished with copies of their constitution and regulations.

It gave him much pleasure to inform the Grand Lodge that his note met with a willing and hearty response from nearly every jurisdiction addressed.

On motion of the V. W. Grand Secretary, seconded by the W. Assistant Grand Director of Ceremonies, it was

"Unanimously Resolved, That the thanks of the Grand Lodge of New Brunswick be extended to the Grand Secretaries of the respective Grand Lodges for their brotherly courtesy."

The Centennial of the Introduction of Freemasonry into New Brunswick was celebrated July 1st, 1884, and consisted of an imposing procession formed by different Masonic bodies in the City of St. John and the Province of New Brunswick. About 500 Freemasons, accompanied by seven bands of music, appeared in the ranks. The procession marched through the principal streets and passed the location of the first lodge in the city, which was on Britain Street near Charlotte, thence to the Mechanics' Institute where interesting services were held, consisting of an address by M. W. Grand Master John Valentine Ellis, in which he detailed the history of the Craft in the Province of New Brunswick up to that time. He also referred to it in his address at the 18th Annual Communication of the Grand Lodge of New Brunswick, held at the Masonic Temple, St. John, on the 28th day of April, A. L. 5885, as follows:

> "The most interesting local event of the year was the celebration on 1st July last of the Centenary of the introduction of Freemasonry into New Brunswick. The arrangements were under the directions of a committee of the Masonic organizations in St. John, and the whole of the proceedings interested not only the fraternity but the public generally. I deemed the matter of sufficient importance to justify the calling of an Emergent Communication; and Grand Lodge had the satisfaction of having present a large representation of the Craft in the Province, and the pleasure of receiving a visit from the Grand Master of Nova Scotia, M. W. Bro. Lieut.-General J. Wimburn Laurie, R. W. Bro. William Taylor, Past Grand Master and our representative in the sister Province, with other Brethren from Nova Scotia, and many whom it was a pleasure to greet from the neighboring State of Maine. A Memorial Medal in commemoration of the event was struck by the Centenary Committee, and, with the concurrence of the Board of General Purposes, I gave permission for the Medal to be worn as one of our Jewels, until Grand Lodge should take action in the matter. A permanent regulation thereon should be by constitutional enactment. It is a most agreeable reflection that our fraternity was able to command the services on such an occasion of so able and eloquent an orator as the V. W. and Reverend Bro. D. McRae, D.D., Past Grand Chaplain, whose masterly address can never be forgotten by those who heard it. In this brief reference I must not overlook the services of Bro. J. Macgregor Grant, who, as Mayor of the City, not only participated in the proceedings at the Mechanics' Institute, but extended generous and courteous hospitalities to representatives of Grand Lodge and to the eminent visiting Brethren."

R. W. Bro. B. Lester Peters, P.G.M., and Representative of the Grand Lodge of Nova Scotia, introduced M. W. Bro. Lieut.-General J. W. Laurie, Grand Master of Masons in Nova Scotia, and R. W. Bro. William Taylor, Past Grand Master of Nova Scotia, a Representative of this Grand Lodge at the Grand Lodge of Nova Scotia, both of whom were received with the Grand Honors.

M. W. Grand Master the Hon. John Valentine Ellis, on behalf of Grand Lodge, cordially welcomed these distinguished representative Masons to Grand Lodge on such an auspicious occasion, to which they both replied in fitting terms.*

On behalf of and of and in the name of the Centennial Committee the Grand Master invested both visitors with the Medal which had been struck in commemoration of the Centennial.

New Brunswick is divided into five Masonic districts, with a District Deputy Grand Master over each, viz.: No. 1, City and County of St. John and Counties of Kings and Queens; No. 2, Counties of Westmoreland and Albert; No. 3, Counties of Kent, Northumberland, Gloucester and Restigouche; No. 4, Counties of York (except the town of McAdam), Carleton, Victoria, Madawaska and Sunbury; No. 5, County of Charlotte and the town of McAdam.

The following is a list of lodges under the Grand Lodge of New Brunswick:

Albion Lodge No. 1, N.B.R., was organized September 5th, 1825, under a dispensation dated August 20th, 1825, issued by the Provincial Grand Lodge of Nova Scotia. It was formally constituted under its warrant dated January 23rd, 1826, by R. W. Bro. Benjamin L. Peters, Deputy Grand Master.

St. John's Lodge No. 2, constituted April 5th, 1802, in the Mallard House, King Street, under virtue of a warrant issued by the Provincial Grand Lodge of Nova Scotia.

Hibernian Lodge No. 3, St. John, originally constituted under warrant No. 30; was granted by the Masonic Grand Lodge of Ireland.

*M. W. Bro. John Valentine Ellis passed peacefully to rest on the 10th of July, 1913. Bro. Ellis was brought to light in the lodge of Social and Military Virtues, Montreal, now the Lodge of Antiquity, No. 1 on the Register of Quebec. Removing to St. John, he affiliated with Hibernia lodge. From that he demitted, and affiliated with Carleton Lodge, then on the English registry. There his abilities soon became apparent. He was several times Master of that Lodge, and as such was one of the active founders of the Grand Lodge of New Brunswick, which he served as Grand Master for six years. "The history of his Grand Lodge career is the history of the Grand Lodge of New Brunswick." Bro. Ellis was a man of commanding ability and untiring energy. He was active in all branches of Masonry. His loss to New Brunswick is irreparable, and will be deeply mourned not only throughout Canada but beyond its borders.

Sussex Lodge No. 4, Dorchester, first opened under a dispensation issued at Halifax, N.S., 1st April, 1840, by R. W. Bro. the Hon. Alex. Keith, Prov. Grand Master.

St. Mark's Lodge No. 5, St. Andrew's, constituted 5th November, 1845, under a warrant granted by the authority of the Grand Lodge of England.

Solomons Lodge No. 6, Fredericton, united in 1879 with St. Andrew's Lodge No. 29, and forms what now constitutes Hiram Lodge No. 6.

Sussex Lodge No. 7, St. Stephen, was originally constituted April 29th, 1846, under a warrant from the Grand Masonic Lodge of Ireland.

Carleton Union Lodge No. 8, St. John West, constituted under a warrant granted 21st March, 1846, under the authority and sanction of the United Grand Lodge of England.

Midian Lodge No. 9, Clifton, Kings Co., now dormant, was constituted January 26th, 1847, under a warrant granted 18th May, 1846, by the United Grand Lodge of England.

The Union Lodge of Portland No. 10, St. John, was constituted under a warrant granted November 3rd, 1846, under the authority and sanction of the United Grand Lodge of England.

Woodstock Lodge No. 11, Woodstock, was originally opened August, 1847, under a dispensation from R. W. Bro. the Hon. Alex. Keith, Prov. Grand Master, and subsequently in the month of August, 1848, under authority and sanction of the United Grand Lodge of England.

St. George Lodge No. 12, St. George, Charlotte Co., N.B., was constituted 27th February, 1855, under a warrant from the United Grand Lodge of England.

Corinthian Lodge No. 13, Hampton, was constituted 11th November, 1854, under a warrant granted 11th July, 1854, by the United Grand Lodge of England.

This lodge first met in Norton, as set forth in the warrant. After meeting there in 1857, a removal was made to the village of Hampton, and again in September, 1872, it changed its quarters to Hampton Station, where it continues to meet.

Alley Lodge No. 14, Upper Mills, St. Stephen, was first opened August 5th, 1855, under a dispensation issued by R. W. Bro. Hon. Alex. Keith; was formally constituted 10th July, 1856, under a warrant dated 26th February, 1856, granted under the sanction and authority of United Grand Lodge of England.

Howard Lodge No. 15, Hillsborough, Albert Co., was first opened 12th April, 1855, by virtue of a dispensation issued 31st March, 1855, by R. W. Bro. Alex. Keith, and afterwards formally constituted by R. W. Bro. James Robertson under a warrant granted 4th April, under sanction and authority of United Grand Lodge of England.

Lodge St. Andrew's No. 16, Richibucto, was constituted February 7th, 1856, under a dispensation issued by R. W. Bro. Hon. Alex. Keith. It was formally constituted 4th March, 1858, under a warrant dated 2nd February, 1857, by the authority and sanction of the Grand Lodge of Scotland.

Northumberland Lodge No. 17, Newcastle, was opened 10th March, 1857, by virtue of a dispensation by R. W. Bro. Balloch, Dep. Prov. Grand Master of New Brunswick, and was formally constituted 11th August, 1857, under a warrant issued by the United Grand Lodge of England.

Miramichi Lodge No. 18, Chatham, N.B., was first opened 18th January, 1859, by a dispensation issued by R. W. Bro. Alex. Balloch, and was formally constituted 6th July, 1859, under a warrant granted 23rd January, 1859, by the sanction and authority of the United Grand Lodge of England.

Leinster Lodge No. 19, St. John, now defunct, was opened under a warrant granted 7th October, 1859, by the M. Gr. L. of Ireland, Duke of Leinster being Grand Master.

Salisbury Lodge No. 20, Salisbury, opened 3rd August, 1858, under dispensation issued by R. W. Bro. Alex. Balloch, and formally constituted 5th June, 1860, by virtue of a warrant granted 7th February, 1860, under sanction and authority of the United Grand Lodge of England.

Zion Lodge No. 21, Sussex, Kings Co., N.B., was first opened 10th April, 1863, by virtue of a dispensation issued by R. W. Bro. Alex. Balloch, and formally constituted 25th November, 1862, by R. W. Bro. Robert Thomson Clinch, Dep. Prov. Grand Master, under warrant granted 30th April, 1863, by the authority and sanction of the United Grand Lodge of England.

New Brunswick Lodge No. 22, St. John, was erected by R. W. Bro. Robt. T. Clinch under a warrant granted by the authority and sanction of the United Grand Lodge of England.

Keith Lodge No. 23, Moncton, was erected 27th January, 1853, by virtue of a dispensation of R. W. Bro. Alex. Keith, Prov. Grand Master of N. S. and N. B., under a warrant granted in February, 1855, by the authority of the United Grand Lodge of England.

Zetland Lodge No. 24, Shediac, was constituted in February, 1861, by a dispensation issued by R. W. Bro. A. Balloch, and formally constituted 20th March, 1862, by R. W. Bro. D. B. Stevens, Prov. S. G. W., under a warrant granted 30th October, 1861, by the authority of the United Grand Lodge of England.

Restigouche Lodge No. 25, Dalhousie, was erected 10th November, 1868, by M. W. G. M. in person, assisted by a staff of Grand Lodge officers, by virtue of a warrant dated 24th September, 1868, under the authority of the Grand Lodge of New Brunswick. This was the first lodge constituted under an original warrant issued by the Grand Lodge of New Brunswick.

Victoria Lodge No. 26, Milltown, N.B., was erected 18th January, 1870, under authority of a warrant granted under sanction and authority of Grand Lodge of New Brunswick.

St. John's Lodge No. 27, Bathurst, was constituted under warrant dated 5th February, 1861, granted by the Grand Lodge of Scotland.

Lebanon Lodge No. 28, Sackville, was constituted under a dispensation issued by M. W. Bro. Wm. Wedderburn, G.M., and formally constituted 28th November by G. M., under the sanction and authority of the Grand Lodge of New Brunswick.

St. Andrew's Lodge No. 29, Fredericton, which afterwards joined with Solomons Lodge and constituted Hiram Lodge, Fredericton, was constituted 14th July, 1858, under a warrant granted by the Grand Lodge of Scotland.

St. Martin's Lodge No. 30, St. Martin's, was opened 5th February, 1872, under a dispensation issued by M. W. Bro. Wm. Wedderburn, and was formally constituted under authority of a warrant issued by the Grand Lodge of New Brunswick, 25th September, 1872.

Benjamin Lodge No. 31, Andover, was constituted by virtue of a dispensation issued by M. W. Bro. R. T. Clinch, and formally constituted under authority of warrant issued by the Grand Lodge of New Brunswick.

Campbellton Lodge No. 32, Campbellton, began its existence under a dispensation issued by M. W. Bro. R. T. Clinch, and was formally constituted 21st September, 1877, by virtue of a warrant granted under sanction and authority of the Grand Lodge of New Brunswick.

Alexandria Lodge No. 33, was first opened 4th April, 1877, under a dispensation issued by M. W. Bro. R. T. Clinch, and formally constituted 28th February, 1878, under a warrant issued by Grand Lodge of New Brunswick.

Albert Lodge No. 34, was opened 23rd January, 1879, under a dispensation issued by M. W. Bro. Robt. Marshall, and formally constituted 17th January, 1879, by Grand Master, under sanction and authority of a warrant issued by the Grand Lodge of New Brunswick.

Carleton Lodge No. 35, Florenceville, was instituted by M. W. Bro. Thomas Walker, M.D., July 15th, 1898.

Ashlar Lodge No. 36, McAdam, was instituted by M. W. Bro. J. Gordon Forbes, November 15th, 1900.

Steven Lodge No. 37, Petitcodiac, was instituted by M. W. Bro. A. T. Trueman, May 13th, 1902.

Mananook Lodge No. 38, Grand Manan, was instituted by M. W. Bro. Edwin J. Everett, October 11th, 1905.

Colebrook Lodge No. 39, Grand Falls, was instituted by M. W. Bro. Edwin J. Everett, October 9th, 1906.

Bethel Lodge No. 40, Edmundston, was instituted by M. W. Bro. Henry S. Bridges, November 5th, 1909.

Tweedie Lodge No. 41, Moncton, was instituted by M. W. Bro. Henry S. Bridges, October 13th, 1911.

GRAND MASTERS.

Benjamin Lester Peters _____1867-68-69
William Wedderburn _____1870-71
John Valentine Ellis _____1872-73-74, 1884-85-86
Robert T. Clinch _____1875-76-77
Robert Marshall _____1878-79-80
Benjamin Stevenson _____1881-82
William F. Bunting _____1883
James McNichol Jr. _____1887-88
Thomas Walker, M.D. _____1889-90-91-92-93-94, 1897-98
J. G. Forbes _____1889-1900
Arthur T. Trueman _____1901-02-03
Edwin J. Everett _____1904-05-06
John S. De W. Chipman _____1907-08
Henry S. Bridges_____1909-10-11
Frederick J. G. Knowlton _____1912-13
H. V. B. Bridges, LL.D. _____1915

THE GRAND LODGE OF NOVA SCOTIA.

Compiled by OSBORNE SHEPPARD from the
writings of the late

M. W. BRO. WILLIAM ROSS (Senator)
Past Grand Master of the Grand Lodge of Nova Scotia.

THE earliest trace of Masons or Masonry on the American continent is afforded by a letter now in the archives of the New England Historic-Genealogical Society, written by Dr. Charles T. Jackson of Boston, a celebrated chemist and geologist. In his letter he says he discovered—whilst making a mineralogical survey of Nova Scotia—a stone on which had been roughly but deeply cut a square and compasses, and the figures 1606.

Thomas C. Haliburton, better known to Americans as "Sam Slick," was born in Windsor, Nova Scotia, in 1796. He became Chief Justice of Common Pleas in 1829, and Judge of the Supreme Court of Nova Scotia in 1840. In 1842 he removed to England, became a Member of Parliament, and died in office in 1865.

In 1829 he published a volume, entitled "Historical and Statistical Accounts of Nova Scotia." In Vol. II. of that work, pp. 155-157, he gives the following account of the stone described by Dr. Jackson:

"About six miles below the ferry is situated Goat Island, which separates the Annapolis Basin from that of Digby, and forms two entrances to the former; the western channel though narrow is deep, and generally preferred to others. A small peninsula extending from the Granville shore forms one of its sides. On this point of land the first piece of ground was cleared for cultivation in Nova Scotia, by the French. They were induced to make this selection on account of the beauty of its situation, the good anchorage opposite to it, the command which it gave them of the channel, and the facility it afforded of giving the earliest notice to the garrison at Port Royal of the entrance of an enemy into the Lower Basin. In the year 1827 the stone was discovered upon which they had engraved the date of their first cultivation of the soil, in memorial of their formal possession of the country. It is about two feet and a half long, and two feet broad, and of the same kind as that which forms the substratum of Granville Mountain. On the upper part are engraved the square and compass of the Free Mason, and in the centre, in large and deep Arabic figures, the date 1606. It does not appear to have been dressed by a mason, but the inscription has been cut on its natural surface. The stone itself has yielded to the power of the climate, and both the external front and the interior parts of the letters have alike suffered from exposure to the weather; the seams on the back part of it have opened, and from their capacity to hold water, and the operation of frost upon it when thus confined, it is probable in a few years it would have crumbled to pieces. The date is distinctly visible, and although the figure 0 is worn down to one-half of its original depth, and the upper part of the latter 6 nearly as much, yet no part of them is obliterated; they are plainly discernible to the eye, and easily traced by the finger. At a subsequent period, when the country was conquered by the English, some Scotch emigrants were sent out by Sir William Alexander, who erected a fort on the site of the French cornfields, previous to the treaty of St. Germain's. The remains of this fort may be traced with great ease; the old parade, the embankment and ditch have not been disturbed, and preserve their original form. It was occupied by the French for many years after the peace of 1632, and, near the eastern parapet, a large stone has been found, with the following monumental inscription: 'LEBEL, 1643'."

It is certain that the stone bears a date very near the earliest named by any authority for the settlement of that region, so celebrated by historians and poets. Aside from the fact that it affords the earliest footprint of Masonry upon the continent, the locality has other claims upon the attention of the Fraternity.

Sir William Alexander, of Menstrie, received charters for the whole of Nova Scotia, in 1621—1625—1628, and settled a Scotch colony at Port Royal, which his people, under David Kirk, captured in 1628 from the French. The son, Sir William Alexander, Jr., was left in command of the Colony. He remained until the peace of 1632 compelled him to return the possession to France, whereupon his son returned with most of his settlers to England.

Sir William, known as "Lord Alexander," was, July 3, 1634, admitted a Fellow of the Craft in the Edinburgh Lodge, and was one of the earliest gentlemen, or Speculative Masons, as we call them, on record in Scotland. It is not improbable that he was initiated by some of the brethren whom he found at Annapolis, and was afterward "admitted a Fellow of the Craft" at Edinburgh.

The records of the St. John's Grand Lodge, of Massachusetts, have the following entry under date of 1740:—

"Omitted in place That Our Rt Worshl Grand Master Mr Price Granted a Deputation at ye Petition of sundry Brethren, at Annapolis in Nova Scocia to hold a Lodge there, and Appointed Majr Erasms Jas. Philipps, D.G.M., who has since at ye request of sundry Brethren at Halifax, Granted a Constitution to hold a Lodge there, and appointed The Rt. Worshl. His Excellency Edwd. Cornwallis, Esqr., their First Master."

Erasmus James Philipps was made in "The First Lodge" of Free and Accepted Masons in Boston, New England, November 14, 1737. He was a nephew of Richard Philipps, Governor of Nova Scotia from 1719 until 1749. When Erasmus settled in Nova Scotia is uncertain. He was present at a meeting of the Governor's Council held in Annapolis on the 22nd of March, 1740. He is named, under date of September 4, 1740, as a member of a royal commission to settle the boundaries between the Province of Massachusetts Bay and the Colony of Rhode Island.

There is now in the archives of the Grand Lodge of Massachusetts a document, believed to be in the handwriting of Brother Philipps, of which the following is a copy:—

"Halifax the 12th June 1750.

"Sir:—At a meeting of true and Lawfull brothers and Master Masons Assembled at Halifax in order to Consult on proper measures for holding and Establishing a Lodge at this Place It was unanimously resolved on that a Petition should be sent to You who we are informed is Grand Master for the Province of Nova Scotia in Order to obtain Your Warrant or Deputation to hold and Establish a Lodge at this Place according to the Antient Laws & Customs of Masonry & that said Petition should be signed by any five of the Brethren then Assembled.

"We therefore the undernamed Subscribers pursuant to the above resolution do most humbly Crave and desire Your Warrant to hold and Establish a Lodge as aforesaid according to the Antient Laws and Customs of Masonry as practised among true and Lawfull Brethren and this we Crave with the utmost dispatch and beg leave to subscribe ourselves Your true and Loving Brethren.

"Copy P.
"Eras. Jas. Philipps,
"P. G. M."

" Ed. Cornwallis
" Wm. Steele
" Robert Campbell
" Willm. Nesbitt
" David Haldane."

Hon. Edward Cornwallis, son of Charles, the third Baron Cornwallis, was born in 1712—twin brother of Frederick, who was Archbishop of Canterbury, and uncle of Lord Cornwallis of Yorktown fame. He was gazetted as Governor of Nova Scotia, May 9, 1749. He sailed in the "Sphinx," sloop of war, May 14th, and arrived at Chebusto, now Halifax harbor, on the 21st of June. The settlers, 2576 in number, embarked some time after, and arrived off the harbor on the 27th of June, 1749.

Of the signers of the above petition, William Steele is described as a brewer and merchant. Robert Campbell and David Haldane were lieutenants in the army. William Nesbitt was one of the clerks of the governor.

The library of the Grand Lodge of Massachusetts contains a work, now very rarely to be found, entitled "Ahiman Rezon of the Grand Lodge of Nova Scotia." It opens with "A concise Account of the Rise and Progress of Free Masonry in Nova Scotia, from the first Settlement of it to this Time,"—1786.

"From Europe the Royal Art crossed the Atlantic with the first Emigrants and settled in various parts of America. It is said to have been known in Nova Scotia, while in the hands of the French. But however this may be, it is certain that as soon as the English took possession of it, they took care to encourage this charitable institution. They saw that it had a tendency to relieve distress and to promote good order. By this early attention to it, discovered in the first planters, it had the happiness to rise into repute with the rising Province, as the ivy climbs around the oak, contributing to its beauty, shade and magnificence.

"As early as the year 1750, which was as soon almost as there were any houses erected in Halifax, we find a number of the Brethren met together with Governor Cornwallis at their head, 'Deeming it,' as they expressed it, 'for the good of the fraternity that Masonry should be propagated in the province, and that there was a necessity of encouraging it in this place.'

"Erasmus James Philipps, Esq., of Annapolis Royal, was Provincial Grand Master at that time. And they agreed to petition him for a Warrant to hold a Lodge at Halifax, and that his Excellency might be Master of it. This warrant was received on the 19th of July; and on the same evening Lord Colvil and a number of Navy Gentlemen were entered Apprentices in this Lodge. It had also the honour of making many of the principal inhabitants and most of the Gentlemen holding considerable offices in the Province; and it was in this Lodge that our present Senior Grand Warden, the Right Worshipful and Honorable Richard Bulkeley, Esq., was made a Master Mason.

"Governor Cornwallis, indeed while he resided in the Province was Master of this Lodge, and governed it by a Deputy, according to the custom prevailing in Scotland. He was succeeded in the Government and in the Chair by Governor Lawrence, who enjoyed both till his death. . . . .

"On March the 18th, 1751, the second Lodge was formed at Halifax. On this occasion Brother Murray acted as Deputy Grand Master, and Brother Nesbitt, the late Attorney-General, as Senior Grand Warden, in installing the officers. . . .

"At this time our R. W. Brother Philipps probably acted only under a deputation: For we find a Grand Warrant dated seven years after this, from the Right Worshipful and Honorable William Stewart, Earl of Blessington, Grand Master of England, constituting Erasmus James Philipps, Esq., Provincial Grand Master of Nova Scotia, and of the territories thereunto belonging.

"Grand Master Philipps was succeeded in his high office by his Honour Jonathan Belcher, Esq., Lieutenant Governor of the Province. But the Province being in its infancy, and having to struggle with many difficulties unfavourable to the cultivation of the Arts, the Grand Warrant, after the death (1776) of the R. W. Brother Belcher, lay dormant for many years; a misfortune severely felt by the Craft."

What is called the "Deputation" under which Brother Philipps acted was issued by the Provincial Grand Master of Massachusetts, under authority of the "Modern" Grand Lodge of England. The Earl of Blessington was Grand Master of the "Ancients," and it is probable that the "Grand Warrant" named was thrust upon Brother Philipps by the recently organized Grand Lodge of "Ancients," without any request on his part, and probably never was used by him.

The Lord Colvill, who was "entered Apprentice" in the first lodge in Halifax, on the 19th of July, 1750, "on the same evening" when its "warrant" was received from Provincial Grand Master Philipps, was soon ordered to Boston, with the other "Navy Gentlemen." It appears by our records that he was "voted a member" of the "First Lodge in Boston on the 24th of October, 1750, raised in the Masters' Lodge November 2nd, and on the 11th of January following (1750 O.S.) he represented the "Second Lodge' 'in Grand Lodge, as Master. He was very constant in his attendance upon the meetings of all these bodies. On the 24th of June, 1752, he was appointed

Deputy Grand Master by Right Worshipful Thomas Oxnard, and held the Feast at the Grey Hound Tavern, in Roxbury.

This distinguished brother seems to have won the hearts of the profane, as well as of his brethren. On the 12th of May, 1752, the inhabitants of Boston, "in Publick Town Meeting Assembled at Faneuil Hall," passed a vote of thanks to him, as commander of His Majesty's Ship "Success," for "his Conduct and good Services," which had "given great satisfaction to the Town." At a meeting on the 22nd, the selectmen returned his answer, in which he declared himself "extreamly sensible of the Honour done him by the Metropolis of America," and expressed the hope that the Commissioners of Admiralty might at some future time return him "to a country which had already given him such marks of Esteem and Regard."

At the quarterly communication of the Grand Lodge, held on the 10th of July, Deputy Grand Master Colvill presided. On the 13th of October Grand Master Oxnard officiated, and

"Presented our Right Worshipfull Bro. McDaniel with the D. G. M.'s Jewell in the Room of our Right Worshipfull Bro. Lord Colvill, who has gone for England."

Before his departure he presented to the "Second Lodge" a copy of Field's Bible, printed in Cambridge, England, in 1683. When the "First and Second" lodges were united under the title of St. John's Lodge of Boston, this Bible became the property of that body, and is still carefully preserved in its archives.

EARLY NOVA SCOTIA LODGES.

Virgin Lodge commenced its meetings at Halifax on February 18th, 1782, under a dispensation by the two warranted lodges, 155 and 211, then at a lodge of quarterly communication held January 21st, 1782, and worked under such dispensation until October, A.D. 1784, when a warrant was granted to the body by the Grand Lodge of Nova Scotia (R. W. Bro. John George Pyke, Provincial

Grand Master) under the title of Artillery Lodge, No. 2, on the Registry of Nova Scotia, under which warrant the lodge continued working until September 22nd, 1800, when the body, by the permission of the Grand Lodge of Nova Scotia, resumed its original name of Virgin Lodge. In 1828 the warrants issued by the Provincial Grand Lodge of Nova Scotia established in September, 1784) were called in by H. R. H. the Duke of Sussex(then M. W. Grand Master of the United Grand Lodge of England; and the old warrant of 1784 having been given up in October, 1829, a new warrant was granted to the lodge by the Grand Lodge of England, under the title of Virgin Lodge, No. 829, on the Registry of England; and in October, 1833, the number of the lodge was changed by the Grand Lodge of England to No. 588; and in July, 1863, was again changed by the Grand Lodge of England to No. 396, R.E.

In the Archives of the Grand Lodge of Nova Scotia are copies of warrants from 1783 down to the present time with the respective names of the Grand Masters who followed each other on the roll of time. These ancient warrants on parchment, with their old-fashioned seals of wax, stamped into a leaden mould, tell the early history of many lodges now erased. From 1784 to 1820 there were 34 lodges under one Provincial Grand Lodge, proving the widespread hold that Freemasonry had in the early history of the province. Many of these lodges, from written files of letters cared for, contain facts of Masonic interest sufficient to form an historical paper in itself. Take for instance the most interesting and continuous Masonic history of any Lodge within this province, that of St. Andrew's Lodge, No. 1, one of the living Lodges that has continued without a break since its origin in March, 1768, and has never failed to meet on the first Tuesday of each month. St. John Lodge, chartered June 3rd, 1780, by the Duke of Atholl, then known as No. 161, but now as No. 2 in the register of the Grand Lodge of Nova Scotia.

From the formation of the Provincial Grand Lodge,

September 24th, 1784, there were continuous applications for charters to form lodges.

Temple Lodge No. 7, was chartered on the 11th day of October, 1784; Hiram Lodge No. 10, March 3rd, 1785, to meet at Shelburne; St. George's Lodge No. 11, November 22nd, 1784. We must mention that Annapolis Royal Lodge, now No. 33, was chartered 27th January, 1795, with Daniel Kendrick, M.D., W.M.; Francis Ryerson, S. W., and Robert Wolsley, J.W., to hold their Lodge meetings in the house of Brother Frederick Sinclair. Another Lodge was chartered in Sydney, C.B., 27th August, 1800, named Harmony Lodge—William McKinnon, W.M., William Cox, S.W., and George Moir, J.W.

On November 13th, 1758, Provincial Grand Master Jeremy Gridley, of Boston, granted a dispensation to R. W. Bro. Edward Huntingford to hold a Lodge in His Majesty's 28th Regiment, to be called Louisburg Lodge 28th Regt., so early did Masonry spring up in Cape Breton after the fall of Louisburg. This regiment was at Quebec with Wolfe the following year, under Colonel Richard Gridley, receiving a pension and a grant of land for his distinguished services at Quebec in 1759.

In 1808 Admiral Murray, of the White Squadron, was Master of St. Andrew's Lodge, No. 1. In 1813 thirty shillings was voted to George Grigason, an American prisoner of war at Dartmouth. In 1819, when Grand Master Pyke retired from that position he stated: "In having my conduct approved by the oldest Lodge of the Province, is truly gratifying to me."

May 22nd, 1820, St. Andrew's Lodge joined a procession to lay the corner stone of Dalhousie College, which ceremony was performed according to ancient custom and Masonic usage by the Earl of Dalhousie. On July 26th, 1825, this Lodge marched with Grand Lodge and Earl Dalhousie to break ground of the Shubenacadie Canal. This Lodge was permitted under all the changes to retain its original charter, and is in possession of many interesting relics, such as the punch bowl, so much admired on account of its age and interesting history, a gift from His Royal Highness the Duke of Kent, a chair, and other things of historic value.

An incident of importance connected with the Masonic acts of the Duke of Kent was that he laid the corner stone of Freemason's Hall in Halifax in 1800, and that stone bearing this inscription, is preserved in a glass case, and reads:

"In the name of God in the reign of George III, His Royal Highness Prince Edward, Duke of Kent, Commander in Chief of British North America, Grand Master of Lower Canada, in behalf of Richard Bulkeley, member of His Majesty's Council, Grand Master of Nova Scotia, laid the foundation stone of Freemasons' Hall, 5th June, A.D. 1800, and of Masonry 5800."

In 1813 the only Lodges carried forward on the Union Roll were Nos. 155 and 211 (now 1 and 2, N.S.), and the Prov. Grand Lodge continued to exist as before, electing its Grand Master yearly, paying tribute to none, and exacting the respect due to any independent Grand Lodge, until 1822, when its proceedings were styled irregular by the Grand Master of England. John Albro, the Prov. Grand Master at that time, was annually re-elected until 1829, when he received a Patent from England, and in the same year seventeen Lodges—Nos. 828-44—were removed from the local to the general list. Nineteen others were added to the English roll between 1840 and 1868. Scotland entered the field in 1827, and Ireland in 1845. From the latter country only two warrants were received, but under the former a Province was erected, by ten of whose daughter Lodges a Grand Lodge was established, June 21, 1866. This, on June 24, 1869, formed a Union of the Lodges then working in the province, under the Grand Lodges of England, Nova Scotia and Scotland, into one Supreme Grand Lodge—twenty-five Lodges on each side, and one Scottish one, or fifty-one in all, taking part in the regular organization of the Grand Lodge of Nova Scotia. A single (English) Lodge adhered to its original allegiance, of which the Grand

Master of Nova Scotia remarks (1880)—"working side by side with us, a healthy emulation is produced, and both parties are the better for it."

M. W. Bro. Duncan Cameron Frazer, Lieutenant-Governor of Nova Scotia, who was Grand Master in 1892-1893, died September 27th, 1910.

M. W. Bro. the Hon. William Ross, who was Grand Secretary from 1889 to 1900, and Grand Master in 1903, died at Ottawa, March 17th, 1912. He was beloved and honoured, not only by members of our Fraternity, but by all mankind. His loss to Nova Scotia is irreparable.

During the year 1914 the Grand Lodge suffered the loss by death of two Past Grand Masters. M. W. Bro. John W. Rhuland, who had attained the age of eighty years, died in Manitoba and was buried there. He was Grand Master in 1896. M. W. Bro. Thomas Trenaman, M.D., died in April, 1914. He was Grand Master in 1901.

On the roll are 75 Lodges, with a membership of over 7,000.

FREEMASONRY IN CAPE BRETON.
BY BRO. ANGUS G. McLEAN
Past D. D. Grand Master District No. 9 Nova Scotia.
Past Prov. Grand Prior of S. G. Priory of Canada.

ALTHOUGH forming part of the Province of Nova Scotia, we are separated from the Mainland by the Strait of Canso, which is about fifteen miles long, and less than a mile in width in some parts. Cape Breton is about 110 miles in length from North to South, and about 90 miles in width from East to West. It is the Easternmost part of the Dominion of Canada. It is divided into four Counties, viz.: Cape Breton, Inverness, Richmond and Victoria, and contains a population of 122,084. It is Masonically divided into two Districts:—No. 9 comprising the Counties of Inverness, Richmond and Victoria, and No. 10 the County of Cape Breton. These Districts are under the supervision of two District Deputy Grand Masters.

In the year 1786 the first lodge in Cape Breton was organized in Sydney, the Charter of which is now in possession of the Grand Lodge of Nova Scotia. The name of this Lodge was "Cape Breton," No. 16. The records of this Lodge from 1811 to 1826 are in possession of St. Andrew's Lodge No. 7, Sydney, and form most interesting reading. On the 27th of August, 1800, another Lodge, called "Harmony," No. 28, was organized in Sydney.

On the 24th of January, 1814, the W. M. of Cape Breton Lodge, No. 16, received information of the union of the two Grand Lodges of Ancient and Modern Masons of England. After the reading of the letter containing this information "the brethren responded with three cheers, with the honors of Masonry." The following officers were elected in 1814:—Bros. John Battersby, Robert McComb, Beth Welton, John Laraway and John Maloney. The descendants of some of these still reside in

Sydney. There is no record of any meeting of either Cape Breton or Harmony Lodges, from the end of 1814 to 1816. In 1818, "it was unanimously agreed by the members of Cape Breton Lodge, No. 16, that the members of Harmony Lodge, No. 28, be admitted as joining members of this body, under the regulations and agreeable to the resolution of October 7th, 1818." On the third Tuesday of November, 1818, Harmony Lodge, No. 28, joined Cape Breton Lodge, No. 16. After the year 1826 there is no record of any meeting of this Lodge having been held.

The next Lodge organized in Cape Breton was St. Andrew's, now No. 7, on the Registry of the Grand Lodge of Nova Scotia. The first meeting of which there is any record, was held in Sydney, December 19th, 1843. The following officers were present, viz.; *W. M.*, Bro. Rauna Cossit, P.M.; *S. W.*, Bro. M. Florian, P.M.; *J. W.*, Bro. Thos. Kirk, P.M.; *Secretary-Treasurer*, Bro. Charles Dodd, P.M.; *Tyler*, Bro. Howie, P.M.

Being all Past Masters it is presumed they had been members of Cape Breton Lodge, No. 16. The next communication of St. Andrew's Lodge was held on St. John's Day, December 27th, 1843. "The brethren sat down to a sumptuous repast." St. Andrew's Lodge was chartered on the 29th of August, 1844, by the Grand Lodge of England, of which Thomas Dundas, Earl of Zetland, was then Grand Master. It was numbered 732, and worked under this number until the 22nd of September, 1863, when the number was changed to 499.

Up to the year 1869, the different Lodges in the Province of Nova Scotia (including Cape Breton) received their Charters and were working under the Grand Lodges of England, Scotland and Ireland respectively. All these Lodges, with the exception of one Lodge in Halifax, agreed to form a Grand Lodge for the Province of Nova Scotia, and on the 24th day of June, 1869, the Grand Lodge of Nova Scotia was formed with fifty-one Subordinate Lodges. All these Lodges were at that time renumbered.

At the time of the formation of the Grand Lodge of Nova Scotia, there were six Subordinate Lodges in Cape Breton, as follows:—

St. Andrew's No. 7, Sydney, Chartered Aug. 29, 1844.
Royal Albert No. 19, North Sydney, Chartered March 13th, 1868.
St. Marks No. 35, Baddeck, Chartered March 20, 1866.
Thistle No. 36, Port Morien, Chartered April 26, 1866.
Tyrian Youth No. 45, Glace Bay, Chartered June, 1867.
Solomon No. 46, Port Hawkesbury, Chartered March 13th, 1868.

The following Lodges have been organized in Cape Breton since the formation of the Grand Lodge of Nova Scotia in 1869:—

Morian No. 55, Port Morien, Chartered Mar. 4th, 1870.
Richmond No. 64, Arichat, Chartered June 5th, 1872.
Sircom No. 66, Whycocomah, Chartered June 4, 1873.
Mariners No. 80, Louisburg, Chartered April 6th, 1892
Inverness No. 83, Inverness, Chartered June 9, 1904.
Sydney No. 84, Sydney, Chartered June 15th, 1905.
Royal Oak No. 85, Sydney Mines, Chartered June 12th, 1907.
Maple Leaf, New Waterford, Chartered June, 1912.

Morien Lodge, No. 55, Amalgamated with Thistle Lodge No. 36, in 1869. Richmond Lodge No. 64, ceased working and surrendered its Charter in June, 1891.

CAPITULAR MASONRY.

On the 5th day of June, 1877, Prince of Wales Chapter No. 10, R. N. S. Royal Arch Masons of Sydney was Chartered. Maple Leaf Chapter No. 15, R. N. S. Royal Arch Masons was instituted at Glace Bay July 13th, 1903.

KNIGHTS TEMPLAR.

Cape Breton Preceptory No. 43, G. R. C., was instituted at Sydney in 1905, Chartered August 9th, 1906.

THE GRAND LODGE OF PRINCE EDWARD ISLAND.

Compiled by OSBORNE SHEPPARD from Grand Lodge Records.

IN the year 1797 a number of Masons residing in the Island St. John (in 1798 the Legislature passed an Act changing the name of Prince Edward Island in honour of Duke of Kent), petitioned the "Provincial Grand Lodge of the Most Ancient and Honourable Fraternity of Free and Accepted Masons of the Province of Nova Scotia in North America," for a Warrant of Constitution. The petition was favorably received and a charter granted to St. John's Lodge, No. 26, on the 9th day of October, 1797, signed by Richard Bulkeley, Grand Master; Duncan Clark, Deputy Grand Master; James Clarke, Senior Grand Warden; John Bremner, Junior Grand Warden, and John Selby, Grand Secretary, to open a lodge at the house of Alexander Richardson, or elsewhere in Charlottetown, on the second Tuesday in each calendar month, and on all seasonable times and lawful occasions, appointing Ebenezer Nicholson, Worshipful Master; William Hillman, Senior Warden, and Robert Lee, Junior Warden. The then Lieutenant-Governor, Edmund Fanning, was a member of the Lodge, and on the 27th day of December, 1797, presented to it a copy of the Holy Bible, still a part of its furniture. After the union of the two Grand Lodges in England the Lodge was given a new number, 833, and continued as the sole Lodge in Prince Edward Island 'till 1827, when Sussex Lodge was created. It ceased work and was erased in 1837. In 1858 a new Lodge, Victoria, was organized under a Warrant of Constitution received from the Grand Lodge of Scotland. Later on the following Lodges were erected under authority of the Grand Lodge of England: King Hiram, St. Eleanors, 1858; St. George's, Georgetown, 1861; Mount Lebanon, Summerside, and Alexandra, Port Hill, 1863; Zetland, Alberton, 1867; True Brothers, Tyron, 1869.

PROVINCIAL DEPUTIES.

From 1797 to 1869 the Lodges holding under authority of the Grand Lodge of England were subject to the authority of the District Deputy Grand Master of Nova Scotia. In the latter year the Lodges in Nova Scotia erected an independent Grand Lodge, the then District Grand Master, the Honourable Alexander Keith, being elected its first Grand Master. He thereby vacated the office held by him under the Grand Lodge of England, leaving the fraternity in Prince Edward Island without a provincial head or one in authority to grant dispensations when required. The matter being brought to the notice of the Grand Lodge in England, the Right Honourable, the Marquis of Ripon, Grand Master of England, in January, 1871, appointed Right Worshipful Adam Murray, District Grand Master for Prince Edward Island.

GRAND LODGE OF PRINCE EDWARD ISLAND.

On the 23rd June, 1875, delegates, representing the eight Lodges in the province, met in Charlottetown, and organized the Grand Lodge of Prince Edward Island, and on St. John's Day (June 24th) the Honourable John V. Ellis, Grand Master of New Brunswick, assisted by his Grand Officers, installed the Honourable John Yeo as Grand Master, 1875 to 1880. The other Grand Officers being installed at the same time. Since that period the following have presided as Grand Masters, viz.: Neil MacKelvie, J. W. Morrison, D. Darrach, S. W. Crabbe, T. A. McLean, R. McNeil, M.D., J. L. Thompson, Leonard Morris, J. A. Messervey, R. MacMillan, John Muirhead, W. R. Ellis, Benjamin Rogers, Sr., Chas. H. S. Sterns, W. K. Rogers, D. F. MacDonald, W. P. Doull, W. S. Stewart, Judge H. C. MacDonald, Rev. T. F. Fullerton, and George S. Inman.

There are 15 Lodges, with a membership of 799.

Royal Arch Masonry is under the Grand Jurisdiction of Nova Scotia.

There is a Council of the Cryptic Rite under the Supreme Grand Council of the Maritime Provinces at Kensington.

The Order of the Temple was established through the efforts of Past Grand Master Dr. R. MacNeill. Prince Edward Preceptory, No. 35, being opened by R. Em. Sir Knight J. B. Nixon, of Toronto, with others, under Dispensation dated Nov. 12, 1895, receiving its Warrant of Constitution from the Great Priory of Canada, dated September 6th, A.D. 1896.

The A. & A. S. Rite was also introduced by Ill. Bro. R. MacNeill, 33°, who was appointed Deputy for the Province.

Albert Edward Lodge of Perfection was constituted by Ill. Bro. John A. Watson, 32°, of St. John, N.B., as Special Deputy, on the 23rd day of September, 1896, under Dispensation granted by M. Ill. Bro. J. W. Murton, 33°, Sovereign Grand Commander of the Supreme Council of the A. & A. S. Rite for the Dominion of Canada, dated August 10th, 1896.

A Chapter of Rose Croix was instituted in due course (May 19, 1898), followed in 1909 by a Consistory of the thirty-second degree, opened on the sixth day of July, under patent granted by Sovereign Grand Commander Hon. J. M. Gibson, 33°, dated April 12th, 1909.

THE GRAND LODGE OF MANITOBA.
BY JAMES A. OVAS, 33°
P. G. M., and Grand Secretary of the Grand Lodge of Manitoba.

THE first Lodge of Ancient, Free and Accepted Masons to organize in what is now the Province of Manitoba, was by authority of M. W. Bro. A. T. C. Pierson, Grand Master of the Grand Lodge of Minnesota, under a dispensation dated the thirteenth day of September, 1863, coming by way of Pembina, Dakota Territory, to Fort Garry (now Winnipeg), in what was then known as the Red River Settlement.

In his address to the Grand Lodge of Minnesota, at the eleventh Annual Communication, held at the City of St. Paul, on the twenty-seventh day of October, 1863, M. W. Bro. Pierson, Grand Master, says: "About the middle of last month I received an application signed by W. Bros. C. W. Nash, J. L. Armington, A. T. Chamblin, Charles H. Mix, and either others, who were en route for Pembina, Dakota Territory, for a Dispensation authorizing them to open and work a Lodge. Pembina is the most northern point in the territory of the United States, a great central point where concentrates a large amount of emigration, and of travel between the two oceans. The want of a Lodge at that place has been long felt and often expressed; and as the brethren named were active, well-informed and discreet Masons, the first two former Masters, and the latter Wardens of Lodges within this jurisdiction—and as they expected to remain in that region for at least two years, I granted a Dispensation to establish a Lodge at Pembina.

The Lodge held its first meeting about the middle of January, 1864, and during the few months it remained active in Pembina, several residents of Fort Garry and vicinity made application, were accepted and received the three degrees of Freemasonry, among whom were Bros. A. G. B. Bannatyne, W. B. Hall and William Inkster.

In the early part of 1864, application was made to M. W. Bro. Pierson, Grand Master, for a continuance of the Dispensation and for authority to transfer it to Fort Garry. This was granted, as in his address to the Grand Lodge at the twelfth Annual Communication, held in the City of St. Paul, on the twelfth day of October, 1864, the M. W., the Grand Master, reports as follows: "I also renewed the Dispensation of Northern Light Lodge, removing it to the Red River Settlement."

The first meeting of the Lodge in Fort Garry, was held on the eighth day of November, 1864, in a room over the trading house of Bro. A. G. B. Bannatyne, described by W. Bro. Schultz, in a letter to the Grand Lodge of Manitoba, in 1895, thus: "And a novelty it was indeed in this country at that time. It was spoken of far and wide, and the description, which did not decrease in detail, or increase in accuracy as to what was done therein, was listened to with much curiosity, and in some cases with awesome wonder which was enhanced by the jocoseness of Bro. Bannatyne's clerks, who spoke knowingly of the whereabouts and propulsive propensities of the goat, and who pointed out from the room below (to wit, the trading house) exactly in what part of the up-stairs room the W. M. hung his hat while the Lodge was at work. The lodge room itself was made as tasteful as the circumstances of that day would admit." etc. W. Bro. John Schultz, was the first W. Master; Bro. A. G. B. Bannatyne, Senior Warden; Bro. William Inkster, Junior Warden.

The three principal Officers mentioned above remained in their respective offices until the twenty-third day of December, 1867, when Bro. A. G. B. Bannatyne, was elected W. Master; Bro. Thomas Bunn, Senior Warden; Bro. John Bunn, Junior Warden, but am unable to find any record of their installation.

The Dispensation was continued year by year by the Grand Lodge of Minnesota, until the year 1867, when a Charter was granted with the No. 68, the Committee on Lodges, U.D., reporting as follows: "From Northern Light

Lodge, U.D., located at Fort Garry, no late returns or records have been received. In this the Committee deem it proper to present the following facts: Fort Garry is situated on the northern confines of the State, several hundred miles from St. Paul, and far outside of the usual mail or transportation facilities, the mails being carried at long intervals by dog trains, through the intervening wilderness, and often lost in transit. Transportation is mostly confined to the spring months. These facts may reasonably account for the non-representation and non-receipt of the records and receipts of the Lodge. The Lodge was originally organized under letter of Dispensation, granted in 1863, to our present M. W. Grand Master, and others, by G. M. Bro. A. T. C. Pierson, and has been continued by dispensation of successive Grand Masters to the present time, and it would seem that the time has arrived when the Lodge should be relieved from its anomalous position. The Committee have had the fullest assurance from responsible sources that the brethren comprising Northern Light Lodge, U.D., are men of excellent character, of good Masonic attainments, and of undoubted ability to carry on the work of the Order. After considering these facts they have arrived at the conclusion that it is wrong to make the remote position and consequent inability of these brethren to communicate with the Grand Lodge at its Annual Communication a reason for depriving them of the benefit of a Charter; and therefore recommend that a Charter be granted to them, to be issued as soon as they have made their returns to, and settled their accounts with, the Grand Secretary, to the satisfaction of the Grand Master."

The Lodge was never constituted under the Charter, as during the troublesome times of 1868-9 the members becoming scattered it eventually ceased to exist. In his address at the Annual Communication in 1869, M. W. Bro. C. W. Nash, Grand Master, makes the following reference: "The Lodges which were chartered at the last Grand Communication have all been properly constituted and the officers installed, either in person or by proxy, except Northern Light Lodge No. 68, at Fort Garry, British America. The charter of this Lodge remains in the possession of the Right Worshipful Grand Secretary. The great distance of Fort Garry from an organized Lodge has rendered it impracticable to constitute the Lodge and install its officers." R. W. Bro. William S. Combs, Grand Secretary, at the same session reports as follows: "The charter issued by the Grand Lodge, at its session in 1867, to Northern Light Lodge No. 68, has not been called for by the proper officers. I anticipate, however, that the same will be attended to very soon, as I have been in correspondence with the brethren at Fort Garry." Thus the pioneer Lodge of the great Canadian Northwest, after four years of activity, terminated its existence.

On the twenty-first day of November, 1870, a Dispensation was issued by M. W. Bro. Alexander A. Stevenson, Grand Master of the Grand Lodge of Canada, to Bro. Robert S. Patterson, W. Master; Bro. Norman J. Dingman, Senior Warden; William N. Kennedy, Junior Warden, and five others, to form and hold a Lodge designated Winnipeg Lodge, which was afterwards changed by permission of the Grand Lodge to Prince Rupert's Lodge, in the City of Winnipeg, Province of Manitoba. The Lodge was instituted on the tenth day of December, 1870, a Charter granted on the thirteenth day of July, 1871, and the Lodge regularly constituted and consecrated as Prince Rupert's Lodge, No. 240, G.R.C., and the officers installed, Bro. William N. Kennedy, succeeding Bro. Norman J. Dingman, who had removed from the jurisdiction, as Senior Warden, and Bro. Matthew Coyne, succeeding Bro. William N. Kennedy, as Junior Warden.

On the fourth day of January, 1871, a Dispensation was issued by M. W. Bro. Alexander A. Stevenson, Grand Master of the Grand Lodge of Canada, to Bro. John Frazer, W. Master; George Black, Senior Warden; Thomas Bunn, Junior Warden, and four others, to form and hold a Lodge designated Manitoba Lodge, which was afterwards changed by permission of the Grand Lodge to Lisgar Lodge, at Lower Fort Garry, in the Province of Manitoba. The Lodge was instituted on the twentieth day of February, 1871, a Charter granted on the thirteenth day of July, 1871, and the Lodge regularly constituted and consecrated as Lisgar Lodge No. 244, G.R.C., and the officers installed, Bro. George Black succeeding Bro. John Fraser, as W. Master, Bro. Thomas Bunn, succeeding Bro. George Black, as Senior Warden, and Bro. William J. Piton, succeeding Bro. Thomas Bunn, as Junior Warden. Subsequently permission was granted to remove the Lodge from Lower Fort Garry, to Selkirk, Manitoba.

On the nineteenth day of September, 1872, a Dispensation was issued by M. W. Bro. William M. Wilson, Grand Master of the Grand Lodge of Canada, to Bro. James Henderson, W. Master; Arthur H. Holland, Senior Warden; Bro. Walter F. Hyman, Junior Warden, and nine others, to form and hold a Lodge designated Ancient Landmark Lodge, at Winnipeg, in the Province of Manitoba. The Lodge was instituted on the sixteenth day of December, 1872, a Charter granted on the ninth day of July, 1873, and the Lodge regularly constituted and consecrated as Ancient Landmark Lodge, No. 288, G.R.C., and the officers installed.

No more Lodges were instituted up to 1875, but during this year a far more important step was decided on, namely, the formation of the Grand Lodge of Manitoba. The preliminary steps were taken April 28, 1875, by issuing the following circular:

"To the Worshipful Masters, Past Masters, Wardens,
Officers and other Brethren of the several Lodges of A. F. and A. M., in the Province of Manitoba:

Brethren—At an influential meeting of brethren hailing from the different constitutionally chartered Lodges of the Province, held in the City of Winnipeg, on the twenty-eighth day of April, A.L. 5875, it was, after mature deliberation, unanimously resolved that a circular be forwarded to all the Lodges in this Province, requesting them to be duly represented at a convention to be held in the Masonic Hall, in the City of Winnipeg, on Wednesday, the twelfth day of May, 5875, at three o'clock P.M., for the purpose of taking into consideration the present state of Masonry in this Province, and to proceed, if decided, to form a Grand Lodge for the Province of Manitoba.''

To some, no doubt, this undertaking must have been entered into with many misgivings. For three Lodge with a membership of only 210, to sever their connection with such a strong organization as the Grand Lodge of Canada, and undertake directing the affairs of a Grand Lodge in a new country sparsely inhabited, must have seemed to many a stupendous undertaking, but it serves to show the character of the men who carried out this project to a successful issue, and there is no finer trait known to mankind than the honor and respect accorded to men who have risen above the adverse and obscure conditions and won. From the proceedings of the convention held on the twelfth day of May, 1875, I quote the following resolutions, all of which were carried unanimously: ''That we, the Representatives of the three Warranted Lodges, being all the Lodges in this Province, in Convention assembled, Resolve, That 'The Most Worshipful, the Grand Lodge of Manitoba, A. F. and A. M.,' be and is hereby formed upon the Ancient charges and constitution of Masonry.

''That in severing our connection from the Grand Lodge of Canada, we desire to express our most profound gratitude to that venerable body for the kind consideration and attention they have always displayed towards us both as Lodges and individually, and we most ardently desire that the same parental feeling may always be entertained towards us by our Mother Grand Lodge, which we will remember with pride and affection.

"That the Lodges in the Province be numbered on the Grand Register according to their seniority, viz:—Prince Rupert's Lodge, to be No. 1, Lisgar Lodge to be No. 2, Ancient Landmark Lodge, to be No. 3.

"That a committee of three be appointed to assist the M. W. Grand Master in preparing the address to Sister Grand Lodges and that R. W. Bro. James Henderson, Grand Senior Warden, R. W. Bro. John Kennedy, Grand Treasurer, and R. W. Bro. Rev. Canon O'Meara, Grand Chaplain, be that committee." In his address to the Grand Lodge at the first Annual Communication, held on the fourteenth day of June, 1876, M.W. Bro. W. C. Clarke, Grand Master, says:—"The usual address to the Sister Grand Lodges was sent to all the Grand Bodies on the American continent, that to the European Grand Bodies being deferred till after this communication, and I am happy to inform this Grand Lodge that in no single case has any fault been found with the constitutionality of our procedure, but that in some instances I have been congratulated on behalf of the formers of Grand Lodge by high Masonic authorities on the entire correctness of the steps which have been taken and the result attained. It is my pleasing duty to congratulate you upon the marked success which has so far attended your efforts in the interest of the royal craft." The Mother Grand Lodge of Canada was first in extending fraternal intercourse under date of the fourteenth day of July, 1875. As the country became settled Lodges were formed in the different towns in the Province and the Northwest Territories, the Grand Lodge having extended its jurisdiction over the Districts of Alberta, Assiniboia, Saskatchewan and the Yukon Territory, until the twelfth day of October, 1905, when the Lodges on the Grand Register numbered 104, with a membership of 5,725, on which date eighteen Lodges in the Province of Alberta met at the City of Calgary and formed the Grand Lodge of Alberta. M. W. Bro. William G. Scott, Grand Master, was present and installed the Officers of the new Grand Lodge, and was elected an Honorary Past Grand Master. At the Annual Communication of the Grand Lodge, held in the City of Winnipeg, on the thirteenth day of June, 1906, fraternal recognition was extended, with the most kindly greetings and the wish that success and prosperity would attend them, the first daughter Grand Lodge of this Grand Body. On the ninth day of August, 1906, twenty-nine Lodges in the Province of Saskatchewan met at the City of Regina and formed the Grand Lodge of Saskatchewan, the second daughter Grand Lodge from this Grand Body. M. W. Bro. John McKechnie, Grand Master, and M. W. Bro. James A. Ovas, P.G.M., Grand Secretary, were present and installed the Officers of the new Grand Lodge, and were elected Honorary Past Grand Masters. At the Annual Communication of the Grand Lodge, held in the City of Winnipeg, on the twelfth day of June, 1907, fraternal recognition was extended, and the same good wishes expressed that had been extended to their sister Grand Lodge of Alberta. At this Communication Yukon Lodge No. 79, Dawson City, and White Horse Lodge No. 81, White Horse, in the Yukon Territory, applied for permission to surrender their Charters and to be allowed to apply to the Grand Lodge of British Columbia, for affiliation. The principal reason advanced being, "that the Province of British Columbia is adjacent and contiguous to the Yukon Territory and bound to it by commercial and other relations, causing continual intercourse between residents of both Districts." The petition was duly considered by the Board of General Purposes and, upon their recommendation, granted by Grand Lodge, leaving on the Grand Lodge Register 57 Lodges, with a membership of 3,724, which has increased to date (1914) to 76 Lodges, with a membership of 6,299.

THE GRAND LODGE OF SASKATCHEWAN.
BY HARRY H. CAMPKIN, 33°.
Past Grand Master of the Grand Lodge of Saskatchewan.

IT was in the early part of the year 1879 that a few Masons of the Prince Albert Mission found that they had a sufficient number to apply for a Dispensation, and on the 28th day of March of that year met in the Hudson's Bay Company's old store to discuss the movement.

The nearest Grand body was at Winnipeg, 650 miles to the east, and at that there was no railway communication, only trail and boat service for the transportation of mail and goods, and as many of the members present were from Eastern Canada, or "The Old Land," and at that time they were not sure which ritual had been adopted by the Grand Lodge of Manitoba, they decided to petition the Grand Lodge of Canada for a Dispensation for the formation of Kinistino Lodge, naming therein Bro. Young as the first W. M.; Bro. J. McKenzie as S. W.; and Bro. Duck as J. W.

The names of the brethren signing the application were Charles Mair, John F. Kennedy, Joseph M. Coombs, A. E. Porter, Edward Stanley, George Tait, John L. Reid, with the three named as officers.

The Dispensation was granted on the 22nd day of May, A.D. 1879, but it was in the latter part of the year that the regalia and supplies were received, so the first meeting was held on the 3rd of October, the Entered Apprentice Degree being worked on the 5th of December, Bros. Thomas McKay, Justice Duncan Wilson and Thomas E. Baker being the candidates.

Owing to the distance that many of the members resided from the Mission, the very scattered population, the very great difficulties of travel and transportation, the Lodge had a very hard struggle for life, and at the end of the second year the membership was but twenty-eight.

The Grand Lodge of Canada granted a Warrant of Constitution on the 14th day of July, A.D. 1880, and shortly after that date negotiations were entered into by the Grand Lodge of Manitoba with a view of Kinistino Lodge coming into and under their jurisdiction. This was consummated on the 9th day of November, A.D. 1883, Kinistino Lodge being assigned No. 16 on the Register of the Grand Lodge of Manitoba.

Kinistino was the first Masonic Lodge within the large area that now comprises the jurisdiction of the Grand Lodges of Saskatchewan and Alberta. In 1883 a Lodge was started at Battleford, about 140 miles to the southwest of Prince Albert, and one at Edmonton.

Wascana Lodge was formed on the 6th day of March, 1883, and located at Regina, then the capital of the North West Territories. The charter members were: Bros. Jas. H. Benson, A. G. M. Spragge, John A. Kerr, Arthur Osborne, John Secord, W. D. Firstbrook, F. W. Evetts, T. C. Johnstone, James Bole, D. A. Johnston, J. S. Laidlaw, W. J. Lindsay, Thomas Barton, and C. H. Barker, and the first Officers were: Bros. J. H. Benson, W.M.; A. G. M. Spragge, S.W.; and J. A. Kerr, J.W

The first meetings were held in a building owned by the Presbyterian Church, and later in a Hall on Broad Street. In March, 1885, they met in a larger hall on Scarth Street, then in a room at the corner of Rose and South Railway, which was destroyed by fire in 1889. In August, 1890, the Lodge occupied the third floor of the brick block on Scarth Street, where they remained until the completion of the Masonic Temple in 1907. During the early years this Lodge had a struggle for life, owing chiefly to the unsettled condition of the country and members not being permanently located.

In 1884-85 Lodges were formed and are still in existence at Moose Jew, No. 26; Fort Qu'Appelle, No. 32; Indian Head, No. 33; Qu'Appelle, No. 34; and Moosomin, No. 35.

A few years later Lodges were started and are still in existence at Whitewood, No. 47; Maple Creek, No. 56; Greenfell, No. 57; Royal Northwest Mounted Police, (2nd at Regina), No. 61; Yorkton, No. 69; Duck Lake, No. 72; Sintaluta, No. 80; Carnduff, No. 88; Saskatoon, No. 89; Carlisle, No. 91; Melford, No. 95; Battleford, No. 96; Weyburn, No. 103; Arcola, No. 104; Rosthern, No. 105; Lloydminster, No. 106; Wolseley, No. 107; all numbers from the Grand Register of Manitoba.

Five Masonic Temple Companies have been formed, and own the buildings in which meetings are held, viz.: Moose Jaw, Regina, Saskatoon, Prince Albert, and Qu'Appelle, and each have palatial quarters and splendid equipment.

The Grand Lodge of Saskatchewan was formed on August 9th, 1906, being comprised of twenty-four Constituted Lodges and five Lodges U.D., all from the Grand Lodge of Manitoba, and was organized from no ill feeling or contentious matter, but from the creation of the Province in a part of the area covered by the jurisdiction of the Grand Lodge of Manitoba and the Northwest Territories.

The initiatory movement for the formation of the Grand Lodge was taken by Wascana Lodge, No. 23, located at Regina, on April 3rd, 1906. In the opinion of that Lodge it was deemed advisable in the best interests of Masonry in the Province to form a new Grand Lodge, but Kinistino Lodge, No. 16, located at Prince Albert, being the oldest Lodge in the Province, was asked to concur, which it gladly did, issuing notices for a Convention to be held at Prince Albert on the 25th of May, following. The Convention was held on that date, and concurred in the resolution passed by Wascana Lodge, and appointed R. W. Bros. Tate and Fawcett to lay the matter before the Grand Lodge of Manitoba at its Annual Communication in June. The Grand Lodge gave every encouragement to the formation of the new Grand Body.

At a Convention called for August 9th, 1906, at Regina, of the 29 Lodges in the Province, 21 were represented by their Officers, and 4 by proxy, and a Constitution was adopted based on that of the Grand Lodge of Manitoba. The following Grand Officers were installed by M. W. Bros. John McKechnie and James A. Ovas, of the Grand Lodge of Manitoba, viz.: H. H. Campkin, Grand Master; C. O. Davidson, Deputy Grand Master; Harold Jaggar, Grand Senior Warden; Rev. W. B. Tate, Grand Junior Warden; Alexander Sheppard, Grand Treasurer; John M. Shaw, M.D., Grand Secretary; Rev. E. Matheson, Grand Chaplain; A. H. Smith, Grand Registrar; C. H. Griffin, Grand Senior Deacon; J. I. Ross, Grand Junior Deacon; John Rutledge, Grand Director of Ceremonies; R. B. Taylor, Grand Organist; W. Barber, Grand Pursuivant; William Barnwell, Grand Tyler. M. W. Bros. John McKechnie, James A. Ovas, and G. B. Murphy, all being Past Grand Masters of the Grand Lodge of Manitoba, were elected Honourary Past Grand Masters of the newly formed Grand Lodge, in recognition of their efforts.

The membership started with about 900, which year by year has steadily increased. At the last meeting of Grand Lodge (1914) the roll showed 5,952 members in good standing in 113 Lodges.

THE GRAND LODGE OF ALBERTA.
BY DR. GEORGE MACDONALD.
P. G. M., and Grand Secretary of the Grand Lodge of Alberta.

THE first Masonic Lodge to be formed in what is now the Province of Alberta was organized in Edmonton as Saskatchewan Lodge No. 17, on the register of the Grand Lodge of Manitoba. Their Charter was granted in the year 1882, but was subsequently surrendered about the year 1890.

The next attempt to establish Masonry in Alberta was made in Calgary in May, 1883, when a notice was issued calling upon all Masons to meet in Bro. George Murdock's store, which then stood on the east bank of the Elbow River, nearly opposite the present site of the barracks of the Royal Northwest Mounted Police. Only five Masons presented themselves at this meeting, namely, Bros. Geo. Murdock, E. Nelson Brown, A. McNeil, George Monilaws and D. C. Robinson. Bros. James Walker and John A. Walker were to have attended, but were unavoidably prevented from being present. At this meeting the unanimous opinion of the brethren present was that the time was not opportune for the formation of a Lodge, as there was no suitable place in which to meet, there were not a sufficient number of Masons to successfully carry on a Lodge, and there was a scarcity of material to work on. After a few months had passed, people began to arrive in greater numbers with the advent of the railway. The C. P. Ry. track was laid through the site of what is now the City of Calgary on the 15th of August, 1883. A few days later the first freight train arrived, bringing with it the printing outfit of the Calgary "Herald." In the first issue of that paper a notice was inserted calling upon all Masons interested in the formation of a Masonic Lodge to meet in George Murdock's shack, east of the Elbow River. A photograph of this shack is still preserved in the archives of Bow River Lodge No. 1. To the surprise of all a large number of Masons assembled. R. W. Bro. Dr. N. J. Lindsay, at that time D.D.G.M. for No. 1 (Essex) District, Grand Lodge of Canada, was elected chairman, and R. W. Bro. George Murdock, Secretary. Meetings were regularly held every Friday night, an attendance register kept and minutes of all proceedings recorded, but no Masonic work was done or examinations made until the petition for a Dispensation was about to be signed.

A petition was forwarded to the Grand Lodge of British Columbia, asking for a Dispensation, the greater number of those signing it having lived in that Province. Discouraged at the long wait for a reply, petition was made to the Grand Lodge of Manitoba. A favorable reply was received from both these Grand Lodges at about the same time. However, on account of the easier communication with Manitoba it was decided to accept Dispensation from their Grand Lodge. This Dispensation was obtained about the 1st of January, 1884, and the first meeting held on the 6th of January. R. W. Bro. Dr. N. J. Lindsay was elected first Worshipful Master. R. W. Bro. Lindsay then attended the meeting of the Grand Lodge of Manitoba, held in Winnipeg on the 11th of February, and at that meeting was elected Junior Grand Warden. At that meeting a charter was granted to Bow River Lodge, Calgary, numbered 28 on the Register of the Grand Lodge of Manitoba. Bow River Lodge is now No. 1 on the Grand Register of Alberta.

At the meeting of the Grand Lodge in Manitoba in 1884 charters were granted to Lodges at Regina, Moosomin and Calgary; these, with the Lodges at Edmonton and Prince Albert, might legally have formed a Grand Lodge for the Northwest Territories, which comprised the Districts of Saskatchewan, Assiniboia and Alberta, all being under one Territorial Government. As even then it was deemed probable that Provincial formations were not far distant, it was recognized that Territorial Grand Lodge would be broken up by the division of the territories into provinces. It was accordingly decided to leave in abeyance any desire to form a Grand Lodge.

The three Districts forming the Northwest Territories have now been divided into two Provinces, Alberta and Saskatchewan, Assiniboia being absorbed by the other two.

Until the formation of the Grand Lodges of Alberta and Saskatchewan, the Grand Lodge of Manitoba claimed jurisdiction over all the Northwest Territories, although in their first Constitution it was declared that the Grand Lodge was formed in and for the Province of Manitoba; they also provided that in the absence of the Grand Master the officer next in rank should assume the duties of that office.

In 1893 Dr. Goggin, of Winnipeg, was elected Grand Master, and Thomas Tweed, of Medicine Hat (District of Assiniboia) was elected Deputy Grand Master. During the year Dr. Goggin was appointed Superintendent of Education for the Northwest Territories and moved to the capital, Regina. This gave rise to a rather peculiar situation, the Grand Master had left the Jurisdiction and the Deputy had been elected from without the Province, and to further add to this peculiar condition the Grand Lodge had decided to hold the Communication of 1894 at Banff, Alberta. To meet this difficulty an amendment to the Constitution was proposed wherein the Grand Lodge would add the Northwest Territories to its Jurisdiction, thus making it the largest Masonic Jurisdiction in America, and the only Grand Lodge that ever extended its boundaries after being once constituted. The proposal was at first opposed, but finally passed.

The political changes which culminated in the division of the old Northwest Territories into the Provinces of Alberta and Sasktachewan on the 1st of September, 1905, precipitated the division of the Manitoba Grand Lodge; for, though it was long considered by many brethren that the large number of Masonic Lodges in the Canadian northwest, and their separation by hundreds of miles from the central authority, necessitated a change, the spirit of loyalty to Manitoba was so strong that nothing short of absolute necessity could change it.

"Provincial Autonomy" was expected in the spring of the year 1905, and accordingly the "Medicine Hat Lodge" No. 31, took the initiative. It was at their request that Bow River Lodge, No. 28 (the oldest Lodge in Alberta), called a convention in Calgary on the 25th of May, 1905, the result being the formation of the "Grand Lodge of Alberta," on October 12th, 1905; when out of eighteen Lodges within the political boundaries, seventeen were represented by 79 delegates, and the change was adopted.

No better exemplification of the beauties of Masonry can be adduced than the fact that W. G. Scott, the M. W. Grand Master of Manitoba, personally undertook the long journey to Calgary, in order to be present and invest the Grand Master of Alberta with authority over this Western Province of Canada—and, on behalf of the Mother Grand Lodge, to facilitate its offspring on arriving at maturity.

Freemasonry is making very satisfactory progress throughout the Province, and at the present time (1914) there are 84 Chartered Lodges with 6,039 members.

THE GRAND LODGE OF BRITISH COLUMBIA.

BY. DR. W. A. DEWOLF SMITH.

Grand Librarian, Grand Historian, and Grand Secretary of the Grand Lodge of British Columbia.

FREEMASONRY in British Columbia traces its descent directly from the Grand Lodges of England and Scotland, and the honor of establishing the first Lodge in the Province belongs to the former. The first Warrant was issued to Bros. J. J. Southgate, Geo. Parkes, and W. Jeffray, authorizing them to hold a Lodge in the City of Victoria. The Warrant was signed by the Earl of Zetland, at that time Grand Master of England, dated March 19th, 1859. For some reason the Warrant did not arrive in the Colony for about a year and it was only on March 20th, 1860, that a notice in the "British Colonist" newspaper informed the Brethren that the long looked for document had at last arrived. Even then there were delays, and it was not until the 28th day of the following August that the Lodge was organized, the name selected being Victoria No. 1,085.

The regular annual meeting of the Lodge was held December 27th, 1860, when a visit was received from the Grand Master of the Grand Lodge of the Washington Territory, M. W. Bro. E. Garfield. The W. M. Treas., and Tyler were elected for the ensuing year, and the day was celebrated by a grand ball in the evening. The ball was held in the Court House, James' Bay, and according to "The British Colonist" the company present was "large and highly respectable." His Excellency, Governor Douglas and the Grand Master of Washington Territory graced the occasion with their presence, and, to again quote from "The British Colonist," "the varied regalia of the Fraternity, combined with the uniforms of the gallant representatives of the Royal Navy, and all set off with the beauty and charms of the fair sex, presented a picture of enjoyment, whilst whirling in the giddy waltz that could not well be surpassed.''

About the time these events were taking place in Victoria, gold was discovered on the Thompson and Fraser rivers, coal had been found at Nanaimo previously. This caused settlements to be established at Nanaimo, at Fort Yale, and at Fort Langley, the last mentioned place being the metropolis of the mainland, although the town was soon afterwards moved to New Westminster, which became the seat of government of British Columbia, while Victoria remained the capital of the colony of Vancouver Island. Cariboo also shared in the excitement, and attracted a large number of men.

It is not surprising, therefore, to learn that shortly after the establishment of Victoria Lodge, a second Lodge was organized, and this time at New Westminster. A meeting to organize a Lodge was held at New Westminster during the winter of 1860, and it was agreed to ask for a Warrant of Constitution from the Grand Master of England, the name selected for the new Lodge being "Union," because the petitioners came from different Grand Lodges. The petition was sent to England, but the Warrant was refused, because, according to the English Constitution, the first office-bearers must be registered in the books of the Grand Lodge of England, and the Brother chosen for the 1st Junior Warden, was a Scotch Mason. Subsequently some of the members of Victoria Lodge, whose names cannot now be ascertained, signed a petition, and a new Junior Warden was selected, the result being that a Warrant was granted, dated 16th December, 1861, and the number was 1,201. Unfortunately the earlier records of Union Lodge were lost in a fire which occurred in 1886, and the details of its organization and early proceedings are wanting.

The gold excitement, and perhaps other reasons, drew a large number of Americans to Victoria, and among them naturally a number of Freemasons. These, being unacquainted with the work practised by Victoria Lodge, desired to organize one which would use American work, and proposed to apply, if they did not actually apply, to the Grand Lodge of Washington for a Dispensation. This did not suit the brethren of Victoria Lodge who held that as this was a British Colony, it was a close preserve for the British Grand Lodges, and on the 24th day of January, 1861, the Lodge passed the following resolution:—

"Wheras, we have been informed that a party in this community has applied to the Grand Lodge of Washington Territory for a Dispensation or Warrant to organize a Lodge of F. & A.M. in this Town, it is therefore

"Resolved, that while we hail the Grand Lodge of Washington Territory, and all other Grand Lodges, as Brethren and Masons, we do not recognize their power to grant Dispensations or Warrants out of the district of their own country, and all Dispensations and Warrants emanating from any other source than the Grand Lodges of the Mother Country in this place we shall hold as clandestine, and all Masons visiting such Lodges cannot be recognized as Masons."

This discouraged the applicants and the project was abandoned. Shortly afterwards, however, a number of brethren decided to apply to the Grand Lodge of Scotland for a Warrant, and asked Victoria Lodge to recommend their petition. The request was received by Victoria Lodge on the 15th day of May, 1862, and was granted, the Brethren being careful, however, to preserve the precedence of the Grand Lodge of England, as may be seen by the tenor of the following resolution:—

"Resolved, that Victoria Lodge No. 1085, cordially responds to the petition of the Brethren desirous to establish a Lodge under the Grand Lodge of Scotland; but in doing so they reserve the precedence of the Grand Lodge of England in general Masonic affairs within the colony, and they communicate this Resolution to the Grand Lodge of England as a matter of record."

In due course a Warrant was granted, and on the 20th day of October, 1862, a meeting was held in the hall of Victoria Lodge to organize the new Lodge, which was known as Vancouver Lodge No. 421 on the Register of Scotland.

Some years then elapsed before a fourth Lodge was organized. During the year 1865 a meeting of Masons was held at Nanaimo, the names of those present being unknown. At this meeting it was decided that a petition for a Warrant for a Lodge, to be held at Nanaimo, should be sent to the Grand Master of England, which was done. The Warrant was expected from England in the spring of the 1866, and as there was no suitable hall in the town, a house was rented at $25 per month. The building was altered to adapt it to Masonic purposes, and the necessary furniture and equipment was procured. Considerable delay occurred, the Warrant having been lost with the steamer carrying the mails between San Francisco and Victoria. A duplicate Warrant was sent for, and eventually reached the colony in the spring of 1867. The meeting to organize the Lodge was held on the 18th day of May, 1867, and its Constitution was attended with considerable ceremony. On the 13th day of May, an Emergent meeting of Victoria Lodge was held, at which the Worshipful Master stated that by virtue of a Dispensation from the Grand Master he was empowered to authorize the Brethren to proceed to Nanaimo in regalia for the purpose of Constituting the new Lodge. They accordingly embarked on the steamer "Sir James Douglas," with several members of Vancouver Lodge, and accompanied by the band of the volunteer Milita. The members of the new Lodge and the visitors from Victoria assembled on the morning of the 15th day of May, Brother Holbrook, of Union Lodge, New Westminster, also being present. Probably because Brother Holbrook had held an office in one of the Provincial Grand Lodges of England (Cheshire) he was requested to take charge of the proceedings, which he did, and the Lodge was duly constituted as Nanaimo Lodge No. 1090.

In 1867 another Lodge was Warranted in Victoria by the Grand Lodge of England, under the name of British Columbia Lodge No. 1187, the date of the Warrant being 26th of July, 1867.

In this year the Grand Master of Scotland appointed a Provincial Grand Master for the Province, the Brother selected for the honour being Worshipful Brother I. W.

Powell. Unfortunately the minutes of the Provincial Grand Lodge are not available, the only record of its meetings that I have been able to find being a small leaflet. R. W. Bro. Powell's Commission was dated the 6th May, 1867, but it was not until December of that year that he called the representatives of his Lodges together and organized a Provincial Grand Lodge. This meeting was held on the 24th day of December, and after the Provincial Grand Lodge had been called to order the Provincial Grand Master addressed the Brethren briefly, stating that he had already granted Dispensations for the formation of two Lodges, Cariboo, at Barkerville, subsequently warranted as No. 469, and Caledonia, at Nanaimo, which afterwards obtained a Warrant No. 478.

The brethren of the English Constitution had at an early date in their history endeavoured to secure the appointment of a District Grand Master, and at various times had passed resolutions and had sent petitions to the Grand Lodge of England urging such appointment. For some time, however, the Grand Master of England hesitated to grant the request. The reason at first given was that no District Grand Master would be appointed until there were at least three Lodges in the colony working under the English Constitution. This difficulty was removed early in 1866 when Nanaimo Lodge was constituted. In July, 1867, the British Columbia Lodge was warranted, making the number of English Lodges four, but still no Patent was granted. Shortly before that date, however, the Grand Master of Scotland had, as already mentioned, appointed a Provincial Grand Master for the colony, and the Grand Lodge of England may have feared that the precedence, so carefully reserved by Victoria Lodge, was in danger of being lost, for in the fall of 1867 a Patent dated 10th September, 1867, was issued through W. Bro. Robert Burnaby, appointing him District Grand Master for the colonies of Vancouver Island and British Columbia.

Although dated September 10th, it is probable that the Patent was not received by Bro. Burnaby until early in 1868, for it was not until the spring of that year that he communicated to several Brethren the fact that the had received the Patent. On the 14th March, 1868, a meeting was held at Bro. Burnaby's residence to make the preliminary arrangements for the formation of a District Grand Lodge, and the District Grand Master announced the names of the Brethren he had nominated as officers.

The Provincial and District Grand Lodges being now in working order, matters proceeded smoothly enough, the Provincial and District Grand Masters being warm personal friends, and each imbued with an ardent desire to promote the welfare of the Craft in general. The only thing that occurred to mar the harmony existing between the two Jurisdictions, was a complaint made by certain Lodges in Victoria that material rejected by them had been accepted by Lodges of the other Jurisdiction. This, however, was strongly denied by the Lodges concerned, and apparently the denial was accepted.

A fourth Lodge under the Grand Lodge of Scotland was formed by Dispensation of the Provincial Grand Master—Mount Hermon Lodge, which was organized at Hastings, in January, 1869. In anticipation of the Dispensation the Brethren of that place had erected "a handsome and commodious hall," and had furnished it with "all the comforts and attractions of a model Lodge room." The Provincial Grand Master was invited to set the Lodge to work, and accordingly proceeded to Burrard Inlet on the 15th of January, 1869, when he instituted the Lodge and installed its officers, at the same time dedicating its hall. The Warrant from the Grand Lodge of Scotland is dated May 3rd, 1869, and the number assigned it was 491.

One other Dispensation for a new Lodge was issued by the Provincial Grand Master for Scotland—that for Quadra Lodge—but no new Lodge was formed under the English Constitution.

After some preliminary meetings the Brethren of Quadra Lodge were called together on the 7th of January, 1871, when the Lodge was constituted and the officers installed by R. W. Bro. I. W. Powell. The Warrant from the Grand Lodge of Scotland probably arrived in due course, but it is doubtful whether the Lodge ever worked under it. It could not have arrived until late in the year, and by that time the formation of an independent Grand Lodge was being proceeded with. The minutes of the Lodge up to and including those of the 1st of December, 1871, are headed

"QUADRA LODGE NO. —
OF SCOTTISH FREEMASONS IN THE PROVINCE OF BRITISH COLUMBIA,"

while following the minutes of this meeting is a "Return of Intrants" pasted into the Minute Book in which the number of the Lodge is given as 508. The next meeting, a regular meeting held on the 8th of December, 1871, has its minutes headed

"QUADRA LODGE NO. 8, ON THE REGISTRY OF BRITISH COLUMBIA."

I infer from this that the Warrant arrived shortly before the formation of the new Grand Lodge, but evidently after the convention to organize the new Grand Lodge had been held. It is probable that the numbers of the various Lodges taking part in the new organization were discussed and allotted at this convention, which would account for the Lodge attaching the number "8" to the Minutes two or three weeks before the Grand Lodge was actually organized.

Thus there were, early in 1871, four Lodges under the English Constitution, and five under the Scotch, governed by a District Grand Lodge of England and a Provincial

Grand Lodge of Scotland respectively. At the head of the District Grand Lodge was R. W. Bro. Robert Burnaby, and under him were the lodges:
> Victoria, No. 783.
> Union, No. 899.
> Nanaimo, No. 1,090, and
British Columbia, No. 1,187.

Over the Provincial Grand Lodge R. W. Bro. I. W. Powell presided, and the Lodges in his charge were:
> Vancouver, No. 421.
> Cariboo, No. 469.
> Caledonia, No. 478.
> Mount Hermon, No. 491, and
> Quadra, U.D., or No. 508, as the case may be.

Some time before this a movement to organize an independent Grand Lodge for the colony had been started, Vancouver Lodge apparently taking the lead. On the 16th of December, 1868, a regular meeting of that Lodge was held, there being present thirty members of the Lodge and seven visitors, three of whom were from Cariboo Lodge and one from Union. A series of resolutions, too long to be given here, were introduced, the mover, W. Bro. R. H. Adams, stating that he would bring them up for action at a subsequent meeting. Briefly, they recite the condition of Freemasonry as it then existed in the Colony; the difficulties that continually occurred because of the distance from the parent Grand Lodge, and the long delays in correspondence; and the desirability of, and the advantages to be secured by the formation of an independent Grand Lodge.

These resolutions were according brought up at a meeting of the Lodge held on the 2nd of January, 1869, and were adopted. They were forthwith communicated to the other Lodges in the Colony, with the suggestion that each Lodge appoint a Committeee to confer with a committee from Vancouver Lodge, as to the best mode of carrying them into effect. They were variously received. Most of the Scotch Lodges at once fell in with the proposal and appointed delegates, Caledonia Lodges refusing to do so. The English Lodges, on the other hand, declined to entertain the proposition, with the exception of Victoria Lodge, which sent the resolutions to the District Grand Master with the request that he lay them before the Grand Lodge of England. This he did in a letter remarkable for its temperate and impartial statement of the case, addressed to the Grand Secretary of the Grand Lodge of England, who was at that time, V. W. Bro. Hervey. The letter received by the District Grand Master in reply, expressed the regret of the Grand Secretary that the Brethren in the Colony should do anything which might tend to lessen the influence they possessed as members of the English Constitution, and the fear that a Grand Lodge of such limited membership, would simply be "the laughing-stock of the Masonic world."

The Provincial Grand Master of Scotland, although he fully recognized the desirability of an independent Grand Lodge, also declined to move in the matter without the consent of the Grand Lodge of Scotland, and accordingly transmitted to his Grand Lodge a copy of the resolutions. If any reply to his communication was received there is no record of it.

Vancouver Lodge, however, seems to have gone ahead with the scheme, and evidently submitted it to a number of Canadian and foreign Grand Lodges, with the view of ascertaining what kind of a reception a new Grand Lodge might expect. Apparently the result was encouraging, for at a meeting held on the 18th of January, 1871, it was announced that all the Grand Lodges communicated with had signified their sympathy with and approval of the project. Thereupon a committee was appointed to arrange for the meeting of a Convention of the Masters, Wardens, and Past Masters of the different Lodges in the Colony.

The Committee accordingly issued a call for a Convention to be held in the City of Victoria on the 18th of March, 1871. Again Victoria Lodge was the only English

Lodge which favoured the movement, and upon receipt of the communication from Vancouver Lodge, forwarded it to the District Grand Master, with a request that the Lodge be allowed to attend the meeting. The District Grand Master submitted the correspondence to the District Board of General Purposes which, after due consideration, decided that the time was not opportune for the formation of an independent Grand Lodge, although such a step might be advisable in the future, and acting on this advice the District Grand Master refused to allowed his Lodges to send delegates to the Convention.

Notwithstanding the aloofness of the English Brethren, the representatives of the Scotch Lodges held the Convention on March 18th, 1871 according to schedule, and decided to form a Grand Lodge for the Colony. There is no record of the meeting, and it is not know who were present. R. W. Bro. I. W. Powell, who, however, was absent from the colony at the time, was elected Grand Master and Bro. H. F. Heisterman, Grand Secretary, and an invitation was sent to and accepted by M. W. Bro. the Hon. Elwood Evans, P.G.M. of Washington, to attend and install the officers of the new Grand Lodge. An invitation to be present was also sent to R. W. Bro. Burnaby, whereupon he instructed the District Grand Secretary to attend the meeting and protest against its proceedings. This he did, and the protest was effectual, for the representatives of Caledonia Lodge returned home with the information that the formation of a Grand Lodge had been indefinitely postponed.

Some time during the summer of 1871, R. W. Bro. Powell returned from England and found the Craft in a state of dissension and discord. Feelings were high, and the two sections of the Craft were hardly on speaking terms. He and R. W. Bro. Burnaby held several consultations on the subject, and after agreeing between themselves that the formation of an independent Grand Lodge was advisable, decided to submit the question to a vote of all the members of their respective Jurisdictions.

It was stipulated and understood by the Brethren that in the event of the Craft voting in favour of an independent Grand Lodge, either Bro. Powell or Bro. Burnaby would be the first Grand Master, and whichever was not elected Grand Master, would be made Past Grand Master.

A circular was accordingly issued by the District and Provincial Grand Masters to their respective Lodges, instructing the Brethren to vote on the question of forming an independent Grand Lodge. The result of the vote was 194 in favour and 28 against the proposition. The result of the vote being so overwhelmingly in favor of forming a Grand Lodge, another Convention was called, and was held in Victoria on the 21st of October, 1871, there being present the representatives of all the Lodges in the Province, with the exception of Union Lodge, which declined to join. Brother James A. Graham, of Quadra Lodge, was appointed Chairman of the meeting, and Brother H. F. Heisterman, of the same Lodge, Secretary. A resolution declaring it expedient to form a Grand Lodge in and for the Province of British Columbia, was carried unanimously, and with great applause, and immediately afterwards another declaring the Grand Lodge of British Columbia to be formed was also carried unanimously. R. W. Bro. I. W. Powell was elected Grand Master, and in consideration of their valuable services R. W. Bro. Burnaby was made an Honourary Past Grand Master, and W. Bro. James A. Graham, an Honourary Past Deputy Grand Master of the new Grand Lodge. After some formal business was transacted, the meeting adjourned, and was called together again on the 26th of December, 1871, when the officers-elect were installed by R. W. Bro. Burnaby.

Nanaimo Lodge and Caledonia Lodge displayed some reluctance to accept Warrants from the new Grand Lodge, fearing that they would be called upon to change their rituals (and in the case of Caledonia Lodge, their clothing). However, a letter from the Grand Master was read in Nanaimo Lodge, and one from the Grand Secretary in Caledonia Lodge, stating that all the Lodges could practice their own rituals so long as they desired, which seemed to dispel the fear of the brethren, and the new Warrants were accepted.

The first special or emergent meeting of Grand Lodge was held in the city of New Westminster on the 30th of July, 1872, the occasion being the laying of the corner-stone of the Mortuary Chapel of the Masonic cemetery at Sapperton. Besides the Grand Lodge officers, there were present about sixty of the Brethren, and the stone was laid in due and ancient form by the Grand Master, M. W. Bro. I. W. Powell.

At the time of this meeting, Union Lodge was still on the English Registry. It shortly afterwards joined the new Grand Lodge, for at the Annual Communication held on December 7th, 1872, the Grand Master expressed his gratification that unification of the Craft had been accomplished by Union Lodge transferring its allegiance. The fraternal feeling displayed by the new Grand Lodge in laying the corner-stone for Union Lodge—and probably the persuasive eloquence of Brothers Powell and Burnaby —no doubt hastened the action of Union Lodge in the matter, for M. W. Bro. Powell stated in his address that it was only a few days after the Emergent meeting that a request for admission to the fold was received from the Lodge. The few months' delay, however, lost Union Lodge its place on the roll, and instead of being No. 2 it had to be content with No. 9.

At this Communication the Grand Master reported that all the Grand Lodges of the Dominion and all those of the United States, with the exception of Indiana, had "extended a hearty recognition and warm welcome" to the new Grand Lodge. Indiana had not refused to recognize them, but was waiting to see what action would be taken by the British Grand Lodges.

At the Annual Communication in 1873 the Board submitted these rules, which provided for the establishment of two funds—a Benevolent Fund and a Widows' and Orphans' Fund. These were to be inaugurated by contributions from each Lodge of $2.00 for every member on its roll, and the same for every Brother affiliated. The support of the funds was provided for by levying an assessment of $3.00 per annum on every member. Of the money so collected, three-fourths was to be devoted to the fund of Benevolence, and one-fourth to the Widows' and Orphan's Fund.

In this year—1873—on the fifth of November, the two Lodges in Nanaimo, Nanaimo No. 3 and Caledonia No. 6, agreed to amalgamate, and their request to be allowed to do so was granted by Grand Lodge on the 8th of December. At the same time the name of the Lodge was changed to Ashlar, the number of Nanaimo Lodge being retained.

Some objection having been made to the date of meeting of Grand Lodge, no Annual Communication was held in 1874, but an Emergent meeting was held at Nanaimo on the 21st of October, of that year, to lay the corner-stone of the new Masonic hall at that place. Although this is called a special Communication of Grand Lodge, it does not appear that Grand Lodge was opened at all. The Grand Master opened Ashlar Lodge, and laid the corner-stone, after which he surrendered the gavel to the W. M. of Ashlar Lodge, who conferred the Entered Apprentice Degree upon a candidate. When this had been done, the Lodge was called to refreshment, to partake of the inevitable banquet, after which labor was resumed and the Lodge drunk the health of the Queen, Prince of Wales, the Grand Master, and of anyone else whose name happened to occur to them. At this meeting, whether one of Grand Lodge or Ashlar Lodge, the announcement was made that the Grand Lodge of England had extended recognition to the new Grand Lodge.

Affairs Masonic proceeded uneventfully until the meeting of Grand Lodge in February, 1878, the Craft holding its own but making no material advance. At this Communication it was announced that the four Lodges in

Victoria had amalgamated into two—Victoria and British Columbia Lodges united to form Victoria-Columbia Lodge, No. 1, and Vancouver and Quadra Lodges joining to make Vancouver and Quadra Lodge, No. 2.

In 1879 another change was made in the time of meeting of Grand Lodge, the date being altered from February to June.

Although application for recognition had been made to the Grand Lodge of Scotland immediately upon the formation of Grand Lodge, that Grand Lodge, for some unknown reason, but in a manner quite consistent with its constant practice, paid no attention to the Communication, and in the addresses of different Grand Masters we find reference to this apparent lack of courtesy. However, in 1880 M. W. Bro. Harrison informed Grand Lodge that the Grand Lodge of Scotland had at last recognized the Grand Lodge of British Columbia—nine years after the request had been made. Even then it was a conditional recognition, Scotland claiming the right

1st. To protect the interests of any of its Lodges which might exist in the Province, and
2nd. To protect the rights of any Lodges which might subsequently be formed in the Province under its authority.

To the first claim, as M. W. Bro. Harrison pointed out, there could be no exception, as no Scotch Lodges remained, but to the second he entered a strong protest, in which he was heartily supported by the committee on his address. The Grand Lodge, too, adopted a resolution denying the right of the Grand Lodge of Scotland, or of any other Grand Lodge, to warrant Lodges in the Province. It is satisfactory to note that the Grand Lodge of Scotland has made no attempt to invade the jurisdiction of the Grand Lodge of British Columbia.

In spite of the expectations of rapid progress which obtained when the Grand Lodge was organized, no attempt was made for some years to institute a new Lodge in the Jurisdiction. In 1881 the Board of General Purposes reported that the preliminary steps had been taken to organize a new Lodge at Yale, which was then a flourishing town. The Board stated that the requirements of the Constitution had been complied with, and recommended that a Warrant be issued. Fifteen brethren joined in the petition for the new Lodge, a Dispensation for which was issued on the 22nd of June, 1881, under the name of Cascade Lodge, No. 10. On the 5th of July, 1881 "a more extended Dispensation" was issued, and on the 29th of October, 1881 by order of the Grand Master, a Warrant was given it. Its existence was of short duration, a fire at Yale and the changes incident to railway construction having made it expedient to return the Warrant to Grand Lodge inside of a year. The Board of General Purposes in 1882, in reporting the fact, stated that in view of the circumstances under which the Warrant had been returned, it had been agreed to issue a new Warrant free of charge to a sufficient number of the original Petitioners at any time during the ensuing twelve months, should it be thought advisable. Unfortunately the happy hour never came, and the first-born of the Grand Lodge died in infancy.

The membership of the Jurisdiction, too, remained practically stationary for a number of years. At the time of its organization in 1871, the Grand Lodge had under its jurisdiction 293 members, and it was not until 1886 that the Grand Master was able to report any substantial gain. In that year the returns showed 333 members on the roll, and the Grand Secretary reported the formation of a new Lodge, this time at Kamloops, under the name of Kamloops Lodge, No. 10, the number of the defunct Lodge at Yale.

In 1886 the Canadian Pacific Railway was completed through to the coast, bringing with it a large number of Eastern Masons and opening the way for many others to come and settle in the Province. From this time the history of the Grand Lodge is one of uninterrupted progress. New Lodges have been added year by year, and the Craft has steadily grown, until now (1914), there are 77 Warranted Lodges in the Jurisdiction, with a membership of 7,176.

STATISTICS CANADIAN GRAND LODGES TO 1914.

	Date of Formation	Number of Lodges	Number of Members
Alberta	1905	84	6,039
British Columbia	1871	77	7,176
Canada in Ontario	1855	446	60,000
Manitoba	1875	76	6,299
New Brunswick	1867	40	3,539
Nova Scotia	1869	73	6,758
Prince Edward Island	1875	15	799
Quebec	1869	66	8,152
Saskatchewan	1906	113	5,952
		987	104,714

THE UNITED STATES OF AMERICA.

Compiled by OSBORNE SHEPPARD from the
writings of the late

ROBERT FREKE GOULD

Historian to the Grand Lodge of England.

THE three oldest Lodges on the Continent of North America are St. John's, at Boston, Massachusetts; Solomon's at Savannah, Georgia, and Solomon's at Charleston, South Carolina. The first of these bodies, all of English origin, was established in 1733, and the last two in 1735. There was formerly in existence a still older Lodge at Philadelphia, with records dating from 1731, and which is presumably referred to—December 8th, 1730—as "one of the several Lodges erected in this Province," by Benjamin Franklin, in the Pennsylvania Gazette. All the evidence points in the direction of this having been an independent Lodge, assembling by inherent right, and acknowledging no higher authority than its own. It has, indeed, been contended, that the Lodge was constituted by Daniel Coxe, to whom a Deputation was granted—June 5th, 1730—by the Duke of Norfolk, as Provincial Grand Master for the Provinces of New York, New Jersey, and Pennsylvania. But all the known facts are inconsistent with the supposition that the powers conferred by this Deputation were ever exercised by Coxe, and even if we concede the possibility of certain official acts having been performed by him, though unrecorded, the conclusion is irresistible, that these could not have occurred until after the formation of the Lodge at Philadelphia, with an Immemorial Constitution, and existing "records dating from 1731." Of this Lodge, which met sometimes as a private, and sometimes as a Grand Lodge, Benjamin Franklin was the Master and Grand Master in 1734.

The first Lodge held under written authority was established by Henry Price, Provincial Grand Master of

New England, at "The Bunch of Grapes" Tavern, in Boston, on August 31st, 1733.

In 1734, Franklin published an edition of the English Book of Constitutions, and entered into a correspondence with Henry Price, "whose deputation and power," he understood, "had been extended over all America," asking the latter to confirm the Brethren of Philadelphia in the privilege of holding a Grand Lodge annually in their customary manner. As Price's reply has not been preserved, what he actually did in response to the application from Franklin, must remain, to a large extent, the subject of conjecture. But there seems no room for doubt that the Lodge (and Grand Lodge) never, until 1749, worked under any sanction which was deemed superior to its own. The authority actually held, as well as the powers exercised by Price, have been much canvassed, but it will be sufficient to state that all the action of the first Provincial Grand Master of New England was recognized in the Mother Country, by the Grand Lodge.

A Master's Lodge, with Henry Price as Master, was founded at Boston, in 1738. On the death of Robert Tomlinson, who succeeded Price—as Prov. G. M. of New England—in 1737, Thomas Oxnard—an Initiate of the first Lodge at Boston—received a patent as Provincial Grand Master of North America, in 1743.

Benjamin Franklin was appointed Provincial Grand Master of Pennsylvania, by Oxnard, in 1749, but in the following year, William Allen, Recorder of Philadelphia, presented a deputation from the Grand Master of England (Lord Byron), appointing him to the same office, and on his authority being duly recognized, nominated Franklin as his Deputy.

At the death of Oxnard, in 1754, a petition was drawn up recommending Jeremy Gridley as his successor. The document states that "Mr. Henry Price, formerly Grand Master, had resumed the chair pro tempore," and closes with the remark, that since the establishment of Masonry at Boston, in 1733, Lodges in Philadelphia, New Hampshire, South Carolina, Antigua, Nova Scotia, Newfoundland, Rhode Island, Maryland, and Connecticut, "have received Constitutions from us."

By the terms of Gridley's patent, which was received in 1755, his authority was restricted to those parts of North America for which no Provincial Grand Master had been appointed.

A self-constituted Lodge at Boston—St. Andrew's—which afterwards numbered among its members some of the most influential men of the city, received a Scottish warrant—granted four years previously—in 1760.

In 1766, there were, in addition to those in Boston, thirty (English) Lodges on the roll of the Province. Of these three were military Lodges, four were in Massachusetts, three in Rhode Island, six in Connecticut, and one each in New Hampshire, South Carolina, Maryland, Virginia, New Jersey, and North Carolina.

In 1767 Gridley died, and in the following year John Rowe was installed as his successor. Immediately afterwards, steps were taken to form a Provincial Grand Lodge under Scotland, and a petition to that effect was drawn up and signed by the Masters and Wardens of St. Andrew's Lodge, and of three Lodges attached to Regiments in the British Army—all four Lodges having a common bond in working according to what was commonly known as the "Ancient System."

The petition was granted in 1769, and a commission was issued appointing Joseph Warren, Grand Master of Masons, in Boston, New England, and within one hundred miles of the same. Two of the Regimental Lodges, which had taken part in the movement, were present at the inauguration of the new governing body, but they were never any more than a nominal part of it, St. Andrew's was really the Provincial Grand Lodge.

In the same year—August 28th—a section of St. Andrew's, calling itself a Royal Arch Lodge, held its first recorded meeting, and the minutes contain the earliest account of the conferring of the degree of a Knight Templar that has yet been discovered either in manuscript or print.

By a further Scottish patent—dated March 3rd, 1772—Warren was appointed Grand Master for the Continent of America. The body over which he presided began to issue charters in 1770, and at a later period (1782) adopted the title of the "Massachusetts Grand Lodge," its rival, under John Rowe, retaining the appellation of "St. Johns."

Returning to Pennsylvania, in 1758, the so-called Ancients gained a foothold in Philadelphia, and from that date the Lodges under the older sanction began to decline. A Provincial warrant was received from the Ancient or Schismatic Grand Lodge of England in 1764. By the Grand Body so established many warrants were granted for Lodges in other States as well as in Pennsylvania. All the other Lodges formed in the Province before the invasion of the Ancients soon after ceased to exist.

In what is now the State of New York, no trace of any Lodge, created before the administration of George Harrison, has been preserved. This worthy was appointed Provincial Grand Master in 1753, and during the eighteen years he held office granted warrants to a large number of Lodges, five of which still exist, and head the roll of the existing Grand Lodge of New York. One of these, Mount Vernon, No. 3, was originally constituted by the members of Lodge No. 74 in the Second Battalion of 1st Foot, who, on leaving Albany, in 1759, gave an exact copy of their Irish Warrant to some influential citizens which was exchanged for a Provincial Charter in 1765.

Masonry came into Virginia from several distinct sources. The earliest Lodge is said to have been founded at Norfolk by Cornelius Harnett in 1741, and, with good show of reason, it has been suggested that the Provincial commission was superseded by a deputation, or "constitution" from the Grand Lodge of England in 1753. To Port Royal Kilwinning Cross Lodge—whose name indicates its source of origin—has been assigned the date of 1755. Other charters were issued from Scotland—by the Grand Lodge—in 1756 and 1758, to Lodges at Blandford and Fredericksburg. The latter had previously existed as an independent Lodge, but for what period is uncertain. Washington was initiated in this Lodge on November 4th, 1752, and in the following year—December 22nd, 1753—we find among its records the earliest known minute referring to the actual working of the Royal Arch degree.

In what were then the other colonies of British North America, Lodges gradually sprang into existence, either under direct or delegated authority from the Mother Country.

A charter for holding a Lodge "by the stile and title of Grant's East Florida Lodge," was issued by the Grand Lodge of Scotland in 1768. But this, after the fashion of the "Ancients" (whose influence was shortly to become paramount in the New World), appears to have been regarded as an instrument authorizing the meetings of a Provincial Grand Lodge. Accordingly, on May 3rd, 1771, this "Grant's Lodge," acting as a Grand Lodge, issued a charter to ten persons at Pensacola, who, "for some time past had been members of Lodge No. 108 of the Register of Scotland, held in his Majesty's Thirty-first Regiment of Foot, as the said Regiment was about to leave the Province." The new Lodge—St. Andrew's No. 1, West Florida—continued to work at Pensacola until the cession of Florida to the Spaniards, when it was removed to Charleston, South Carolina. It will be seen that the founders of the first Stationary (though in the light of subsequent events it may be more appropriate to say Civil) Lodge in Florida, were all members of an Army or "Travelling" Lodge, attached to a British Regiment. It is also not a little remarkable that one and the same Military Lodge, should have been in the first instance "Modern" (1750), next Scottish (1761), then "Ancient" (1802), and finally "Scottish" once more (1805), without any break of continuity in its existence.

During the Revolution, communication with the Mother Grand Lodges in North and South Britain was largely interrupted, and in most cases wholly ceased. When hostilities commenced, there were Provincial Grand Lodges, in real or nominal existence, in Massachusetts (for New England), New York, Virginia, South Carolina, North Carolina, and Georgia, under the Regular Grand Lodge of England; in Pennsylvania under the "Ancients" and in Massachusetts under the Grand Lodge of Scotland.

The first man of distinction to lay down his life in the cause of American Independence was Joseph Warren, the Scottish Provincial Grand Master, and leader of the "Ancients" in Massachusetts, who was killed at the battle of Bunker Hill, where, though commissioned as a Major-General, he fought as a Volunteer. Among the Provincial Grand Masters of the "Moderns," whose sympathies were enlisted in the opposite direction, were John Rowe, whose action paralysed the St. John's Grand Lodge at Boston; William Allen, of Pennsylvania, who attempted to raise a regiment for the British Army; Sir Egerton Leigh, of South Carolina, who, foreseeing the approaching storm, left for England in 1774; and Sir John (son of the more famous Sir William) Johnson of New York, who cast in his lot with the Royalists at the commencement of the war.

The death of Joseph Warren raised a constitutional question of much perplexity. What was the status of the Grand Lodge after the death of the Grand Master? It was disposed of by the election of Joseph Webb to the position of "Grand Master of Antient Masonry" in the State of Massachusetts. This, if we leave out of consideration the Lodge (and Grand Lodge) at Pennsylvania in 1731, was the first sovereign and independent Grand Lodge in America, and the second was the Grand Lodge of Virginia, which was established in the following year.

Many Military Lodges were in active existence during the war, the most renowned being American Union, which received a charter from John Rowe (of Boston), and was attached to the "Connecticut line." On December 27th, 1779, at Morristown, New Jersey, the Lodge celebrated the Festival of St. John. There were present a large number of members and visitors—among the latter being General Washington. A form of petition to the several Provincial Grand Masters, to be signed on behalf of the Army Lodges and the Masons in each military line, for the appointment of a Grand Master for the United States of America, was approved. Accordingly, at "a convention Lodge from the different lines of the Army and the departments, held in due form under the authority of American Union Lodge, at Morristown, the sixth day of March, in the year of Salvation, 1780," a duly appointed committee presented their report. Washington was naturally designated for the office of Grand Master, and it would seem that the representatives of the Army Lodges hoped that the movement, if successfully carried out, would obliterate all distinction between "Ancient" and "Modern" Masons.

In New York, prior to the War, Masonry was a monopoly of the "Moderns," but when the British Army occupied New York City, with it came "Ancient" Masonry. A Provincial Grand Lodge was organized in 1782 by three stationary and six Army Lodges. Of the latter, one was Scottish and one Irish. but the remaining seven were "Ancient" Lodges.

Within seven years after the close of the War of the Revolution, the system of Grand Lodges with Territorial jurisdiction was firmly established. It became an accepted doctrine, that the Lodges in an independent State had a right to organize a Grand Lodge; that a Grand Lodge so created possessed exclusive jurisdiction within the State; and that it might constitute Lodges in another State in which no Grand Lodge existed, and maintain them until a Grand Lodge should be established in such State.

The following independent Grand Lodges, created in accordance with these principles, existed in 1790:—In Massachusetts (two, St. John's and Massachusetts), New

Hampshire, Connecticut, New York (Ancient), Pennsylvania (Ancient), New Jersey, Maryland, Virginia, North Carolina, South Carolina (two, Ancient and Modern), and Georgia.

For some time after the Revolutionary period, there were two methods of working, as there had been before, but as the "Ancients' 'and "Moderns" assimilated in each jurisdiction, one mode was adopted, which embraced more or less the peculiarities of both systems. Gradually, in States where there were two Grand Lodges, they amalgamated. A union of the rival bodies at Boston was effected in 1792. In the two other leading jurisdictions, all opposition to the "Ancients" had simply melted away. The Grand Lodges established by the Schismatic Grand Lodge of England in Pennsylvania and New York simply declared their independence, the former in 1786, and the latter in the following year. In Pennsylvania there were no "Moderns" left to either conciliate or coerce, but in New York the Lodges under the older English sanction (which survived the period of the Revolution) one by one fell into line and became component parts of the Grand Lodge.

The fiercest contest between the "Ancients" and the "Moderns' was in South Carolina. For nearly twenty years each party had a Grand Lodge in active operation, and the contest was maintained for many years after the Union in England.

In 1800, there were in the United States, 11 Grand Lodges, having 347 subordinate Lodges, and a membership of 16,000.

During the first quarter of the nineteenth century the history of the American Craft was uneventful, but a storm then arose that well-nigh swept the great Fraternity from the land. William Morgan, a mechanic from Batavia, New York, who was reported to be about to publish a volume disclosing the secrets of the Freemasons, was kidnapped and carried off. What his fate was has never been ascertained.*

*Vide page 44, A. T. Freed's article.

An Anti-Masonic party was formed in New York, and the excitement gradually spread into other States. With the full belief that it would sweep the old political divisions out of existence, a candidate for the Presidency was nominated in 1832. The other candidates (of the two recognized parties), Andrew Jackson and Henry Clay, were Masons and Past Grand Masters. In the result, the former was elected by an overwhelming majority, the Anti-Masons only carrying the State of Vermont. This was a death-blow to political Anti-Masonry.

In the United States there have been many fierce and embittered contests, but no other has approached in intensity that which was carried on for several years by the Anti-Masons.

No society, civil, military, or religious, escaped its influence. The hatred of Masonry was carried everywhere, and there was no retreat so sacred that it did not enter. This, of course, was disastrous to the growth of the Institution. Masonic work almost ceased, most of the Lodges suspended their meetings, and many of them surrendered their charters.

Eventually, however, the tide of popular feeling began to turn. Dormant Lodges were revived. Surrendered charters were restored.

The most important of the National Conventions which have been summoned from time to time in order to consider matters common to, or affecting the whole of the jurisdictions, appears to have been that held at Baltimore, on May 8th, 1843. Fifteen Grand Lodges were represented. It was in session for ten days. With great unanimity a system of work and lectures was adopted. It was settled at this meeting, and the usage has since prevailed, that the business of the Lodges should be conducted in the third degree. The issuing of Grand Lodge certificates was recommended to the Grand Lodges.

Brigham Young, with about 1,500 other Mormons, was expelled from Masonry by the Grand Lodge of Illinois, in 1844. Six years later—at the close of the first half of the century just expired—there were, in the United States, 28 Grand Lodges, having 1,835 subordinate Lodges, with a membership of 66,142.

During the Civil War more than a hundred Military Lodges were chartered by the Grand Lodges of the North and South, but the experience gained during that great conflict was decidedly opposed to their utility.

The American Rite, consists of nine degrees, viz:— 1—3, Entered Apprentice, Fellow Craft and Master Mason, which are given in Lodges, and under the control of Grand Lodges; 4—7, Mark Master, Past Master, Most Excellent Master, and Royal Arch, which are given in Chapters, and under the control of Grand Chapters; 8, 9, Royal Master, and Select Master, which are given in Councils and under the control of Grand Councils. To these, perhaps, should be added three more degrees, namely, Knight of the Red Cross, Knight Templar, and Knight of Malta, which are given in Commanderies, and are under the control of Grand Commanderies.

There are also the degrees of the Ancient and Accepted Scottish Rite, which attract the most influential section of the Craft, and the degree of Sovereign Grand Inspector General (33°) may be described as the innermost sanctuary of the Masons of the United States.

The three degrees of the Craft are erroneously referred to in America as the York Rite, an expression for which the origin must be sought in the assumption of the term, "York Masons" by the "Ancients" in the year 1756.

There is, or may be, a Grand Lodge, Grand Chapter, Grand Council, and Grand Commandery in each State, whose jurisdiction is distinct and sovereign within its own territory. There is no General Grand Lodge, or Grand Lodge of the United States; but there is a General Grand Chapter, Grand Council, and Grand Encampment, to which the Grand Chapters, Grand Councils, and Grand Commanderies are subject.

STATISTICS U. S. A. LODGES TO 1914.

	Date of Formation	Number of Lodges	Number of Members
Alabama	1821	553	27,548
Arizona	1882	21	2,324
Arkansas	1832	562	20,962
California	1850	366	53,179
Colorado	1861	126	16,758
Connecticut	1789	110	25,378
Delaware	1806	22	3,436
District of Columbia	1810	30	9,924
Florida	1830	205	12,051
Georgia	1786	654	40,458
Idaho	1867	64	4,413
Illinois	1840	824	130,778
Indiana	1818	557	70,014
Iowa	1844	521	49,550
Kansas	1850	411	42,412
Kentucky	1800	591	42,139
Louisiana	1812	226	16,885
Maine	1820	203	30,294
Maryland	1787	117	16,650
Massachusetts	1777	249	67,938
Michigan	1844	428	74,964
Minnesota	1853	262	30.411
Mississippi	1818	373	20,073
Missouri	1821	636	61,522
Montana	1866	91	7,500
Nebraska	1857	262	21,122
Nevada	1865	24	1,939
New Hampshire	1789	80	10,782
New Jersey	1786	194	38,674
New Mexico	1877	43	3,361
New York	1787	826	186,179
North Carolina	1771	434	23,969

U. S. STATISTICS—Continued.

	Date of Formation	Number of Lodges	Number of Members
North Dakota	1889	107	9,130
Ohio	1808	546	96,075
Oklahoma	1892	448	26,181
Oregon	1851	141	13,260
Pennsylvania	1786	490	110,620
Rhode Island	1791	37	8,833
South Carolina	1787	259	16,165
South Dakota	1875	142	10,730
Tennessee	1813	457	28,081
Texas	1837	881	63,394
Utah	1872	19	2,355
Vermont	1794	103	13,847
Virginia	1777	325	24,566
Washington	1858	194	19,542
West Virginia	1865	147	16,710
Wisconsin	1843	274	29,243
Wyoming	1874	34	3,190
		14,669	1,655,509

THE LADY MASON.

Compiled by Osborne Sheppard from the records of Richard Spencer, the famous Masonic Bibliophile.

MRS. Elizabeth Aldworth, about the year 1735, received the first and second degrees of Freemasonry in Lodge No. 44, at Doneraile, in Ireland. The circumstances connected with this singular initiation were first published in 1807, at Cork, and subsequently republished by Spencer, the celebrated Masonic bibliophile, in London. It may be observed, before proceeding to glean from this work the narrative of her initiation, that the authenticity of all the circumstances was confirmed on their first publication by an eye-witness to the transaction.

The Hon. Elizabeth St. Leger was born about the year 1713, and was the youngest child and only daughter of the Right Hon. Arthur St. Leger, first Viscount Doneraile, of Ireland, who died in 1727, and was succeeded by his eldest son, the brother of our heroine. Subsequently to her initiation into the mysteries of Freemasonry she married Richard Aldworth, Esq., of Newmarket, in the county of Cork.

Lodge No. 44, in which she was initiated, was an aristocratic Lodge, consisting principally of the gentry and wealthy inhabitants of the country around Doneraile. The communications were usually held in the town, but during the Mastership of Lord Doneraile, under whom his sister was initiated, the meetings were often held at his Lordship's residence.

It was during one of these meetings at Doneraile House that this female initiation took place, the story of which Spencer, in the memoir to which we have referred, relates in the following words:

"It happened on this particular occasion that the Lodge was held in a room separated from another, as is often the case, by stud and brickwork. The young lady, being giddy and thoughtless, and determined to gratify her curiosity, made her arrangements accordingly, and, with a pair of scissors, (as she herself related to the mother of our informant), removed a portion of a brick from the wall, and placed herself so as to command a full view of everything which occurred in the next room; so placed, she witnessed the two first degrees in Masonry, which was the extent of the proceedings of the Lodge on that night. Becoming aware, from what she heard, that the brethren were about to separate, for the first time she felt tremblingly alive to the awkwardness and danger of her situation, and began to consider how she could retire without observation. She became nervous and agitated, and nearly fainted, but so far recovered herself as to be fully aware of the necessity of withdrawing as quickly as possible; in the act of doing so, being in the dark, she stumbled against some furniture. The crash was loud; and the Tiler, who was on the lobby or landing on which the doors both of the Lodge room and that where the honorable Miss St. Leger was, opened, gave the alarm, burst open the door and, with a light in one hand and a drawn sword in the other, appeared to the terrified lady. He was soon joined by the members of the Lodge present, and luckily; for it is asserted that but for the prompt appearance of her brother, Lord Doneraile, her life would have fallen a sacrifice to what was then esteemed her crime. The first care of his Lordship was to resuscitate the unfortunate lady without alarming the house, and endeavor to learn from her an explanation of what had occurred; having done so, many of the members being furious at the transaction, she was placed under guard of the Tiler and a member, in the room where she was found. The members re-assembled and deliberated as to what, under the circumstances, was to be done, and for over an hour she could hear the angry discussion and her death deliberately proposed and seconded. At length the good sense of the majority succeeded in calming, in some measure, the angry and irritated feelings of the rest of the members, when, after much had been said and many things proposed, it was resolved to give her the option of submitting to the Masonic ordeal to the extent she had witnessed, (Fellow Craft), and if she refused, the brethren were again to consult. Being waited on to decide, Miss St. Leger, exhausted and terrified by the storminess of the debate, which she could not avoid partially hearing, and yet, notwithstanding all, with a secret pleasure, gladly and unhesitatingly accepted the offer. She was accordingly initiated.''

Sister Aldworth lived to a ripe old age and never forgot the lessons of charity and fraternal love she received on her unexpected initiation into the esoteric doctrines of the Order. ''Placed as she was,'' says the memoir we have quoted, ''by her marriage with Mr. Aldworth, at the head of a very large fortune, the poor in general, and the Masonic poor in particular, had good reason to record her numerous and bountiful acts of kindness; nor were these accompanied with ostentation—far from it. It has been remarked of her, that her custom was to seek out misery and poverty, and with a well-directed liberality, soothe many a bleeding heart.''

ORIGIN OF THE EASTERN STAR.
BY MADELEINE B. CONKLIN, P.M.W.G.M.

THE Order of the Eastern Star, unlike many other orders, does not claim to have existed in any prehistoric age; like all women, our age is uncertain. Masonic historians seem to experience great difficulty in determining our origin, although they all take a lively interest in us. The eminent Masonic chronologist, Mackey, tells us that the Adoptive Rite was established in England, in the seventeenth century, under the patronage of Queen Henrietta Maria, daughter of King Henry IV of France and wife of King Charles I of England. After the execution of that unfortunate monarch, the Queen escaped to France, introducing the Rite there in 1730, under the name of "Macconneire d'Adoptione." After many changes and as late as 1838, this same Adoptive Rite was known as "The Five Jewels of the Orient."

In our rapidly increasing progress, we have no time to spend in idle retrospection of such uncertainty, for we care not whether we were rocked in the cradle of our infancy by the wives of King Solomon or the French Queen. If, as Mackey tells us, we are an offspring of that ancient Adoptive Rite, then we are indeed glad of the many changes which have taken place in the Order, incident to progress.

We have, however, conclusive proof, that in 1850, Robert Morris, the "Poet Laureate of Free-Masonry," outlined and founded our present system, and communicated the degrees to his wife. Later Robert Macoy, of New York, revised the manuscript, and put it into book form, known as the "Book of Mosaics," consisting of one hundred and ninety-eight pages, from which, after many changes, our present Ritual was compiled. Morris states positively, that his ideas were original, and that the "Five Heroines of the Order" were chosen to more clearly represent to the minds of the wives, mothers, daughters, widows and sisters of Master Masons, "Five Great Principles of Free-masonry." Be that as it may, most of us at least, prefer to believe that the "Eastern Star" was discovered by an American astrologist, in the blue sky of Freedom, and that its first rays shone over the "Land of the Free and the Home of the Brave."

The progress of the Order of the Eastern Star has exceeded the fondest hopes and desires of its founder. The Order has passed through the crucible of opposition and prejudice, but like the Masonic Fraternity, it has come forth shining with increased brilliancy.

Although no part of Free-Masonry, yet it is related to it by the dearest ties; and into the warp of the Masonic Mantle of all Fraternal Charity, you will find woven, "the woof of woman's tenderness, the devotion of the wife, the affection of the daughter, the unchanging love of the mother, the grief of the widow and the confiding faith of the sister."

The Order of the Eastern Star is built upon the enduring principles of Fidelity, Constancy, Purity, Hope and Benevolence, and is dedicated to Truth, Charity and Loving Kindness. It scatters sunshine, relieves distress, comforts the bereaved, cares for the sick and dying, admonishes its members to sacredly preserve their lips from slander and evil speaking, and raises the standard of moral purity, by teaching its men to be more manly and its women to be more womanly.

The Order of the Eastern Star, is the best systematized, most progressive and largest Woman's Charitable Fraternal Organization in existence. It is composed of affiliated Master Masons in good standing, their wives, mothers, daughters, widows and sisters. Here they join with the Masonic brothers in promulgating the principles of Brotherly Love, Relief and Truth.

As the Star in the East shone forth to guide the Wise Men to Bethlehem, so have the rays of our Star shone forth, until they have given warmth and light to every spot on earth, where the banner of the Red, White and Blue has been unfurled. England, Scotland, India and Canada have also been glorified by its piercing rays.

There is no question but what the Order of the Eastern Star has come to stay, and the longer it stays the more friends it will have and the better you will like it. It does not solicit members, but welcomes all the worthy that knock at its doors, and asks to be written as "One who loves his fellow men!"

The Order of the Eastern Star teaches morality, charity, heroism, self-denial and immortality. It opens the way to great possibilities for doing good, and affords ample opportunity of extending the reign of "Peace on earth, good will to men."

THE EASTERN STAR.
BY BROTHER ROBERT MORRIS
Masonic Poet-Laureate.

If there be lacking anything within this starry group,—
If there is place for other grace amidst the radiant troupe,—
I'll not go back on history's track to find a model clear,—
But crave your light, dear ladies bright, who grace my birthday here;
    And so I'll fill the measure of the Eastern Star!

The sparkling eye, the fairy form, they shall my muse inspire;
The singing tongue, the sacred song, awake my humble lyre;
The tripping feet in mazes fleet their mystic spell shall cast,
And all shall say, "The present day is better than the past!"
    And so I'll add new splendor to the Eastern Star!

From mothers here and maidens dear I'll borrow many a grace,—
In all this earth there is no worth like that a woman has;
Last at the Cross,—in lingering hope by Jesus, the adored;
First at the Grave,—in eager haste to magnify their Lord;
    From these I'll take fresh brilliance for the Eastern Star!

In each home circle, where the wife keeps household lamp alight,—
From sister's vigilant eye that guides the brother's steps aright,—
From mother's knee where childhood learns its one effectual prayer,—
If I indeed a lesson need I'll find that lesson there,
    And it will give rare glory to the Eastern Star.

Lastly, I'll seek the happy dead,—that grave, I know it well,
How fondly loved my Ella was, ah me, no words can tell,—
I know the answer that will come from you bright maiden blest,
"They who with Jesus suffer here shall have eternal rest."
    This overfills the radiance of the Eastern Star.

WHAT IS FREEMASONRY?

"A Jew entered a Parsee temple and beheld the sacred fire. 'What!' said he to the priest, 'do you worship fire?' 'Not fire,' answered the priest, 'it is an emblem to us of the sun and of his genial heat.' 'Do you then worship the sun as your God?' asked the Jew. 'Know ye not that this luminary also is but a work of the Almighty Creator?' 'We know it,' replied the priest, 'but the uncultivated man requires a sensible sign in order to form a conception of the Most High, and is not the sun, the incomprehensible source of light, an image of that invisible being who blesses and preserves all things?' 'Do your people, then,' rejoined the Israelite, 'distinguish the type from the original? They call the sun their God, and, descending even from this to a baser object, they kneel before an earthly flame! Ye amuse the outward but blind the inward eye; and while ye hold to them the earthly, ye draw from them the heavenly light! Thou shalt not make unto thyself any image or likeness.' 'How do you designate the Supreme Being?' asked the Parsee. 'We call him Jehovah Adonai; that is, the Lord who is, who was, and who will be,' answered the Jew. 'Your appellation is grand and sublime,' said the Parsee, 'but it is awful too.' A Christian then drew nigh and said, 'We call Him Father!' The Pagan and the Jew looked at each other and said, 'Here is at once an image and a reality; it is a word of the heart.' Therefore they all raised their eyes to Heaven, and said, with reverence and love, 'Our Father,' and they took each other by the hand, and all three called one another 'brother'."

FREEMASONRY—THE UNIVERSAL BROTHERHOOD.

Compiled by OSBORNE SHEPPARD from the writings of the late
M. W. BRO. JOHN HAMILTON GRAHAM, LL.D.
The First, and for nine years, Grand Master of the Grand Lodge of Quebec.

FREEMASONRY is a Universal Fellowship. It knows no distinctions but those of worth and merit. It is founded upon the equality of man in his inherent and inalienable rights. Its great aim is the amelioration, in all things, of the individual the family, the neighborhood, the State, the Nation, and the race. Utilizing the past, it acts in the living present, and strives after a glorious future. Envious of none, it gladly welcomes the coöperation of all who love their fellow-men.

Freemasons are free men. Each seeks admission into the Fraternity of his own free-will. If admitted, he receives instruction common to all. He exercises and enjoys, in equality, the perfect freedom of the Order; and he may withdraw therefrom at will.

Freemasonry is a system of symbolic architecture. The grand superstructure to be erected is the temple of humanity. Therein, labor is nobility and all is dedicated to work and worship. Man, the rough ashlar, is symbolically taken from the quarry of life,—is hewn, squared, polished, and made well-fit for his place in the great living temple whose chief foundation stones are truth and right; whose main pillars are wisdom, strength, nad beauty; whose adornments are all the virtues; the key-stone of whose world-o'erspanning arch is brotherhood; and whose Master Builder is The Great Architect of the Universe.

Freemasonry is a system of human culture. It inspires a desire for, inculcates a knowledge and teaches the use of, all the liberal arts and sciences, Chief among these is the science of mathematics. Geometry, its most important branch, is the basis of the Craftsman's art. It is taught to be of a divine or moral nature, enriched with the most useful knowledge, so that while it proves the wonderful properties of nature, it demonstrates the more important truths of morality. It teaches a knowledge of the earth, and sun, and moon, and stars, and of the laws which govern them. Above all, it teaches the Craftsman to adore and serve, the Grand Geometrician of the Universe.

Freemasonry is a peculiar system of morality veiled in allegory, and illustrated by symbols. It instils the sacred duties of brotherly love, relief, and truth; of prudence, temperance, fortitude, and justice; of benevolence, and charity; of forbearance and love; of gratitude and mercy; of patriotism, loyalty, and tolerance; of honesty and fidelity; of diligence, courtesy, and regard for others' welfare; of self-care and self-culture; to seek peace, and to assuage the rigors of conflict; and, in all things, to do not to others what one would they should not do to him.

It inculcates all the mutual duties and obligations of man in all the relations of life; of the ruler and the ruled; of the master and the servant; the employer and the employed; the high and the lowly; the rich and the poor; the learned and the unlearned; the teacher and the taught; the strong and the weak; the parent and the child; the old and the young; the hale and the infirm; and it inculcates the practice of every moral virtue, and every duty which man owes to himself, to his neighbor, and to the Most High.

Freemasonry is a social Order. The Craft are called from labor to refreshment. Temperance presides. Polite courtesy, pleasing address, and social intercourse are cultivated; the bonds of friendship are strengthened; and to refreshment of the body, are joined the feast of reason and the flow of soul.

Freemasonry is a system of willing obedience and rightful rule. Order is its first law. The Master commands according to the constitution; the brother obeys. He who best works, becomes best fitted to preside over and instruct his fellows. Preferment is founded upon worth and personal merit. Cheerful, lawful obedience and rightful rule have in Freemasonry their noblest union and fruition.

In the jurisprudence of the Craft, law, equity, and human welfare are united. Its supreme end is the wellbeing of man. The Craftsman is taught not to palliate or aggravate offences; but in the decision of every trespass, to judge with candor, admonish with friendship, and reprehend with mercy.

Freemasonry is a comprehensive system of government founded upon the rights of man, and exercised and enjoyed in the perfection of loyalty, union, efficiency, and harmony. Its mission is peace, progress, and prosperity.

Freemasonry is not a religion or a system of religion. It is a centre of union of good and true men of every race and tongue, who believe in God and practise the sacred duties of morality.

Freemasonry is a system of human philosophy. It is a school of learning; a college of builders. To the artist and the artisan; to the poet and philosopher; to the theorist and the utilitarian; to the speculative and the operative; to the man of business and the savant; to the prince and the peasant; to the ruler and the ruled; to the resident and the traveller; to the old, the middle-aged, and the youth, Freemasonry is alike congenial, instructive and beneficent. Therein all meet upon the Level, work by the Plumb, and part upon the Square. The grand mission of Freemasonry is peace, prosperity, uprightness, enlightenment, and unlimited good-will.

The fact that throughout the British Empire, and among free and enlightened peoples, so many of those in every grade of society, who are most vitally interested in conserving, ameliorating, and perpetuating what is most valuable and beneficial in the present civil, military, and political order of things are active and prominent members of the Craft, proves that Freemasonry is a thoroughly patriotic and loyal institution. The fact that so many of the adherents, and leaders even, of so many religious creeds and denominations belong to the Order shows beyond question that Freemasonry is a most tolerant institution. The fact that so many men of more than ordinary ability and culture are zealous Freemasons is proof that there is much in and pertaining to the Fraternity which is worthy the attention of the best and most brilliant intellects.

The fact that so many good and pious men are devoted Craftsmen demonstrates that, in their opinion, and from their experience, Freemasonry is an institution honoring to God and beneficial to man. The fact of its age, and its world-wide prevalence shows, that as to its moral principles;—its social order; its system of jurisprudence and government; its stability and permanence; its educating influence; its adaptability to the condition, needs, and aspirations of a free and progressive people; its humanizing efficacy; its non-partisan character; its practical and voluntary charity, it contains within itself the elements of a true, universal brotherhood, destined to exist and prosper, world without end.

SYMBOLISM.
ENTERED APPRENTICE.

The First or Entered Apprentice Degree is intended to symbolize man, helpless and ignorant, entering into the world; also youth groping in mental darkness for intellectual light.

QUALIFICATION.

Every Candidate for initiation must believe in the existence of a Supreme Being and future state; he must be of good moral character, and mature age, and able to conscientiously answer the following questions in the affirmative:

DECLARATION.

"Do you seriously declare, upon your honor, that, unbiased by friends against your own inclination, and uninfluenced by unworthy motives, you freely, and voluntarily offer yourself a candidate for the mysteries and privileges of Freemasonry?"

"Do you seriously declare that you are solely prompted to solicit those privileges by a favourable opinion conceived of the Order, a desire of knowledge, and a sincere wish to render yourself more extensively serviceable to your fellow-creatures?"

"Do you also seriously declare, upon your honor, that you will cheerfully conform to the ancient usages and established customs of the Fraternity?"

THE PREPARATION.

The Candidate is required to close his eyes on the past, and think of the dark mysterious future. This blindness is emblematical of our ignorance, and of the designs of the great Architect of the Universe being beyond the utmost stretch of the Human Mind. Yet the study of Nature will develop intellectual light, dispel ignorance;

and the more it is studied the loftier and more comprehensive will be our ideas of the great Creator and First Cause of all things.

Equality.—As Masonry does not regard, or admit any person on account of rank or fortune, he should divest his mind of all selfish and worldly considerations, and lay aside the trinkets and trappings of the outward world, and for a time become poor and penniless; so that he may remember, when asked to assist a Brother in distress, that Masonry received him in poverty, and that he should then embrace the opportunity of practising that virtue, Charity.

His Sincerity of purpose and purity of mind are symbolized by the left * * * being made bare; in token of implicit or unreserved Confidence, the right * * * is uncovered; so also in token of Humility is the left * * * made bare, to bend before the Great Author of his existence; and to follow the ancient custom of the Israelites, he will be prepared to slip the shoe from off his foot, as a testimony or token of Fidelity (Ruth iv. 7). The Cable Tow, with a running noose, is emblematical of the Dangers which surround us in this life, especially if we should stray from the paths of duty. It will also remind the initiated to submit, while he is in ignorance, to being guided by those whom he knows to be enlightened.

THE INITIATION.

"Ask and it shall be given you; seek, and you shall find; knock, and it shall be opened unto you."—Matt. vii. 7.

The knocks at the door denote Peace, Harmony, and Brotherly Love. Before the ceremony of Initiation begins, the Candidate is informed that Freemasonry is an institution founded on the purest principles of Morality—i.e., on Truth, Brotherly Love, and Charity; and requires a cheerful compliance, to maintain the established usages and customs of the Order. The moment we enter the world, and draw the first breath of life, the Sword of Justice is pointed to our heart, and will sooner or later overtake us;

so in Masonry, at our first entrance we are taught to be cautious, and trust in God.

Prayer.—Vouchsafe Thine aid, Almighty Father, and Supreme Architect of the Universe, to our present convention; and grant that this Candidate for Freemasonry may dedicate and devote his life to Thy service, so as to become a true and faithful Brother among us. Endow him with a competency of Thy Divine Wisdom, that, assisted by the lessons of our Moral Science, he may be better enabled to display the beauty of true Godliness, to the Honor and Glory of Thy Holy Name. Amen.

THE PILGRIMAGE.

Where the blessing of God is invoked, the Candidate may fear no danger, but arise, and follow his enlightened guide, who will enable him to travel safely through the dark emblematic pilgrimage of ignorance, and overcome the obstructions and difficulties which beset the way of knowledge.

This part of the ceremony symbolizes the progress of human intelligence, from a state of ignorance, to the highest state of civilization and mental enlightenment. During the time of this part, in some lodges the 133rd Psalm is read, to impress the Candidate and Brethren with a feeling of Brotherly Love.

THE BIBLE.

No Lodge exists without the acknowledged Bible, and would, without, be illegal and unwarrantable.

The hand placed on the Bible, which is properly called the greatest light of Masonry, and attention called to its teachings, will remind us of the obligations we owe to God and our fellow-men.

The Holy Bible, the inestimable gift of God to man, is the wonder of books. Its teachings are the basis of morals and religion, and it is the book of universal appeal.

The historian, the poet, the philosopher and the legislator have found in it an inexhaustible mine of treasures.

It is the Bible which reveals to us the glories of immortality for within our mortal tenement there burns an undying flame, lit by the hand of God Himself.

THE SECRECY AND VOWS OF FIDELITY.

Having completed the symbolic journey in search of enlightenment, Vows of Fidelity or Secrecy are required; but these are voluntary, and the Candidate must be assured, before taking them, that there is nothing in those Vows incompatible with his civil, moral, or religious duties. The Veil of Secrecy which shrouds Freemasonry has attracted the attention of the uninitiated more than anything else; and by their conjectures have attributed to it many erroneous notions, some of which none but the most ignorant could believe—such as using incantations, and raising unearthly-like beings, or performing some waggish mischief on the Candidate. The writer has often seen a Candidate enter the Lodge trembling with fear, and has known of others who, after being partly prepared, became so suspicious or afraid of some evil that they would not proceed, even though assured by members to the contrary. But some may naturally reason in their own mind: "If the objects and pretensions of Freemasonry be honest and praiseworthy, what need is there for an obligation of secrecy? If it be really a system of morality, and has a tendency to elevate the mind, or be a benefit to mankind, why not make it free to all? And charity being boasted of as one of its characteristic features, is it not Masons' bounden duty, as charitable men, to make it known without fee or price, instead of binding the members by obligations to secrecy?" The only answer which we can give to these questions is, That nature is shrouded in mystery; and mystery has charms for all men. Whatever is familiar to us, however novel, beautiful, or elevating, is often disregarded, unnoticed, or despised; whilst novelty, however trifling or devoid of intrinsic value, will charm and captivate the imagination, and become the fuel of curiosity, which cannot bear to be ignorant of what others know. And so Freemasonry, taking the example of Nature, veils its beauties in mystery, and illustrates them by symbols. In support of this, we will conclude this part by quoting two distinguished modern writers:

"Thoughts will not work, except in silence; neither will virtue work, except in secrecy. Like other plants, virtue will not grow unless its roots be hidden, buried from the light of the sun. Let the sun shine on it—nay, do but look at it privily thyself—the roots wither, and no flowers will glad thee."—Thomas Carlyle, "Sartor Resartus."

"God has put the veil of secrecy before the soul for its preservation; and to thrust it rudely aside, without reason, would be suicidal. Neither here, nor, as I think, hereafter, will our thoughts and feelings lie open to the world."—H. W. Beecher, "Life Thoughts."

THE ENLIGHTENMENT.

"The light shineth in darkness; and the darkness comprehendeth it not."—John i. 5.

"And God said, let there be light, and there was light."— Gen. i. 3.

This particular part of the ceremony symbolizes the victory of Knowledge over Ignorance, and the impression intended to be made on the mind of the Candidate on first beholding the Thee Great Lights of Masonry, is to make him recollect that the light of Wisdom is beautiful, and that all her paths are peace.

" 'Tis the Great Spirit, wide diffused
Through everything we see,
That with our spirits communeth
Of things mysterious—life and death,
Time and Eternity!

"The people that walked in darkness have seen a great light: they that dwell in the land of the shadow of death; upon them hath the light shined."—Isaiah ix. 2.

THE **** **** ****

The three great Lights are the Holy Bible*, Square, and Compasses. The Bible to govern our faith and practice, being the gift of God to man for that purpose; the Square to regulate our actions; and the Compasses to keep us in due bounds with all mankind.

THE **** ****

Are three burning Candles or Tapers, emblematical of the Spirit of God, whereby His chosen people are enlightened, and are also meant to represent, the Sun, to rule the day, the Moon to govern the night, and the Master to rule and direct his Lodge. They are also emblematical of the Master and his Wardens, and are placed in the east, south, and west; as the sun rises in the east, so the Worshipful Master is placed in the east, to open his lodge, and enlighten the brethren in Masonry.

The Junior Warden represents the sun at its meridian in the south, and as it is then the beauty and glory of the day, it is his duty to call the brethren from labor to refreshment, see that they do not convert the time thereof into intemperance, but to regulate them so that pleasure and profit may be enjoyed by all.

The Senior Warden represents the sun in the west at the close of the day, and it is his duty to see that the Brethren are all satisfied, and that they have their just dues, before closing the Lodge by command of the Master.

THE SECRETS.

Having been converted into one of the Sons of Light, and taught to be cautious, the Candidate may be intrusted

---

*The Bible is used among Masons as the symbol of the Will of God, however it may be expressed. And, therefore, whatever to any people expresses that will may be used as a substitute for the Bible in a Masonic Lodge. Thus, in a Lodge consisting entirely of Jews, the Old Testament alone may be placed upon the altar, and Turkish Masons make use of the Koran. Whether it be the Gospels to the Christian, the Pentateuch to the Israelite, the Koran to the Mussulman, or the Vedas to the Brahmin, it everywhere Masonically conveys the same idea—that of the symbolism of the Divine Will revealed to man.

with the Secrets belonging to this degree, which consist of a S * * a G * * or T * *, and a Word. For these the reader is referred to W. M. of his lodge; but it would be well to remember that all squares, levels, and upright lines allude to the Obligation, and are proper signs by which to know a Mason.

THE INVESTURE.

After the reciprocal communication of the marks which distinguish us as Masons, the Candidate is invested with a LAMBSKIN OR WHITE APRON. It is the Emblem of Innocence, the Badge of a Mason, and the Bond of Brotherhood; and, when worthily worn as such, will give pleasure to himself and honor to the Fraternity; and be of more value than the diadems of Kings, or the pearls of Princesses; and it should remind him that purity of life and rectitude of conduct are necessary to gain admission to the Celestial Lodge, where the Supreme Architect presides.

CHARGE AFTER INVESTURE.

You are never to put on that Badge if you are at variance with any Brother in the Lodge; if so, either or both of you must retire, so that the harmony of the assembly be not disturbed by your unseemly strife. When haply your differences are reconciled, you may return and clothe yourselves, and "dwell together in unity," for brotherly love is regarded as the strongest cement of the Order.

THE FOUNDATION STONE.

Of every Masonic edifice is, or ought to be, placed in the north-east corner of the building; and the newly initiated Brother is made to represent that stone, and there receives his first lesson on Moral Architecture, teaching him to walk and act uprightly before God and man; as well as for special reasons, a striking illustration of brotherly love and charity, which he is unable, in his present condition, to bestow. (I. Kings vi. 7.) But charity is the principal of all social virtues, and the distinguishing characteristic of Masons. Let the feelings of the heart, guided by reason, direct the hand of Charity:

THE WORKING TOOLS

Are the twenty-four inch Gauge, the Common Gavel, and the Chisel. Their use in operative Masonry is obvious, and requires no explanation; but as speculative or Free Masons, we see them applied to our morals, thus—

THE TWENTY-FOUR INCH G****

Is emblematical of the twenty-four hours of the day, which ought to be devoted to the service of God by a proper division of our time, for pray, labor, refreshment, and sleep.

THE COMMON G****

Is the emblem of Reason, and of labor being the lot of man. By reasoning and examining ourselves, we see the necessity of breaking off and divesting our consciences of all vice, thereby fitting our minds, as living stones, for that spiritual building eternal in the heavens.

THE C****

Points out to us the advantages of Education, by which means alone we are rendered fit members of regularly organised Society.

THE JEWELS.

A Lodge has Six jewels, three movable and three immovable.

The immovable jewels are the Square, Level and Plumb Rule. They are termed immovable because they are assigned to particular stations in the Lodge—the Square in the East, the Level in the West, and the Plumb Rule in the South; and although the brethren occupying those stations may from time to time be changed, still the jewels will always there be found.

The Square teaches morality; the Level, equality; and the Plumb Rule, justness and uprightness of life and conduct.

The movable jewels are the Rough Ashlar, the Perfect Ashlar, and the Tracing Board.

THE ROUGH ASHLAR.

Represents man in his natural state, ignorant, unpolished, and vicious, like a precious stone surrounded by a dense crust, its beauty unseen till the rough surface is removed.

THE PERFECT ASHLAR

Represents him in a high state of civilization, with his mind divested of all vice, and prepared for that house, not made with hands, eternal in the heavens, which, by a liberal and virtuous education, our own endeavors, and the grace of God, we hope to attain.

BROTHERLY LOVE, RELIEF AND TRUTH

Are the three great Tenets or Principles of a Freemason.

BROTHERLY LOVE

Is the strongest cement of the Order, and without it the Fraternity would soon cease to exist. By it we are taught to regard the whole human species as one family, to aid, support, and protect each other.

RELIEF

Flows from brotherly love, and it is a duty incumbent on all men to soothe the unhappy, relieve the distressed, and restore peace to their troubled minds.

TRUTH

Is a divine attribute, and the mother of Virtue; and the first lesson we are taught in Masonry is to be fervent and zealous in the pursuit of truth, and to dispense it freely.

THE LODGE-ROOM AND ITS ACCESSORIES.

The Lodge-room is a representation of the world; and a properly constructed Lodge should be situated due east and west, for which we assign three Masonic reasons— First, the sun rises in the east, and sets in the west; second, Learning originated in the east, and extended to the west; third, The Tabernacle in the Wilderness was so situated (Exodus chaps. xxvi. and xxvii.), to commemorate the miraculous east wind (Exodus xiv. 21), and being symbolic of the universe, was the type of a Freemason's Lodge.

ITS FORM

Being an oblong square, or double cube, is emblematical of the united powers of Darkness and Light.

ITS DIMENSIONS

Embrace every clime; in length, from east to west; in breadth, between the north and south; in depth, from the surface of the earth to the centre; and in height, from earth to heaven; denoting the universality of its influence.

W***, S***, AND B***

Are the three great pillars on which the Lodge-room is supported. Wisdom to contrive, govern, and instruct; Strength to support; and Beauty, to adorn. The W.M. in the east represents * * * *, the S.W. in the west represents * * * *, and the J.W. in the south represents * * * *. Their situations, forming a triangle, is emblematical of their unity in forming one Government; they also represent Solomon, King of Israel, for wisdom; Hiram, King of Tyre, for his assistance in building the Temple; and Hiram

Abiff, for his cunning or beautiful workmanship. These three great pillars are represented by the three principal orders of Architecture, i.e., the Doric, Ionic, and Corinthian. The Ionic column represents Wisdom, because it wisely combines strength with grace. Strength is represented by the Doric, being the strongest and most massive of the orders. Beauty is represented by the Corinthian, being the most beautiful and ornamental.

THE COVERING

Of a Freemason's Lodge is the Celestial Canopy, or the starry-decked Heavens, The sun, moon, and stars are emblems of God's power, goodness, omnipresence, and eternity.

THE FURNITURE

Consists of the Holy Bible, Square, and Compasses. The Bible is the symbol of God's Will, and is dedicated to His service; the Square to the Master, being the emblem of His office; the Compasses are dedicated to the whole Craft, being emblematical of the limits which ought to circumscribe our conduct, that we may live with honor, and be respected by a large circle of good friends, and make our exit from the stage of life in the humble hope of being rewarded with a Crown of Glory.

THE ORNAMENTS

Are the Mosaic Pavement, the Tessellated Border, and Blazing Star.

THE MOSAIC PAVEMENT

Reminds us of the bounteous liberality of our Father in heaven, who has spread the earth with a beauteous carpet, and wrought it, as it were, in Mosaic work. It also represents the world chequered over with good and evil, pain and pleasure, grief with joy; today we walk in prosperity, tomorrow we totter in adversity; but, united in the Bond of Brotherhood, and walking uprightly, we may not stumble.

THE TESSELLATED BORDER

Of the Mosaic Carpet may be likened to the wavy ocean, which skirts the land, and by indenting it adds beauty to the earth; but it is emblematically intended to represent the many blessings and comforts with which we are surrounded in this life, but more especially those which we hope to enjoy hereafter.

THE BLAZING STAR

Is the first and most exalted object that demands our attention in the Lodge, and is the emblem of PRUDENCE, which should shine conspicuously in our conduct, and be the guiding star of our lives, instructing us to regulate our actions by the dictates of reason and experience, to judge wisely, and determine with propriety, on everything that tends to our present or future happiness. Its proper place is in the centre of the Lodge, so as to be ever present to the eye, that the heart may be attentive to the dictates, and steadfast in the laws of Prudence.

THE TASSELS.

These cords which adorn the four corners of the Tessellated Border are emblematical of the Cardinal Virtues—viz., Prudence, Fortitude, Temperance, and Justice.

FORTITUDE

Is that virtue which enables us to bear the adversities of social life, encounter danger, resist temptation, and keep us in the practice of Virtue.

TEMPERANCE

Sets bounds to our desires, frees the mind from the allurements of vice, and renders our passions tame and governable. The health of the body, and the dignity of man, depend upon a faithful observance of this virtue.

JUSTICE

Is the boundary of Right, and the cement of Civil Society. Without the exercise of this virtue, social intercourse could not exist; might would usurp the place of right, and universal confusion ensue. Justice commands you to "Do unto others as you would that others should do unto you." Let Prudence direct you, Fortitude support you, Temperance chasten you, and Justice be the guide of all your actions.

THE THEOLOGICAL LADDER

Which Jacob saw in his vision, extending from earth to heaven, represents the way of salvation, the many steps composing it representing as many moral virtues, the principal being Faith, Hope, and Charity. It rests on the volume of the Sacred Law, which strengthens our Faith, and creates Hope in Immortality; but Charity is the chief of all social virtues, and the distinguishing characteristic of the Order; and the Mason possessed of that virtue in its widest sense may be said to wear the brightest jewel that can adorn the Fraternity. The Sacred Volume is represented on the Tracing Board as resting on the vortex of a circle, which is embordered by two perpendicular parallel lines, representing Moses and King Solomon; or (in Christian Lodges) St. John the Baptist and St. John the Evangelist, who, in Masonry, it is understood, were parallels, and exemplary of those virtues which Masons are taught to reverence and practice.

THE CIRCLE

Represents the Boundary Line of a Mason's conduct; and in going round the circle, we necessarily touch upon these lines, and the Holy Scriptures, which point out the whole duty of man; and they who circumscribe their conduct by those examples, and the precepts therein contained, cannot materially err. There is a point within the circle referring to the Glorious Throne of God, the great Architect and Creator of the Universe, who is Almighty, of infinite Wisdom, and whose Being extends through boundless space, enjoying alone the attributes of Immortality and Eternity! This symbol of God is almost universal in His works.

THE LEWIS

Which is dovetailed into the Perfect Ashlar, denotes Strength, to support us in all our lawful undertakings. It also denotes the son of a Mason, whose duty it is to support his aged parents, when they are unable to labor or bear the burden of cares, gathered upon them in their journey through life.

CHARGE TO NEWLY ADMITTED BROTHER.

You have now passed through the ceremony of your Initiation, and been admitted a member of our ancient and honorable Institution. Knowledge and virtue are the objects of our pursuit; and the Great Architect of the Universe is our Supreme Master. On Him we rely for support and protection, and to His will we ought to submit, while we work by the unerring rule He has given to guide us. By having said so much, we do not mean you to understand that Masons arrogate to themselves everything that is great, good, and honorable. By no means. The gates of knowledge, and the paths of truth and virtue, are open to all who choose to enter and walk therein; but this much may be affirmed of Masonry, that the moral lessons which it teaches favor us with peculiar advantage, which, if duly studied and practiced, would exalt us above the rest of mankind.

As a Mason, you are bound to be a strict observer of the moral law, as contained in the Holy Writings, and to consider these as the unerring standard of Truth and Justice, and by their divine precepts to regulate your life and actions. Therein is inculcated your duty to God, your neighbor, and yourself; to God, in never mentioning His name but with that reverential awe which becomes a creature to bear to his Creator, and to look upon Him as the source of all good, which we came into the world to enjoy, to love, and obey; to your neighbors, by acting on the Square, and doing unto them as you would wish them to do unto you; to yourself, in avoiding all irregularity and intemperance, or debasing your dignity as a man, and a Mason. A zealous attachment to these duties will ensure public and private esteem.

As a citizen, you should be exemplary in the discharge of your civil duties, true to your government, and just to your country, yielding obedience to the laws which afford you protection.

As an individual, be careful to avoid reproach or censure; let not interest, favor, or prejudice bias your integrity, or influence you to be guilty of any dishonorable action; and, above all, practice benevolence and charity, so far as you can without injury to yourself or family. But do not suppose that Masonry confines your good offices to the Fraternity only, or absolves you from your duty to the rest of mankind,—it inculcates Universal Benevolence, and extends its benign influence to the whole world. Your frequent attendance at our meetings we earnestly solicit, yet it is not meant that Masonry should interfere with your necessary avocations; but in your leisure time, that you may improve in Masonic Knowledge, you should converse with well informed Brethren, who will be as ready to give as you to receive instruction. Finally: you are to keep sacred and inviolable the mysteries of the Institution, as these are to distinguish you from the rest of the community; and if a person of your acquaintance is desirous of being initiated into Masonry, be careful not to recommend him unless you are convinced he will conform to our rules, that the honor and reputation of the Institution may be firmly established.

Your attention to this charge will lead us to hope that you will estimate the real value of Freemasonry, and imprint on your mind the dictates of Truth, Honor, and Justice.

FELLOW CRAFT.

In the pursuit of Knowledge, the intellectual faculties are employed in promoting the glory of God, and the good of man. In this Degree the young Mason is represented as having attained the age of Manhood, and laboring to overcome the difficulties which beset him in the attainment of the hidden mysteries of learning and science, to which he is introduced and enjoined to study, so that he may see knowledge rising out of its first elements, and be led, step by step, from simple ideas, through all the windings and labyrinths of Truth, to the most exalted discoveries of the human Intellect.

PRAYER AT OPENING.

Let us remember that wherever we are or whatever we do the All-Seeing Eye is upon us; and while we continue to act together as faithful craftsmen, let us never fail to discharge our duty towards Him with fervency and zeal. Amen.

THE WORKING TOOLS.

Of this Degree are the P***, L***, and S***.

THE P****

Is the emblem of Justness and Uprightness, and admonishes us to hold the scales of Justice in equal poise, and make our conduct coincide with the line of our duty, which is to walk uprightly before God and man.

THE L****

Is the emblem of Equality, and reminds us that we are descended from the same stock, partake of the same nature, and share the same hope. In the sight of God all men are equal; and the time will come when all distinctions but that of goodness shall cease, and Death, the grand leveller of human greatness, reduces all to the same state.

THE S****

In this Degree is a very important instrument, as none can become a Fellow Craft without its assistance. It is the emblem of Morality and Virtue, reminding us to square our actions, and harmonize our conduct by the unalterable principles of the moral law as contained in the Holy Bible, and we are obligated to act upon the Square with all mankind, but especially with our Brethren in Masonry.

THE JEWELS.

The Three Symbolic or precious Jewels of a Fellow Craft are Faith, Hope and Charity.

FAITH IN GOD.
"For humble Faith, with steadfast eye,
Points to a brighter world on high."
HOPE IN IMMORTALITY.
"Daughter of Faith! Awake, arise, illume,
The dread unknown, the Chaos of the tomb."
CHARITY TO ALL MANKIND.
"Secures her votaries unblasted fame,
And in celestial annals 'graves their name."

THE TWO PILLARS.

Names B*** and J*** placed at the porch or entrance to King's Solomon's Temple are described in I. Kings vii. 15-22, II. Kings xxv. 17, Jer. lii. 21-23, as being eighteen cubits high; but, in 2 Chron. iii. 15-17, they are said to have been "thirty and five cubits high." This discrepancy is supposed to have arisen by the aggregate height of both Pillars being given in Chronicles, and allowing half a cubit of each to be hidden in the joining holes of the Chapiters. The Chapiters on the top were of molten brass, and five cubits in height. Although another discrepancy seemingly exists in 2 Kings xxv. 17, where it is said that they were only three cubits, but if we allow two cubits for the "wreathen work and pomegranates" described, they will amount to five cubits. The net work denotes Unity; the lily work, Peace; and the pomegranates, from the exuberance of their seed, Plenty. The Chapiters were also surmounted by two pommels or globes (1 Kings vii. 41; 2 Chron. iv. 12), which, according to Masonic tradition, were the archives of Masonry, and contained the maps and charts of the celestial and terrestrial bodies, denoting the universality of Masonry, and that a Mason's charity should be equally extensive, bounded only by Prudence, and ruled by Discretion, so that real want and merit may be relieved, and the knave prevented from eating the bread which Virtue in distress ought to have. Pillars of such magnitude, strength, and beauty could not but attract the attention of those who beheld them, and impress upon their minds the idea of strength and stability which their names imply, and will be remembered by every Mason. The destruction of these immense pillars, the magnificent temple, and city, is significant of the weakness and instability of human greatness, and that our strength can only be in God; and faith in Him is the only foundation on which we can build our future temple of happiness to stand firm for ever. 2 Sam. xii. 17; 1 Kings ix. 3-7.

THE WINDING STAIR.

Having passed the pillars of the porch, the Candidate, seeking for more light by the mysteries contained in the Second Degree, must approach the east by a supposed Winding Stair, symbolically leading from the ground floor to the Middle Chamber of Masonry. The only reference to it in Scripture is in 1 Kings vi. 8.

Before entering the Middle Chamber, where, as Masons, we are told that the Fellow Craft went to receive their wages, they had to give a certain password, in proof that they were not imposters. This password was instituted at the time when Jephtha put the Ephraimites to flight, and slew forty and two thousand at the different fords and passes of the river Jordan (Judges xii. 1-7). The word S**** means the ford of a river, or an ear of corn, and is depicted on the Tracing Board by an ear of corn near a stream of water; but, as speculative Masons, it is the lesson which this symbol is intended to illustrate that we have to consider, for, by historical facts and natural reasons, we cannot suppose that legend as rehearsed in the Lodge-room is anything more than a philosophical myth. Masonic Symbolism shows the Candidate as always rising towards a higher state of perfection. In the First Degree we have the Theological Ladder, impressing this idea; in the Second Degree, we have the Winding Staircase, symbolizing the laborious ascent to eminence in the attainment of the hidden mysteries of learning and science. The Symbolic Staircase is composed of three, five, seven, or other unequal number of steps.

The Three Steps represent youth, or the Degree of the Entered Apprentice,viz.—1st, his being born to Masonic life; 2nd, his ignorance of the world in his childhood; 3rd, the lessons which he receives in his youth to prepare his mind for the instruction which is given in the succeeding Degrees; they also allude to the three supports, Wisdom, Strength, and Beauty.

The Five Steps allude to Manhood, or the Fellow Craft Degree, the Five Orders of Architecture, and the Five Human Senses.

The Seven Steps refer to Old Age, or the Third Degree; the seven Sabbatical Years, seven Years of Famine, seven Golden Candlesticks, seven Planets, seven Days of the Week, seven Years in Building the Temple, seven Wonders of the World, &c., but more especially to the seven liberal Arts, and Sciences. The total number of Steps, amounting in all to fifteen, is a significant symbol, for fifteen was a sacred number among the Orientals, because the letters of the holy name JAH, were, in their numerical value, equivalent to fifteen; the Fifteen Steps of the Winding Stair are therefore symbolic of the name of God; and hence a figure, in which the nine digits were so disposed as to count fifteen either way when added together perpendicularly, horizontally, or diagonally, constituted one of ther most sacred talismans.

Masons are indebted for the symbol of odd numbers to Pythagoras, who considered them more perfect than even ones; therefore, odd numbers predominate in Masonry, and are intended to symbolize the idea of perfection.

In ancient times it was considered a fortunate omen, when ascending a stair, to commence with the right foot, and find the same foot foremost at the top; and this is said to be the reason why ancient temples were ascended by an odd number of steps.

It is then as a symbol, and a symbol only, that we study the legend of the Winding Staircase; to adopt it as an historical fact, the absurdity of its details stares us in the face. What could be more absurd than to believe that eighty thousand craftsman had to ascend such a stair, to the narrow precincts of the Middle Chamber, to receive their wages in corn, wine, and oil? Taken as an allegory, we see beauty in it, as it sets before us the picture of a Mason's duty,—to be ever on the search for knowledge, even though the steps in the attainment of it are winding and difficult; but by study and perseverance we will gain our reward, and that reward more precious than either money, corn, oil, or wine.—2 Chron. ii. 15.

Having passed into the Middle Chamber, the attention of Fellow Crafts is drawn to the letter placed conspicuously in the centre of it, to denote Geometry, the science on which this Degree is founded, but it refers more especially to G∴T∴G∴G∴O∴T∴U∴.

CORN, WINE, OIL,
Are emblematical of
PLENTY, CHEERFULNESS, PEACE.

ARCHITECTURE.

Architecture is the art of building edifices, either for habitation or defence, and with respect to its objects, may be divided into three branches—Civil, Military, and Naval. Nature and necessity taught the first inhabitants of the earth to build huts to shelter them from the rigor of the seasons, and inclemency of the weather; and, after attaining what was useful and necessary, luxury and ambition caused them to ornament their buildings.

THE ORDERS OF ARCHITECTURE.

The Origin of the Orders of Architecture is almost as ancient as human society. At first the trunks of trees were set on end, while others were laid across to support the covering, hence, it is said, arose the idea of more regular architecture, the trees on end representing columns, the girts or bands which connected them express the bases and capitals, and the brest-summers laid across gave the hint of entablatures, as the coverings ending in points did of pediments. This is the hypothesis of Vitruvius. Others believe that columns took their rise from pyramids, which the ancients erected over their tombs, and the urns which enclosed the ashes of the dead represented the capitals, while a brick or stone laid thereon as a cover formed the abacus. The Greeks, however, were the first to regulate the height of their columns on the proportion of the human body, the Doric representing a strong man; the Ionic, a woman; and the Corinthian, a girl.

The various Orders took their names from the people among whom they were invented, and are thus classed—The Tuscan, Doric, Ionic, Corinthian, and Composite. Scamozzi uses significant terms to express their character; he calls the Tuscan, the Gigantic; the Doric, the Herculean; the Ionic, the Matronal; the Corinthian, the Virginal; the Composite, the Heroic.

THE TUSCAN

Is the most simple and solid; its column is seven diameters high, the capital, base, and entablature having few mouldings or ornaments.

THE DORIC

Is said to be the most ancient and best proportioned of all the orders; it has no ornaments on base or capital except mouldings. The height is eight diameters, and its frieze is divided by Triglyphs and Metopes; the oldest example extant is at Corinth.

THE IONIC

Bears a kind of mean proportion between the more solid and delicate orders; the capital is ornamented with volutes, and its cornice with denticles. The column is nine diameters. Michael Angelo gives it a single row of leaves at the bottom of the capital.

THE CORINTHIAN

Is ten diameters high, and its capital is adorned with two rows of leaves and eight volutes, which sustain the abacus, and the cornice is ornamented with denticles and modillions. Vitruvius relates the following narrative of its invention:—"Collimachus, accidentally passing the tomb of a young lady, he perceived a basket of toys, covered with a tile, placed over an ancthus root, having been left there by her nurse. As the branches grew up, they encompassed the basket, till, arriving at the tile, they met an obstruction, and bent downwards. Struck with the beauty of the arrangement, he set about imitating the figure, the basket representing the base of the capital; the tile, the abacus; and the bending leaves, the volutes." Foliated capitals of much greater antiquity than any discovered in Greece, are, however, to be found in Egypt and Asia Minor; and Villalpandus says "that it took its origin from an Order in Solomon's Temple, the leaves whereof were those of the palm tree."

THE COMPOSITE

Is so called because it is composed of the other orders; the column is ten diameters high, and its cornice has denticles, or simple modillions.

There are, however, many other styles of architecture. The Teutonic is distinguished by semi-circular arches, and massive plain columns.

The Gothic is distinguished by its lightness and profuse ornament, pointed arches, and pillars, carved so as to imitate several conjoined. The Egyptians, Chinese, Hindoos, Moors, &c., have each their own styles of ornamental buildings, and splendid specimens are to be seen in their several countries.

THE FIVE SENSES

An analysis of the human faculties is next given in this Degree, in which the five external Senses particularly claim attention, as they are the root or foundation of all human knowledge. It will be seen by a careful consideration of the functions of the Five Senses, that sensation and reflection are the great sources of human knowledge, and that they are the means by which all our first ideas and information are acquired, because external objects act first on our senses, and rouse us to a consciousness of their existence, and convey distinct impressions to the mind, according to the manner in which they affect us; the mind, storing up and remembering these impressions, assembles them, and compares one with another, and thus we acquire a new and more complex set of ideas, in which we observe variety, uniformity, similitude, symmetry, novelty, grandeur, and reference to an end; and by the mind reflecting upon what passes within itself, creates another set of impressions no less distinct than those conveyed to it by the senses. Sensation is, therefore, the great source of human knowledge, and, at the same time, the boundary beyond which our conceptions cannot reach, for we are unable to find one original idea, which has not been derived from sensation. But we are not to conclude that, because solid and thinking beings are the only ideas of existence which we are able to form, that there may not be a class of being superior to mankind, enjoying other powers of perception unknown to us; we might as well conclude that the want of the ideas of light and color, in a man born blind, would be an argument against the reality or possibility of their existence.

HEARING

Is the sense by which we distinguish sounds and enjoy all the charms of music; by it we are enabled to communicate with each other, and enjoy the pleasures of society, and avoid many dangers that we would otherwise be exposed to.

THE EYE

Is the organ of Sight, and seeing is that sense by which we distinguish objects, forms, colors, motion, rest, and distance or space, &c.

> "The beams of light had been in vain displayed,
> Had not the eye been fit for vision made;
> In vain the Author had the eye prepared
> With so much skill, had not the light appeared."

FEELING

Is the sense by which we acquire ideas of hardness and softness, roughness and smoothness, heat and cold, &c., and is the most universal of our senses.

Those three senses are peculiarly essential to Masons, i.e., to see the Signs, hear the Words, and feel the Grips.

TASTING

Is the sense by which we distinguish sweet from sour, bitter from salt, &c., and enables us to make a proper distinction in the choice of our food.

SMELLING

Is the sense by which we distinguish sweet, sour, aromatic, and fœtid or offensive orders, which convey difference impressions to the mind: and the design of the G** A** O* T** U** is manifest in having located the organ of smell in the nostrils, the channels through which the air is continually passing.

The inconceivable wisdom of the Almighty Being is displayed in the five senses. The structures of the mind, and all the active powers of the soul present a vast and boundless field for philosophical investigation, which far exceeds human inquiry; and are peculiar mysteries, known only to Nature and to Nature's God, to whom we are indebted for every blessing we enjoy. This theme is therefore peculiarly worthy of attention.

The Seven Liberal Arts and Sciences are—Grammar, Logic, Rhetoric, Arithmetic, Geometry, Astronomy, and Music.

GRAMMAR

Embraces the whole science of language, and teaches us to express our ideas in appropriate words.

RHETORIC

Is the art of speaking eloquently, in order to please, instruct, persuade, and command; and is by no means a common or an easy attainment.

LOGIC

Is the art of correct thinking, and directs our inquiries after truth by conceiving things clearly and distinctly, thereby preventing us from being misled by unsound reasoning.

ARITHMETIC

Is the science of numbers, and teaches us to compute or calculate correctly with expedition and ease.

GEOMETRY

Is the science of extension or magnitude, abstractedly considered, and treats of lines, surfaces, and solids; as all extension is distinguished by length, breadth, and thickness. A geometrical point has no parts, neither length, breadth, nor thickness, and is therefore invisible. A line is length without breadth, and a superficies is length and breadth without thickness. The point is the termination of the lines, the line is the termination of the superficies, and the superficies the termination of a body.

By this science, which is the foundation of architecture, and the root of mathematics, man is enabled to measure any place or distance, accessible or inaccessible, if it can only be seen. By it geographers show us the magnitude of the earth, the extent of seas, empires, and provinces, &c.; and by it astronomers are enabled to measure the distance, motions, and magnitudes of the heavenly bodies, and regulate the duration of times, seasons, years and cycles. Geometry is particularly recommended to the attention of Masons, not only as a study of lines, superficies, and solids, but as a method of reasoning and deduction in the investigation of truth, and may be considered as a kind of natural logic. The contemplation of this science, in a moral and comprehensive view, fills the mind with rapture. The flowers, the animals, the mountains, and every particle of matter which surrounds us, open a sublime field for inquiry, and proves the wisdom of God, and the existence of a First Cause.

MUSIC

Is the science of harmonious sounds, and is the effect of vibration, propagated like light, from atom to atom, and depending on the reflection of surrounding bodies and the density of the air.

> Of all the arts beneath the heaven
> That man has found, or God has given,
> None draws the soul so sweet away,
> As music's melting, mystic lay;
> Slight emblem of the bliss above,
> It soothes the spirit all to love."

ASTRONOMY

Is a mixed mathematical science, and the most sublime that has even been cultivated by man. It treats of the celestial bodies, and affords an interesting theme for instruction and contemplation, kindling the mind to praise, love, and adore the Supreme Creator.

THE CHARGE

Being now advanced to the Second Degree of Masonry, we congratulate you on your preferment. As you increase in knowledge, you will improve in social intercourse. In your new character it is expected that you will conform to the principles of the Institution, by steadily persevering in the practice of every commendable virtue. You are not to palliate or aggravate the offences of your Brethren; but in the decision of every trespass against our rules you are to judge with candor, admonish with friendship, and reprehend with justice. The study of the liberal arts, which tends to polish and adorn the mind, is earnestly recommended to your consideration, especially the science of Geometry, which is enriched with useful knowledge; while it proves the wonderful properties of nature, it demonstrates the most important truths of morality, which is the basis of our art. We exhort you to strive, like a skilful Brother, to excel in everything that is good and great; and may you improve your intellectual faculties, and qualify yourself to become a useful member of society, and an ornament to the Craft.

As Moses was commanded to pull the shoes from off his feet, on Mount Horeb, because the ground on which he trod was sanctified by the presence of Divinity, so should a Mason advance to the Third Stage of Masonry, in the naked paths of Truth, with steps of innocence, virtue, and humility.

MASTER MASON.

Represents man saved from the Grave of Iniquity, and raised to Salvation, by faith and the grace of God. In this Degree we look beyond the narrow limits of this world to that celestial sphere—

"Where high the heavenly temple stands,
The house of God not made with hands."

By a proper study of this Degree, we are taught to

"Contemplate when the sun declines,
Our death with deep reflection;
And when again he rising shines,
Our day of resurrection."

OPENING PRAYER.

Oh, thou all-seeing and omnipresent God, from everlasting to everlasting, we pray thee to direct us how to know and serve thee aright, and bow before thy throne of grace, for the forgiveness of our sins, that we may obtain fellowship with thee, and promote the honor and glory of thy most holy name. Amen.

THE SANCTUM SANCTORUM.

A Master Mason's Lodge duly opened represents the Sanctum Sanctorum, or Holy of Holies, of King Solomon's

Temple, where not even kings are allowed to enter unless duly initiated, and raised to that high and sublime privilege, by the help of God, his good name, and the united aid of square and compasses, which represent Virtue, Morality, Friendship, and Brotherly Love.

Having entered, in due form, a Masters' Lodge, that beautiful passage of scripture (Eccl. xii. 1-7), representing the infirmities of old age, should always be remembered as an appropriate introduction to the sublime ceremonies of this Degree, and the lessons taught by our emblematic death, and resurrection to life eternal.

THE SYMBOLIC JEWELS

Of a Master Mason are Friendship, Morality, and Brotherly Love. These he should wear as an adornment to his mind—Morality being practical virtue, and the duty of life; Friendship is personal kindness, which should extend beyond the circle of private connections to universal philanthrophy; and Brotherly Love is the purest emanation of earthly friendship.

THE WORKING TOOLS.

The Working Tools of the Master Mason are all the tools of the Craft indiscriminately, but more especially the Trowel.

THE TROWEL

Which emblematically teaches us to spread the cement of brotherly love, unite in one bond of social union, and diffuse the principle of universal benevolence to every member of the human family.

THE SKIRRET

Is emblematical of the straight and undeviating line of conduct, which directs us in the path which leads to immortality as revealed to us in the volume of the Sacred Law.

THE PENCIL

Reminds us that our words and actions are recorded by the Almighty Architect, to whom we must give an account of them, whenever it is his pleasure to call on us to do so.

THE COMPASSES.

As in Operative Masonry, the Compasses are used for the admeasurement of the architect's plans, and to enable him to give those just proportions which will insure beauty as well as stability to his work; so, in Speculative Masonry, is this important implement symbolic of that even tenor of deportment, that true standard of rectitude which alone can bestow happiness here and felicity hereafter. Hence are the Compasses the most prominent emblem of virtue, the true and only measure of a Mason's life and conduct.

The Compasses peculiarly belong to this Degree, as when properly extended they embrace all the tenets of the Institution, limit our desires, and keep our passions within due bounds, so that we may, as Master Masons, lead a life of physical as well as moral and intellectual integrity.

Before proceeding further with the M. M. Degree it will be necessary to give an outline of the historical, or rather allegorical, legend on which the most important part of this Degree is founded, as it is intended to symbolize our faith in the resurrection of the body, and the immortality of the soul, and give an instance of firmness and fidelity to our duty in contrast with the cunning and deceitful passions which are so pernicious and destructive to all who indulge in them. To assume the story to be literally a historical fact instead of an allegory, would be to rob the impressive ceremony of its beauty, and weaken the effect which is intended to be produced by it on the mind.

The Bible informs us that a person, of the name of Hiram, was employed at the building of King Solomon's Temple (1 Kings vii. 13; 2 Chron. ii. 13-14); but neither the Bible, nor any other authority, except Masonic tradition, gives any further information respecting him, not even of his death; how it occurred, when or where. According to the Masonic legend, it was the custom of Hiram, as Grand Master of the work, to enter the Sanctum Sanctorum every day at high twelve (when the workmen were called from labor to refreshment), to offer up prayers, and adore the God in whom he put his trust. The Temple at length being nearly finished, and the Craftsmen not having obtained the Master's Word, which was only known to King Solomon, Hiram King of Tyre, and H*** A***, *** of them *** to extort it from him, or ***, they being determined to have the Word by any means, so as to enable them to travel into foreign countries and obtain employment. T*** of them, however, repented, and confessed to King Solomon what they had conspired to do. It does not, however, appear that Solomon took any active steps to prevent the * * * * * * * * , for we are told that when he arrived at the Temple all was in confusion, and, on making inquiry as to the cause, he was informed that the Grand Master, H*** A***, was missing, and that there were no plans on the tracing board for them to work by. Recollecting what had been confessed to him that morning, and knowing that H**** had always been punctual and regular, he began to fear that some mischief had been done to him; he then ordered the roll to be called, when three were found to be missing (namely J****, J***, and J***). Solomon immediately caused an embargo to be laid on all the shipping, so as to prevent their escape to a foreign country, and ordered * * * Fellow Crafts to be sent in search of the * * *, and that if they could not be found, the * * * who had confessed were to be considered as the * * *, and suffer accordingly. Those who had been sent west, on coming near the coast of Joppa, heard voices issuing from a cavern in the rocks, and on listening discovered that the * * * had been unable to obtain a passage to Ethiopia, or escape from their own country.

On hearing exclamations, the searchers rushed suddenly upon them, took them prisoners, and conveyed them to Jerusalem, where they confessed their guilt, and were * * *, each according to the * * * passed from his own lips. F * * * Craftsmen were again assembled, and, clothed in white aprons and gloves in token of innocence, were sent, three East, three West, three North, three South, and three in and about the Temple, to search for the body of Hiram, which was discovered in an accidental manner by one who became wearied and sat down to rest on the brow of a hill. On rising, he caught hold of a sprig of A * * *, which easily gave way, and showed that the earth had been recently moved. He called for his companions, who came to his assistance, and discovered the body of their Master very indecently interred. With due respect they again covered the body, and hastened to acquaint King Solomon, who, on hearing the melancholy intelligence, raised his hands, and exclaimed, "Oh *** *** *** *** *** *** ***," and dropped them in such a manner as indicated the grief into which he was thrown. Immediately recovering himself, he commanded the body to be raised and conveyed to Jerusalem, to be interred in a sepulchre, as near the Sanctum Sanctorum as the Jewish law would permit, in honor of his rank and exalted talents.

THE T**** R****

In the foregoing allegory are typical of Deceit, Avarice, and Death, who invaded man's original innocent state, and laid him prostrate in the grave of spiritual death.

The law came to his aid, but failed to raise his corruptible nature.

Idolatry offered her assistance, but also proved a slip, and failed to effect his moral resurrection.

At length the Gospel, "marked with the seal of high Divinity," descended from Heaven, and pronounced the omnific word, which raised him from a spiritual death to everlasting life, robbed death of its sting, and swallowed it up in victory (Isaiah xxv. 8; 1 Cor. xv. 54-57). Thus a

Master Mason represents man, saved from the grave of iniquity and corruption, and raised to the sphere of righteousness and salvation, where peace and innocence forever dwell, in the realms of a boundless eternity.

THE MONUMENT

Erected to the memory of Hiram was a broken column of white marble supporting a book, with a virgin weeping over them, an urn in her left hand, and a sprig of acacia in her right. Father Time standing behind her with his fingers entwined in the ringlets of the virgin's hair.

THE BROKEN COLUMN

Is emblematical of the frailty of man, and all things human. "To everything there is a season, and a time to every purpose under the sun." (Eccl. chap. iii.)

THE OPEN BOOK

Is emblematical of the revealed will of God, and the Book of Nature, open for our investigation.

> " See through this air, this ocean, and this earth,
> All matter quick, and bursting into birth."

THE SPRIG OF ACACIA

With its graceful drooping leaves, like the weeping willow, is an emblem of tender Sympathy and never-dying Affection, and being an evergreen is also emblematical of the immortal Soul that never dies; and this thought is calculated, in the hope of a glorious immortality, to dispel the gloomy contemplation and fear of death.

> "Death cannot come
> To him untimely who is fit to die;
> The less of this cold world, the more of heaven;
> The briefer life, the earlier immortality."

SYMBOLS OR EMBLEMS

Particularly recommended to the attention of Master Masons inculcate many a useful lesson, as showing us how we may become examples in our religious, civil, and moral conduct.

WORKING TOOLS.

The principal working tools of the Operative art that have been adopted as symbols in the Speculative science, confined to Ancient Craft Masonry are, the twenty-four inch gauge, common gavel, square, level, plumb rule, skerrit, compasses, pencil and trowel.

THE MALLET

Is the emblem of Power, morally teaching us to correct irregularities, and reduce man to a proper level.

THE THREE STEPS

Are emblematical of the three Masonic Degrees, or stages of human life—viz., Youth, Manhood, and Old Age; and also of the three periods of our existence—viz., Time, Death, and Eternity.

THE BOOK OF CONSTITUTIONS

Should remind us to be guarded in our Thoughts, Words, and Actions; for the Sword of Almighty Vengeance is drawn to reward iniquity.

THE ALL-SEEING EYE.

Of the Incomprehensible, Omnipotent God! whom the Sun, Moon and Stars obey, and whose being extends through boundless space, and "penetrates the very inmost recesses of the human Heart," must see and know our Thoughts and Actions, and will reward us according to our faithfulness and merits.

THE FORTY-SEVENTH PROBLEM OF EUCLID.

The forty-seventh problem of Euclid's first book, which has been adopted as a symbol in the Master's degree, is thus enunciated:

In any right angled triangle, the square described upon the side subtending the right angle is equal to the squares described upon the sides which contain the right **angle.**

This problem, which is of great use in geometrical solutions and demonstrations of quantities, is said to be the invention of the philosopher Pythagoras, and which, in the joy of his heart, he called Eureka (I have found it), and sacrificed a hectatomb to commemorate the discovery. It is emblematical of the symmetry and beauty of Creation, and the unalterable laws of Divine wisdom and infinite power which govern every atom of the universe. It should remind Masons that they ought to love and study the arts and sciences.

THE HOUR GLASS

Is an emblem of Human Life. The sand in the glass passes swiftly, though almost imperceptibly, away. So do the moments of our lives, till the wave of Time is swallowed up by the billows of Eternity.

THE COFFIN, SKULL, AND CROSS-BONES

Are emblems of the inevitable destiny of our Mortal Bodies. The grave yawns to receive us:

"And creeping things shall revel in their spoil,
And fit our clay to fertilize the soil."

THE SPRIG OF ACACIA

Is an emblem of Immortality.

" The dead are like the stars by day
Withdrawn from mortal eye,
But not extinct, they hold their way
In glory through the sky."

THE ORNAMENTS.

Of this Degree are the Porch, the Mosaic Pavement, and the Dormer.

THE PORCH.

The Porch of the Temple of Solomon was twenty cubits in length, and the same in breadth. At its entrance was a gate made entirely of Corinthian brass, the most precious metal known to the ancients. Beside this gate there were the two pillars **** and ****, which had been constructed by Hiram Abiff, the architect whom the King of Tyre had sent to Solomon. The Entrance to the Holy of Holies, will remind the thoughtful Mason of his emblematic * * *, and that the grave is the porch which all must pass through to the world of spirits, where worthy servants only will find admittance to the Sanctum Sanctorum of that Celestial Lodge where the Grand Master presides.

THE DORMER

Or Window, which gives light to the Sanctum Sanctorum, is emblematical of the Fountain of Wisdom, which enlightens the mind, and dispels the gloomy darkness of ignorance, and instructs us how to die.

"Grant that in life's last hour my soul may crave,
Nor crave in vain, his love to light me through the grave."

CHARGE.

(W.M.)—Brother, your zeal for the institution of Freemasonry, the progress which you have made in the art, and your conformity to the general regulations, have pointed you as a proper object of our favor and esteem. In the character of a Master Mason, you are henceforth authorized to correct the errors and irregularities of Brethren and Fellows and guard them against a breach of fidelity. To improve the morals and correct the manners of men in society must be your constant care. With this virtue, therefore, you are always to recommend to inferiors obedience and submission; to equals, courtesy and affability; to superiors kindness and condescension. You are to inculcate universal benevolence, and, by the regularity of your own behaviour, afford the best example for the benefit of others. The Ancient Landmarks of the Order, which are here entrusted to your care, you are to preserve sound and inviolable, and never suffer an infringement of our rites, or a deviation from established usage and custom. Duty, honor, and gratitude now bind you to be faithful to every trust, to support with becoming dignity your new character, and to enforce by example and precept the tenets of the System. Let no motive, therefore, make you swerve from your duty, violate your vows, or betray your trust; but be true and faithful, and imitate the example of that celebrated Artist whom you have once represented.

By this exemplary conduct you will convince the world that merit has been your title to our privileges, and that on you our favors have not been undeservedly bestowed.

THE ANCIENT LANDMARKS.

The landmarks are twenty-five in number, and are:

1. The modes of recognition. They admit of no variation.

2. The division of symbolic Masonry into three degrees.

3. The legend of the third degree is an important landmark. There is no rite of Masonry, practised in any country or language, in which the essential elements of this legend are not taught. The lectures may vary, but the legend has remained the same. And it should be so, for the legend of the Temple Builder constitutes the very essence of Masonry.

4. The government of the Fraternity by a Grand Master, elected from the body of the Craft, is a fourth landmark of the Order.

5. The prerogative of the Grand Master to preside over every assembly of the Craft, is a fifth landmark.

6. The prerogative of the Grand Master to grant dispensations for conferring degrees at irregular times, is a very important landmark. The statutory law of Masonry requires a month to elapse between the presentation of a petition and the election of a candidate. But the Grand Master has the power to dispense with this probation, and to allow a candidate to be initiated at once.

7. The prerogative of the Grand Master to grant dispensations for opening and holding Lodges is another landmark.

8. The prerogative of the Grand Master to make Masons at sight is a landmark which is closely connected with the preceding one.

9. The landmarks of the Order prescribed that Masons should from time to time congregate together for the purpose of either Operative or Speculative labor, and that these congregations should be called Lodges.

10. The government of the Craft when congregated in a Lodge, by a Master and two Wardens, is also a landmark.

11. The necessity that every Lodge, when congregated, should be duly tyled, is an important landmark of the Institution that is never neglected.

12. The right of every Mason to be represented in meetings of the Craft, is a twelfth landmark. Formerly, these meetings, which were usually held once a year, were called "General Assemblies," and all the Fraternity, even to the youngest Entered Apprentice, were permitted to be present. Now they are called "Grand Lodges," and only the Masters and Wardens of the subordinate Lodges are summoned.

13. The right of every Mason to appeal from the decision of his brethren to the Grand Lodge, is a landmark essential to the preservation of justice. A few Grand Lodges, in adopting a regulation that the decision of subordinate Lodges, in cases of expulsion, cannot be set aside upon an appeal, have violated this landmark.

14. The right of every Mason to visit and sit in every regular Lodge is an unquestionable landmark of the Order. This right has always been recognized as an inherent right which inures to every Mason as he travels through the world. This right may be forfeited, but when admission is refused to a Mason in good standing, who knocks at the door of a Lodge as a visitor, it is to be expected that some good reason shall be furnished for this violation of a right, founded on the landmarks of the Order.

15. It is a landmark of the Order, that no visitor can enter a Lodge without first passing an examination. Of course, if the visitor is known to any brother present to be a Mason in good standing, and if that brother will vouch for him, the examination may be dispensed with.

16. No Lodge can interfere with the business of another Lodge, or give degrees to brethren who are members of other Lodges, except by special dispensation.

17. It is a landmark that every Freemason is amenable to the laws of the Masonic jurisdiction in which he resides. Non-affiliation does not exempt a Mason from Masonic jurisdiction.

18. Certain qualifications of candidates for initiation are derived from a landmark of the Order. These qualifications are that he shall be a man—unmutilated, free born, and of mature age.

19. A belief in the existence of God is one of the landmarks of the Order. The annals of the Order never yet have furnished an instance in which an Atheist was ever made a Mason.

20. Subsidiary to this belief in God, is the belief in a future life. This landmark is not so positively impressed on the candidate by exact words as the preceding; but the doctrine is taught by very plain implications, and runs through the whole symbolism of the Order.

21. It is a landmark that a "Book of the Law" shall constitute an indispensable part of the furniture of every Lodge. The "Book of the Law" is that volume which, by the religion of the country, is believed to contain the revealed will of the Grand Architect of the Universe. Hence, in Christian countries, the "Book of the Law" is composed of the Old and New Testaments; in a country where Judaism was the prevailing faith, the Old Testament alone would be sufficient; and in Mohammedan countries, the Koran might be substituted.

22. The equality of all Masons is another landmark of the Order. This equality has no reference to those gradations of rank which have been instituted by the usages of society. The monarch, the nobleman, or the gentleman is entitled to all the influence which rightly belongs to his position. But Masonic equality implies that we meet in the Lodge upon the level—that on that level we are all travelling to one predestined goal—that in the Lodge genuine merit shall receive more respect than wealth, and that virtue and knowledge alone should be the basis of all Masonic honors, and be rewarded with pre-

ferment. When the labors of the Lodge are over, and the brethren have retired from their peaceful retreat, to mingle once more with the world, each will then again resume that social position, and exercise the privileges of that rank, to which the custom of society entitle him.

23. The secrecy of the Institution is another and most important landmark. The form of secrecy is a form inherent in it, existing with it from its very foundation. If divested of its secret character, it would lose its identity, and would cease to be Freemasonry.

24. The foundation of a speculative science upon an operative art, and the symbolic use and explanation of the terms of that art, for the purpose of moral teaching, constitutes another landmark of the Order.

25. The last and crowning landmark of all is, that these landmarks can never be changed. Nothing can be subtracted from them—nothing can be added to them— not the slightest modification can be made in them. As they were received from our predecessors, we are bound by the most solemn obligations to transmit them to our successors.

MASONIC CALENDAR.

Freemasons, in affixing dates to their official documents, never make use of the common epoch or vulgar era, but have one peculiar to themselves, which, however, varies in the different rites. Era and epoch are, in this sense, synonymous.

Ancient Craft Masons commence their era with the creation of the world, calling it Anno Lucis (A. L.), "in the year of light."

Scottish Rite, same as Ancient Craft, except the Jewish chronology is used, Anno Mundi (A. M.), "in the year of the world."

Royal Arch Masons date from the year the second temple was commenced by Zerubbabel, Anno Inventionis (A. I.), "in the year of discovery."

Royal and Select Masters date from the year in which the temple of Solomon was completed, Anno Depositionis (A. Dep.), "in the year of the deposit."

Knights Templar commence their era with the organization of their order, Anno Ordinis (A. O.), "in the year of the Order."

RULES FOR MASONIC DATES.

Ancient Craft Masons—Add 4000 years to the common era. Thus: 1915 and 400—5915.

Scottish Rite—Add 3760 to the common era. Thus: 1915 and 3760—5675. After September add another year.

Royal Arch—Add 530 years to the vulgar era. Thus: 1915 and 530—2445.

Royal and Select Masters—Add 1000 to the common time. Thus 1915 and 1000—2915.

Knights Templar—From the Christian era take 1118. Thus: 1118 from 1915—797.

THE ROYAL ARCH.

Compiled by OSBORNE SHEPPARD from the writings of

ALBERT G. MACKEY, M.D., 33°.

THE Royal Arch degree is the fourth in the Masonic series, and a Master Mason who has been so for six months is eligible for Exaltation. The principal officers of a Chapter are: Zerubbabel, Haggai and Joshua; three Sojourners and two Scribes—Ezra and Nehemiah,—a Treasurer, and a Janitor. The Chapters in the Maritime Provinces, however, have adopted a ritual somewhat resembling the American and the Principal Officers are called: High Priest, King and Scribe.

The legend or historical basis may vary in the different Rites, but in all of them the symbolical significance of the Royal Arch is identical. The true symbolism of the Royal Arch degree is founded on the discovery of the *Lost Word*. It can never be too often repeated that the WORD is, in Masonry, the symbol of TRUTH. This truth is the great object of pursuit in Masonry—the scope and tendency of all its investigations—the promised reward of all Masonic labor. Sought for diligently in every degree, and constantly approached, but never thoroughly and intimately embraced at length, in the Royal Arch, the veils which concealed the object of search from our view are withdrawn, and the inestimable prize is revealed.

This truth, which Masonry makes the great object of its investigations, is not the mere truth of science, or the truth of history, but is the more important truth which is synonymous with the knowledge of the nature of God—that truth which is embraced in the Sacred Tetragrammaton, or omnific name, including in its signification his eternal, present, past, and future existence, and to which he himself alluded when he declared to Moses: "I appeared unto Abraham, unto Isaac, and unto Jacob by the name of God Almighty; but by my name Jehovah was I not known unto them." The discovery of this truth is then the essential symbolism of the Royal Arch degree, wherever it is practised,—and under some peculiar name the degree is found in every Rite of Masonry,—this symbolism is preserved.

There was a time, undoubtedly, when the Royal Arch did not exist as an independent degree, but was a complementary part of the Master's Degree, which terminates abruptly in its symbolism, and leaves the mind waiting for something that is necessary to its completeness. This deficiency is supplied by the Royal Arch Degree.

It is evident that its establishment as an independent and distinct degree dates at a comparatively modern period. In none of the old manuscripts is there the slightest allusion to it, and Anderson does not make any reference to it in his History of the Order. As late as the year 1758 the Constitutional Grand Lodge (Moderns) had no Royal Arch Degree, for in that year the Grand Secretary declared that "our Society is neither Arch, Royal Arch, nor Ancient," and in the lecture of the third degree prepared by Anderson and Desaguliers it is said "that which was lost is now found," clearly indicating that the Master Mason's word was delivered to the newly raised Master in the latter ceremonies of the third degree, which would preclude the necessity for a Royal Arch Degree.

In the year 1766 Thomas Dunckerley was authorized by the Mother Grand Lodge (Moderns) to inaugurate a new system of lectures and from this date it is probable *the Word* was dissevered from the Third Degree ,and the Royal Arch was evolved as a new and distinct degree. At the union of the two Grand Lodges—Moderns and Ancients—in 1813, the Holy Royal Arch was officially recognized as a part of Ancient Craft Masonry, and so it has ever since remained.

THE BANNERS AND THEIR USE IN THE ROYAL ARCH.

BY REV. GEORGE A. MacLENNAN, B.A.
P. Z. St. Andrew's Chapter, No. 139, R. A. M., G. R. of C.

THE question of the Banners is a very obscure and difficult one, presenting a great variety of opinion, concerning which convincing conclusions are not likely to be reached at any time.

The use of Banners in a Royal Arch Chapter is suggested by Numbers 2:2—"Every man of the Children of Israel shall pitch by his own standard."

The Bible gives us no information as to the form, device or color of these standards. To the Talmud, and particularly to the explanatory Targums, do we turn for assistance. Let us bear in mind, however, that prior to the destruction of the Temple and the dispersion of the Jews that their traditions, the Mishna and the Gamara, or the second law or learning and the commentaries thereon, were handed down orally, but with greatest care. The authoritative committal to writing only dates back to about 190 A.D.

Banners have been used from earliest times to mark tribal encampments, or to direct armed bodies. Banners are frequently represented on the Monuments of Egypt and Assyria. They might be simple bunches of leaves or wisps of grass tied to a pole, or a figured metal receptacle for fire, or a piece of cloth bearing some device usually of a sacred character.

Three words occur in the Hebrew representing respectively (1) the divisional standard, (2) the tribal banner and (3) a signal. Modern critical scholars generally conclude that two banners were implied in Numbers 2:2—the divisional standard and the tribal banner. This is true to the custom of the modern Bedouin.

The historical section of the Talmud represents the devices and colors of the Banners as corresponding to the twelve precious stones of the Breast Plate of the High Priest. The Grand Chapter of England and the Grand Bodies issuing from her have adopted this view.

TRIBAL BANNERS.

While the Bible is silent as to device and color, the Jewish commentators have with a free hand supplied both, arranging their scheme after Jacob's blessing of his sons, Gen. 49; supplemented by Moses' blessing, Deut. 33, and Exodus 28:17-20.

DEVICES UPON THE TRIBAL BANNERS.

There is a large measure of agreement between the Grand Chapters of England, Scotland, Canada and Quebec, and they follow the Talmud.

1. Judah—a lion couchant, with crown and sceptre.

2. Issachar—an ass crouching between two burdens. The Talmud has the Sun and Moon from their supposed influence upon vegetation.

3. Zebulon—a ship.

4. Reuben—a mandrake, rudely moulded into the form of a man, Talmud and Quebec; a man erect, Scotland; wavy lines, after the LXX, translated, "unstable as water," England and Canada.

5. Simeon—Talmud, a city; Scotland, a tower; Quebec, a sword and dagger crossed; England and Canada, a sword or swords. Gen. 34:25; Gen. 49:5. (R. V.)

Levi—When Levi became the priestly tribe, their office and portion became national, they ceased to be numbered. The Talmud associated Levi with the Urim and Thummim.

6. Gad—a troop of horsemen. The Talmud has a camp.

7. Ephraim—The portion of Joseph became the inheritance of his two sons; an ox or bullock charging, symbolical of strength.

8. Manasseh—The Talmud and Quebec have adopted the mythological unicorn, due to a mistranslation of Deut. 33:17. The "reem" was a two-horned ox or ox-antelope noted for the length and strength of its horns; England, Scotland and Canada have adopted the device of a vine beside a wall, after Jacob's blessing of Joseph, Gen. 49:22.

9. Benjamin—a wolf.

10. Dan—The Talmud and Quebec, a serpent; England, an eagle; Scotland, an eagle with a serpent in its talons; Canada, a serpent biting a horse's heel, the horse representing the foreigner. Dan's position being at a gateway of Israel, he was ready, like a serpent coiled in a camel track, to spring upon the enemy.

11. Asher—The Talmud has a female figure and a full-leafed olive tree, the symbol of fertility and abundance. Quebec, Canada, Scotland and England adopted the overflowing cup. Psalms 23:5.

12. Naphtali—a hind let loose.

DIVISIONAL STANDARDS.

The camp of Israel was divided into four great divisions under the tribes of Reuben, Judah, Ephraim and Dan. The devices associated with each a man, a lion, an ox and an eagle, respectively, following the device of the tribal banner, with the exception of Dan. There is an old Hebrew saying that there are four superb creations in the world—the lion among wild beasts, the ox among tame, the eagle among the birds, and man, who surpasses them all. The Cherubim was a favorite with the Hebrews as symbolizing the sanctifying presence of God, in majesty and power, in Israel. The Hebrew saying doubtless suggested to Ezekiel the form of his vision of the Cherubim, a vision in the mind of the companions of 1753, and explaining the adoption of the Cherubim upon the seals of Grand Chapters. The American Rite has adopted these four standards and places them at the veils.

COLOR OF THE BANNERS.

According to the Talmudists this was determined by the color of the stones of the Breast Plate of the High Priest. This presents a question of great difficulty, involving the identification of the stone, its color, its order, and the tribal name with which associated.

There are three sources of information:

(1) Talmudic traditions, oral until about 190 A.D.

(2) The Septuagint (LXX) version of the Old Testament, prepared in Alexandria, Egypt, about 280 B.C.

(3) Modern Egyptological research of Petrie, Myres, and Rabbi Hirsch. This largely supports No. 2.

(1) Talmudic traditions. Quebec has consistently adopted this view, as she has done throughout, with one slight exception (the device of Asher). Puzzled with the conflict of opinion and desirous of some authority to guide her, she conferred with a learned Rabbi in the matter and followed his opinion.

(2) The Septuagint tradition has been adopted by other Grand Chapters, but with a strange want of agreement in the detail of the color scheme, particularly in some subordinate Chapters. My own research has led me to adopt the modern form of the Septuagint tradition.

The names and arrangement of the stones of the Breast Plate occur in Exod. 28:15-17 and 39:8-14. In the margin we find the names of the tribes.

A serious difficulty confronts us at the outset in finding modern stones to correspond with the stones of the Hebrew list. The Talmudists have allowed fancy free play, and the translators of the Authorized Version have clearly adopted some names at random. The Septuagint, translated by Alexandrian scholars from the Hebrew for Hellenistic Jews, at the very heart of the jewel trade of the day, presented a favorable opportunity for a correct identification of the stones and to give the Greek equivalent to the Hebrew names. This identification they made, and modern research upholds their opinion.

The majority of precious stones were unknown to the ancients. Such as they were acquainted with they classified according to color rather than composition or form. Further, only stones which would engrave easily would serve. The diamond, emerald and sapphire, if known, would be too hard. Large stones, not gems, would be proportionate with the rest of the Breast Plate.

In the following table I will place these two views side by side, using Quebec and Canada as illustrations. The difference between Canada, England and Scotland is for the most part one of color shade.

Tribe	Stone	Quebec	Canada	Modern Name and Color
Reuben	Sardius	Red	Scarlet	Red Jasper.
Simeon	Topaz	Green	Yellow	Greenish-yellow Serpentine.
Levi	Carbuncle			Colorless Rock Crystal.
Judah	Emerald	Sky Blue	Crimson	Red Garnet.
Dan	Sapphire	Blue	Green	Lapis Lazuli, blue with reddish-yellow dots.
Naphtali	Diamond	Wine	Blue	Dark Green Jasper.
Gad	Ligure	Grey	White	Brilliant Yellow Quartz or Agate.
Asher	Agate	Pearl	Purple	A Grey and White Agate.
Issachar	Amethyst	Black	Sky Blue	Purple Amethyst.
Zebulon	Beryl	White	Purple	Yellow Jasper.
Joseph	Onyx	Jet Black	Green	Green Felspar or Malachite.
Ephraim	Onyx	Jet Black	Green	Green Felspar or Malachite.
Manasseh	Onyx	Jet Black	Flesh	Green Felspar or Malachite.
Benjamin	Jasper	Combined colors	Green	Green Jasper, with variants of yellow, red and opalescent.

THE STANDARDS.

A baritha on the Tabernacle says that there were four Standards—large and ornamented with colors in white, purple, crimson and dark blue, wrought with embroidered work. Quebec uses the colors of the Tribal Banner of Judah, Reuben, Ephraim and Dan; England and Canada use either crimson, scarlet or green; the American Rite has adopted the suggestion of the baritha; Scotland has but two large Standards, that of Judah being of crimson color and bearing the device of "four-headed animals," and the motto, "In Domino fiducia omnis," that of Reuben being of purple color and bearing for device the signs of the Zodiac.

ARRANGEMENT OF THE TRIBES.

There are two views:

(1) The Talmudic, in which the leading tribe of the Division holds a central position. This is the view of Prof. G. L. Robinson, of Chicago. The encampment was, according to Numbers 2:3—in the form of a hollow square—a strong camp. The Tabernacle was in the centre, and a division protected each side of this square, the Levites forming the inner lines; thus—

In Camp—The Talmudic View.

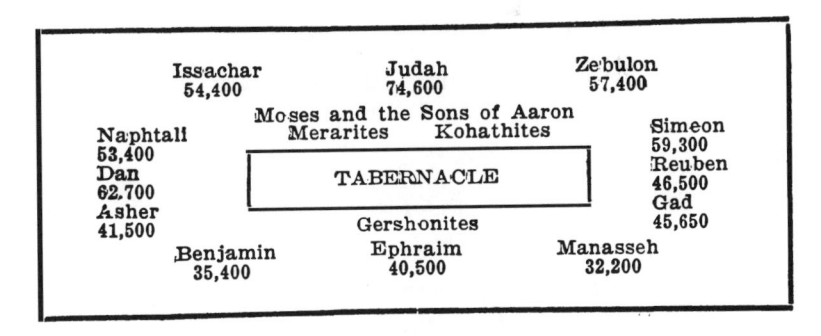

	Issachar 54,400	Judah 74,600	Zebulon 57,400	
		Moses and the Sons of Aaron		
Naphtali 53,400 Dan 62,700 Asher 41,500	Merarites	Kohathites		Simeon 59,300 Reuben 46,500 Gad 45,650
		TABERNACLE		
		Gershonites		
	Benjamin 35,400	Ephraim 40,500	Manasseh 32,200	

(2) The Septuagint view, in which the leading tribe of the division leads, thus—Reuben, Simeon, God; Ephraim, Manasseh, Benjamin.

The line of march, Numbers 10, may have been a "column" or "line." Schick (Leaders of Israel) favors the "column"; military men, having regard to ease of march and strength of defence through an enemy's country, declare the "column" to be very weak and the "line" the best. In "line formation" the order would be something like this:

The Ark, (Num. 10:33; Exod. 33:7).
Judah's Division.   Reuben's Division.
Levites bearing materials of Tabernacle.
Dan's Division.   Ephraim's Division.

The arrangement of the Camp, a quadrilateral, is unsuitable to "labor," so two parallel lines have been substituted, with the tribal banners arranged as in the order of march in Numbers 10. Whether we follow one or other of the above orders we must keep the Divisions together and not separate Judah from his Division or Ephraim from his, as has been done in some arrangements of the Banners.

(1) Talmudic order—
First line—Issachar, Judah, Zebulon; Simeon, Reuben, Gad.

Second line—Naphtali, Dan, Asher; Benjamin, Ephraim, Manasseh.

This (the Talmudic view) is the authorized arrangement of the Grand Chapter Quebec.

(2) Septuagint order—
First line—Judah, Issachar, Zebulon; Reuben, Simeon, Gad.

Second line—Naphtali, Asher, Dan; Benjamin, Manasseh, Ephraim.

THE TRIBAL BANNERS AND THEIR RELATIVE LOCATION IN THE ROYAL ARCH CHAPTER.

BY WALTER J. FRANCIS, C.E.

P. Z., Corinthian Chapter R. A. M., No. 36, G. R. C.
P. Z., Carnarvon Chapter R. A. M., No. 5, G. R. Q.

IN my anxiety to know something more about the banners of the chapter beyond the fact of their being the armorial bearings of the twelve tribes of Israel and the standards of the four divisions of the army of Israel, I made careful inquiry of my instructors and authorities without success. I was at length rewarded with some interesting light through a careful review of the Pentateuch, where two phases of the subject are referred to. In the forty-ninth chapter of Genesis, which describes the death-bed scene of Jacob, one by one the patriarch blesses his sons. He speaks figuratively, and the expressions used by him seem to be the subject of the devices used on the tribal banners authorized for use in the jurisdiction of the Grand Chapter of Canada.

To Reuben he said, "Reuben, thou art my first-born, my might, and the beginning of my strength, the excellency of dignity, and the excellency of power: unstable as water, thou shalt not excel; because thou wentest up to thy father's bed; then defiledst thou it." The banner of Reuben bears a device of wavy lines, to represent water. In other jurisdictions the device is a man, while in Quebec the Grand Chapter authorizes a mandrake bearing some general resemblance to the form of a man.

The two brothers, Simeon and Levi, were taken together, and the words of Israel to them were, "Simeon and Levi are brethren; instruments of cruelty are in their habitations. O my soul, come not thou into their secret; unto their assembly, mine honour, be not thou united: for in their anger they slew a man, and in their self-will they digged down a wall. Cursed be their anger, for it was fierce; and their wrath, for it was cruel: I will divide them in Jacob, and scatter them in Israel.'' The Levites having been subsequently set apart for the ministrations of the tabernacle and not being numbered among the tribes, the words of the prophesy apply remarkably to the device on the banner of Simeon which is a sword and a dagger.

Judah received a blessing in which the lion, kingship and power are dominant. They are typified on his banner as a reclining lion, a crown and a sceptre. ''Judah, thou art he whom thy brethren shall praise: thy hand shall be in the neck of thine enemies; thy father's children shall bow down before thee. Judah is a lion's whelp: from the prey, my son, thou art gone up: he stooped down, he couched as a lion, and as an old lion; who shall rouse him up? The sceptre shall not depart from Judah, nor a law giver from between his feet, until Shiloh come; and unto him shall the gathering of the people be.''

Addressing Zebulun the patriarch said, ''Zebulun shall dwell at the haven of the sea; and he shall be for an haven of ships; and his border shall be unto Zidon.'' The device on the banner of Zebulun is a ship.

To Issachar these words were addressed, ''Issachar is a strong ass couching down between two burdens; and he saw that rest was good, and the land that it was pleasant; and bowed his shoulder to bear, and became a servant unto tribute.''

On the banner of Dan is depicted a serpent attacking a horse which threatens to throw its rider backward. In some jurisdictions the serpent only is used. The words of Jacob to Dan were, ''Dan shall be a serpent by the way, an adder in the path, that biteth the horse heels so that his rider shall fall backward.''

The device on the banner of Gad is a troop of horsemen, referring undoubtedly to the words, ''Gad, a troop shall overcome him: but he shall overcome at the last.''

The wine cups on the banner of Asher derive their origin from Jacob's blessing, "Out of Asher his bread shall be fat, and he shall yield royal dainties."

To Naphtali Israel said, 'Naphtali is a hind let loose: he giveth goodly words." On the banner of Naphtali is a bounding hind.

The words which Israel addressed to Joseph were, "Joseph is a fruitful bough, even a fruitful bough by a well; whose branches run over the wall: The archers have surely grieved him, and shot at him, and hated him: but his bow abode in strength, and the arms of his hands were made strong by the hands of the mighty God of Jacob; even by the God of thy father, who shall help thee; and by the Almighty, who shall bless thee with blessings of heaven above, blessings of the deep that lieth under, blessings of the breasts, and of the womb: the blessings of thy father have prevailed above the blessings of my progenitors unto the utmost bound of the everlasting hills: they shall be on the head of Joseph, and on the crown of the head of him that was separate from his brethren." Later we find that Ephraim and Manasseh were considered as separate tribes. In the forty-eighth chapter of Genesis Jacob took each of the two sons of Joseph as his own. Since the Levites were deputed to serve in the tabernacle and were not numbered among the tribes, the acceptance of Ephraim and Manasseh in this way keeps the number of tribes constant at twelve. The device on the banner of Manasseh is a vine branching over a wall near a well, a reference, doubtless, to the first part of Joseph's blessing, while the latter part of the blessing referring to the riches of the land is referred to in the ox on the banner of Ephraim.

The banner of Benjamin bears a picture of a wolf. The words of Jacob were, "Benjamin shall ravin as a wolf: in the morning he shall devour the prey, and at night he shall divide the spoil."

Regarding the colors of the banners the Law seems to be silent. The order of precedence, however, is well defined.

The two opening chapters of the book of Numbers describe the census of the tribes, their leaders and their order. The tabernacle of the congregation was the vital centre. Specific instructions were laid down regarding the location of the tribes about it, both on the march and at rest.

The Levites who had now lost their identity as an ordinary tribe, not even being counted in the census, were to attend solely to the needs of the tabernacle and were to encamp or march about it. The twelve tribes were divided into four divisions of three tribes each, one division camping on each side of the tabernacle when at rest, and two divisions preceding and following it when setting forward.

Each large standard represents one of the divisions, that of Judah being a lion, Reuben, a man, Ephraim, an ox, and Dan, an eagle. The choice of the devices for the first three seems clear from what has already been noted. The selection of the eagle for the division of Dan is more obscure.

In the division of Judah were included also Issachar and Zebulun. The Judah division, consisting of 186,400 male, twenty years old and upwards, pitched on the east side of the tabernacle and went foremost on the march.

The division of Reuben, 151,450, included Simeon and Gad. It pitched on the south side when resting, while on the march it followed Judah and preceded the tabernacle with the Levites.

With Ephraim were Manasseh and Benjamin, forming the division of Ephraim, 108,100 strong. They encamped on the west side, and followed the tabernacle on the march.

Encamped on the north was the division of Dan, consisting of Dan, Asher and Naphtali, and numbering 157,600 fighting men. On the march the division of Dan brought up the rear.

The order of the banners as used in the work is apparently derived from the positions in the encampment. Diagrammatically the tribes were thus located:

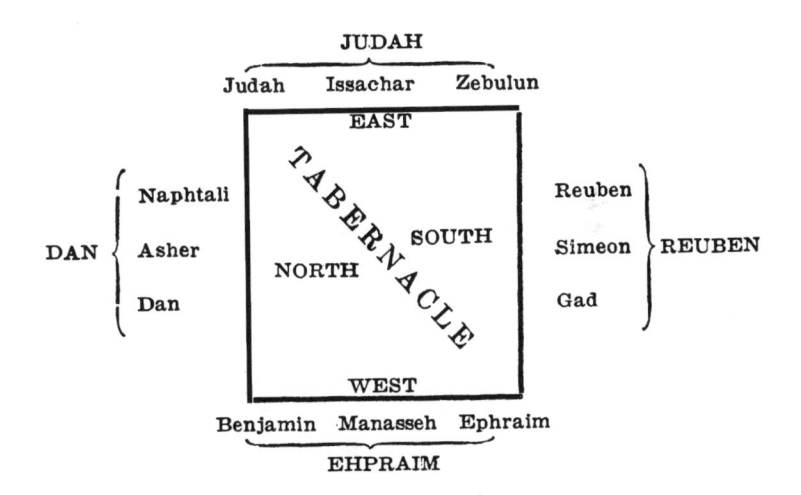

```
                        JUDAH
               ┌─────────────────────┐
              Judah    Issachar    Zebulun
                        EAST
           ┌  Naphtali                     Reuben  ┐
   DAN    ┤   Asher         SOUTH         Simeon   ├ REUBEN
           │                TABERNACLE             │
           └  Dan           NORTH          Gad    ┘
                        WEST
              Benjamin   Manasseh    Ephraim
               └─────────────────────┘
                       EHPRAIM
```

By dividing the camp as nearly as practicable along the centre from east to west, but not breaking up a tribe, we have on the one side Judah, Naphtali, Asher, Dan, Benjamin and Manasseh, while on the other we have Issachar, Zebulun, Reuben, Simeon, Gad and Ephraim, the exact order authorized by the Grand Chapter of Canada.

ROYAL AND SELECT MASTERS.

Compiled by OSBORNE SHEPPARD from the writings of
ALBERT G. MACKEY, M.D., 33°.

ROYAL MASTER.

THE Royal Master is the eighth degree of the American Rite, and the first of the degrees conferred in a Council of Royal and Select Masters. Its officers are a Thrice Illustrious Grand Master, representing King Solomon; Illustrious Hiram of Tyre, Principal Conductor of the Works, representing Hiram Abiff; Master of the Exchequer, Master of Finances, Captain of the Guards, Conductor of the Council and Steward. The place of meeting is called the "Council Chamber," and represents the private apartment of King Solomon, in which he is said to have met for consultation with his two colleagues during the construction of the Temple. Candidates who receive this degree are said to be "honored with the degree of Royal Master." Its symbolic colors are black and red—the former significant of grief, and the latter of martyrdom, and both referring to the chief builder of the Temple.

The events recorded in this degree, looking at them in a legendary point of view, must have occurred at the building of the first Temple, and during that brief period of time after the death of the builder which is embraced between the discovery of his body and its "Masonic interment." In all the initiations into the mysteries of the ancient world, there was, as it is well known to scholars, a legend of the violent death of some distinguished personage, to whose memory the particular mystery was consecrated, of the concealment of the body, and of its subsequent discovery. That part of the initiation which referred to the concealment of the body was called the *Aphanism*, from a Greek verb which signifies "to conceal," and that part which referred to the subsequent finding was called the *euresis*, from another Greek verb which signifies "to discover." It is impossible to avoid seeing the coincidences between the system of initiation and that practised in the Masonry of the third degree. But the ancient initiation was not terminated by the discovery. Up to that point, the ceremonies had been funereal in their character. But now they were changed from wailing to rejoicing. Other ceremonies were performed by which the restoration of the personage to life, or his apotheosis or change to immortality, was represented, and then came the autopsy or illumination of the neophyte, when he was invested with a full knowledge of all the religious doctrines which it was the object of the ancient mysteries to teach—when, in a word, he was instructed in divine truth.

Now, a similar course is pursued in Masonry. Here also there is an illumination, a symbolic teaching, or, as we call it, an investiture with that which is the representative of divine truth. The communication to the candidate, in the Master's degree, of that which is admitted to be merely a representation of or a substitution for that symbol of divine truth, (the search for which, under the name of the true word, makes so important a part of the degree), how imperfect it may be in comparison with that more thorough knowledge which only future researches can enable the Master Mason to attain, constitutes the autopsy of the third degree. Now, the principal event recorded in the legend of the Royal Master, the interview between Adoniram and his two Royal Masters, is to be placed precisely at that juncture of time which is between the *euresis* or discovery in the Master Mason's degree and the autopsy, or investiture with the great secret. It occurred between the discovery by means of the sprig of acacia and the final interment. It was at the time when Solomon and his colleague, Hiram of Tyre, were in profound consultation as to the mode of repairing the loss which they then supposed had befallen them.

We must come to this conclusion, because there is abundant reference, both in the organized form of the Council and in the ritual of the degree, to the death as an event that had already occurred; and, on the other hand, while it is evident that Solomon had been made acquainted with the failure to recover, on the person of the builder, that which had been lost, there is no reference whatever to the well-known substitution which was made at the time of the interment.

If therefore, as is admitted by all Masonic ritualists, the substitution was precedent and preliminary to the establishment of the Master Mason's degree, it is evident that at the time that the degree of Royal Master is said to have been founded in the ancient Temple, by our "first Most Excellent Grand Master," all persons present, except the first and second officers, must have been merely Fellow Craft Masons. In compliance with this tradition, therefore, a Royal Master is, at this day, supposed to represent a Fellow Craft in the search, and making his demand for that reward which was to elevate him to the rank of a Master Mason.

If from the legendary history we proceed to the symbolism of the degree, we shall find that, brief and simple as are the ceremonies, they present the great Masonic idea of the laborer seeking for his reward. Throughout all the symbolism of Masonry, from the first to the last degree, the search for the WORD has been considered but as a symbolic expression for the search after TRUTH. The attainment of this truth has always been acknowledged to be the great object and design of all Masonic labor. Divine truth—the knowledge of God—concealed in the old Kabbalistic doctrine, under the symbol of his ineffable name—and typified in the Masonic system under the mystical expression of the True Word, is the reward proposed to every Mason who has faithfully wrought his task. It is, in short, the "Master's wages."

Now, all this is beautifully symbolized in the degree of Royal Master. The reward had been promised, and the time had now come, as Adoniram thought, when the promise was to be redeemed, and the true word—divine truth—was to be imparted. Hence, in the person of Adoniram, or the Royal Master, we see symbolized the Speculative Mason, who, having labored to complete his spiritual temple, comes to the Divine Master that he may receive his reward, and that his labor may be consummated by the acquisition of truth. But the temple that he had been building is the temple of his life; that first temple which must be destroyed by death that the second temple of the future life may be built on its foundations. And in this first temple the truth cannot be found. We must be contented with its substitute.

SELECT MASTER.

THE Select Master is the ninth degree in the American Rite, and the last of the two conferred in a Council of Royal and Select Masters. Its officers are a Thrice Ilustrious Grand Master, Illustrious Hiram of Tyre, Principal Conductor of the Works, Treasurer, Recorder, Captain of the Guards, Conductor of the Council, and Steward. The first three represent the three Grand Masters at the building of Solomon's Temple. The symbolic colors are black and red, the former significant of secrecy, silence, and darkness; the latter of fervency and zeal. A Council is supposed to consist of neither more or less than twenty-seven; but a smaller number, if not less than nine, is competent to proceed to work or business. The candidate, when initiated, is said to be "chosen as a Select Master." The historical object of the degree is to commemorate the deposit of an important secret or treasure which, after the preliminary preparations, is said to have been made by Hiram Abiff. The place of meeting represents a secret vault beneath the Temple.

A controversy has sometimes arisen among ritualists as to whether the degree of Select Master should precede or follow that of Royal Master in the order of conferring. But the arrangement now existing, by which the Royal Master is made the first and the Select Master the second degree of Cryptic Masonry, has been very generally accepted, and this for the best of reasons. It is true that the circumstances referred to in the degree of Royal Master occurred during a period of time which lies between the death of the Chief Builder of the Temple and the completion of the edifice, while those referred to in the degree of Select Master occurred anterior to the builder's death. Hence, in the order of time, the events commemorated in the Select Master's degree took place anterior to those which are related in the degree of Royal Master; although in Masonic sequence the latter degree is conferred before the former. This apparent anachronism is, however, reconciled by the explanation that the secrets of the Select Master's degree were not brought to light until long after the existence of the Royal Master's degree had been known and recognized.

In other words, to speak only from the traditional point of view, Select Masters had been designated, had performed the task for which they had been selected, and had closed their labors, without ever being openly recognized as a class in the Temple of Solomon. The business in which they were engaged was a secret one. Their occupation and their very existence, according to the legend, were unknown to the great body of the Craft in the first Temple. The Royal Master's degree, on the contrary, as there was no reason for concealment, was publicly conferred and acknowledged during the latter part of the construction of the Temple of Solomon; whereas the degree of Select Master, and the important incidents on which it was founded, are not supposed to have been revealed to the Craft until the building of the Temple of Zerubbabel. Hence the Royal Master's degree should always be conferred anterior to that of the Select Master.

The proper jurisdiction under which these degrees should be placed, whether under Chapters to be conferred preparatory to the Royal Arch degree, or under Councils and to be conferred after it, has excited discussion. There is no doubt that these degrees belonged originally to the Ancient and Accepted Rite, and were conferred as honorary degrees by the Inspectors of that Rite. This authority and jurisdiction the Supreme Council for the Southern Jurisdiction of the Rite continued to claim until the year 1870.

THE ORDER OF THE TEMPLE IN CANADA.

BY M. EM. SIR KNIGHT WILL. H. WHYTE,
Past Supreme Grand Master Knights Templar of Canada.

THERE is an old tradition that the Knights Hospitaller (Knights of St. John and Knights of Malta, alternately so called) were in active existence in the City of Quebec in the 17th and 18th centuries. It is claimed that Champlain, who came to Quebec in 1603, was a Knight of Malta. Montmagny, who was Governor of Quebec from 1636 to 1648, especially was untiring in his efforts to advance the interests of the Order of Malta, but after his recall the Order declined. Captain John Knox, in his journal of the Siege of Quebec under date of 1st October, 1759, describes the chief edifices of the city and refers to the unfinished but imposing house of the Knights Hospitaller. The American Gazetter, published in Italian at Leghorn, 1763, in describing the Town of Quebec, refers to the house of the Knights of Jerusalem, a superb building of square stones and which is said to have cost £40,000 sterling. The Abbe Bois, F.R.S.C., states that the Knights established a bureau in the yard of the Castle of St. Louis, costing 40,000 livres (not pounds). The gable contained a large stone set in the wall, on which was engraved the arms of the Order. The edifice was destroyed by fire during the siege of July, 1759, and the stone which bore a gilt Maltese Cross and the date 1647, remained among the ruins until 1784 when it was unearthed and placed in the wall of the Chateau Yard. This stone is still to be seen in the archway, which faces St. Louis Street of that handsome hostelry the "Chateau Frontenac," now standing on the site of the famous old Chateau St. Louis of many historic memories.

RECORDS IN BOSTON.

1769—The oldest record pertaining to the Order of the Temple on this continent is found in the first meeting recorded of St. Andrew's Royal Arch Chapter of Boston, August 28th, 1769, when one William Davis received the four steps of Excellent, Super Excellent, Royal Arch, and Knight Templar.

RECORDS IN NOVA SCOTIA.

1782—The first records in Canada, so far as known, are from Halifax, in the Province of Nova Scotia, which give the minutes of a chapter of Royal Arch Masons held under warrant of No. 211 on the "Ancient Grand Registry of England," on the 20th September, 1782, and the conferring of the Royal Arch Degree on three candidates, after which, "an assembly or encampment of Sir Knights Templar being formed, the said Brothers, J. G. Pyke, John Clark, and Joseph Peters, were instituted and dubbed Knights of the Most Noble and Right Worshipful Order of the Knights Templar." There are similar records of ten other meetings.

RECORDS IN QUEBEC.

1791—In the old minutes of Albion Lodge No. 2, in the City of Quebec, it is recorded, June 10th, 1791, that Archibald Ferguson, Knight Templar, was present. Letters from H.R.H. Prince Edward, afterward Duke of Kent, Colonel commanding the Royal Fusiliers, and father of Her Most Gracious Majesty Queen Victoria, and dated at Quebec, 27th October, 1792, written to Sir Thomas Dunckerley, Grand Master of the Templar Order in England, states: "Nothing gives me greater pleasure than to hear of the advancement of that Order, which, in my humble opinion is, of all Masonry, the most valuable." Also of date November 20th, 1793, H.R.H. writes: "I shall think myself particularly fortunate when circumstances shall permit my meeting the Knights of Grand Chapter in London." H.R.H., who was Grand Master of the G. L. of

Lower Canada from 1792 to 1812, and resided for some years at both Quebec and Halifax, also held during the latter part of that period the office of Grand Patron of the Order of Masonic Knights Templar. There are many records in the minutes of the old Lodges in the Province of Quebec relating to the Order of the Temple in the beginning of the 19th century.

FIRST WARRANT, KINGSTON, ONT.

1800—In the early days of the Order the degrees were always conferred under a Craft Warrant, but the year 1800 produced the first Templar Warrant in Canada for holding a separate organization for the assembling of the Fratres and conferring the Order of the Temple. This old Templar Warrant is dated 31st October, 1800, and was issued to Sir Knight Companion Christopher Danby as Captain General and signed:

Frederick Hirschfeldt, Grand Master,
John Danley, Generalissimo,
Francis Wycott, Capt. General.
William Mackay, First Captain.
Thomas Sparham, Second Captain.
John McGill, Recorder pro tem.

A list of the members, dated 2nd November, shows a roll of fourteen names. There is also preserved two invocations, one a prayer to be used at the making of Knights Templar, and the other for the closing ceremonies of the Encampment.

SECOND WARRANT, KINGSTON, ONT.

1823—The next record appears to have been a dispensation for an Encampment of Templars at Kingston on the 10th day of March, 1823. This dispensation was granted to Sirs John Butterworth, Thos. Ferguson and William Chestnut, and a constitutional number of Knights Templar and Knights of Malta, in the Town of Kingston, and signed by Ziba M. Phillips, General Grand Master, K.T., K.M. This Encampment was known by the style and title of No. 1 or St. John's in the Town of Kingston, and met in the house of Sir George Millward, known by the sign of the Old King's Head. This body was also known as St. John's Encampment No. 1.

1824—This dispensation was followed by a warrant dated 12th February, 1824, signed by Ziba M. Phillips, G.M., and Phillip F. Hall, Grand Recorder, P.T. The Petitioners all resided in Kingston and were British subjects.

1827—The next document is a letter from Hall the Recorder, to the Grand Encampment at Montreal, and the reply is dated at Montreal, January 24th, 1827, and is signed by Gwyn Owen Radford, Past Grand Master, K.T. and K.M., who writes for the Grand Master, in the absence of the Grand Recorder.

1840—The Order in the Maritime Provinces received its first impetus, by the issuing of a charter by the Supreme Grand Encampment of Ireland, on the 5th April, 1840, to "Hibernian Encampment" No. 318, located at St. Andrews, N.B. This body, however, went out of existence in May, 1860, and its warrant was returned to Ireland.

1843—Frater J. Ross Robertson's history of the Knights Templar of Canada states a warrant was issued by Ziba M. Phillips in 1843 for Victoria Encampment at Smith's Falls, also one from Ireland in 1850 to be attached to Lodge No. 159, Irish Register, at Hawkesbury, Canada West. There is no record of Templar work at this latter place. The warrant is signed by Augustus Frederick, Duke of Leinster, the Supreme Grand Commander of the High Knights Templar of Ireland.

THIRD WARRANT, KINGSTON, ONT.

1854—In the year 1854 the late Col. Wm. McLeod Moore, who had arrived in Canada a few years previously, found that an Encampment had been in existence in Kingston, and that two of the original members, Fratres Samuel Boyden and Robert Sellars, still resided there.

The warrant of 1824 was eventually found and forwarded, accompanied by a petition signed by the two surviving members and other Templars, to England, praying that it might be exchanged for a new one to be called "Hugh de Payens."

This new warrant was issued by Colonel Kemeys Tynte, Grand Master of England, on the 10th March, 1854, with Colonel Moore as First Commander. In July of the same year the Colonel received a patent making him Provincial Grand Commander for the Province of Canada.

From this time dates the revival of the Order of the Temple in Canada.

PROVINCIAL GRAND CONCLAVE.

In the same year (1854) a warrant was issued to open Geoffrey de St. Aldemar in Toronto, dated 8th September, and William de la More the Martyr, at Quebec, was constituted on the 28th July, 1855, with Frater T. D. Harington as Eminent Commander. These three Encampments, on the 7th October, 1855, formed the first governing body of the Order, the "Provincial Grand Conclave" at Kingston, the predecessor of the present Sovereign Great Priory. The Premier Preceptory, Hugh de Payens, of Kingston, installed at its inception and had among its earlier members a number of Knights whose names are very familiar to all Canadian Masons, among them James A. Henderson, Q.C., afterwards Supreme Grand Master of Canadian Templars; S. B. Harman, Thos. D. Harington, Sir Allan Napier MacNab, the Right Hon. Sir John A. Macdonald, afterward Prime Minister of Canada, and Sir Alexander Campbell, the latter three becoming in later years distinguished Canadian statesmen.

1856—On the 22nd April, 1856, a dispensation was issued by the Chapter General of Scotland to a number of Knights resident in Saint John, N.B., under the designation of the Encampment of St. John, No. 48; a charter followed dated February 11th, 1857. John Willis, who in 1827 was a member of the St. John's Encampment No.

1, Kingston, was the first Lieutenant Commander of this body. This Encampment has had a notable existence, and came under the banner of the Sovereign Great Priory in 1897. On the 11th October, 1858, Nova Scotia Preceptory of Halifax was chartered by Convent General, and together with Union de Molay of St. John (founded in 1869) formed a Provincial Grand Priory for Nova Scotia and New Brunswick. This provincial body kept a separate existence until the death of the Provincial Prior, the Hon. Alex. Keith, in December, 1872, when by instructions from the Great Priory of England, they came under the Grand Priory of Canada.

1859—In 1855 a charter had been granted by Ireland for an Encampment in the City of Hamilton, and in April, 1859, a number of Knights Templar resident in that City, petitioned for a charter from England, and forwarded with their petition this warrant or Charter No. 231 from the Grand Encampment of Ireland. A new warrant was issued by Col. Tynte, Grand Master, for Godfrey de Bouillon of Hamilton, to bear date from the Irish warrant, October 25th, 1855. The next warrants were, Richard Coeur de Lion of London, Ont., in 1857; King Baldwin of Belleville, 7th June, 1861; Richard Coeur de Lion of Montreal, 3rd December, 1863; Plantagenet of St. Catharines in 1866, and Plantagenet of Stanstead, 1867. The name of this latter body was subsequently changed to Sussex.

GRAND PRIORY OF CANADA.

1868—The last session of the Provincial Grand Priory was held at Ottawa in 1867 and request forwarded to England that owing to the confederation of the Canadian provinces this year into a Dominion or National body, it was highly expedient to likewise confederate the various Templar organizations into a Supreme Grand Conclave. This was agreed to by England, and at the annual session of the Order in Montreal, in 1868, it met as a Grand Priory, and under the regime of this governing body the following subordinates were given life, viz., in 1869, Hurontario at Collingwood, afterwards removed to Guelph and re-named Victoria; Mount Calvary at Orillia, afterwards removed to Barrie; Geoffrey de St. Aldemar of Toronto, which had been practically dormant for several years, was revived in 1871. Harington was chartered for Trenton, but it practically went out of existence in 1873. In 1872 Gondemar was instituted at Maitland, St. John the Almoner at Whitby, Palestine at Port Hope, and Odo de St. Amand at Toronto. In 1873, William de la More the Martyr, which, upon the removal of the Government to Ottawa, was taken to that city, and had languished in a semi-dormant manner, finally returned its warrant. Sussex this year was moved to Dunham, in 1874 it was removed to Montreal and became dormant, was later on revived and moved back to its first home Stanstead, and in 1900 was finally located in Sherbrooke.

NATIONAL GREAT PRIORY OF CANADA.

1876—In 1876 Grand Priory, after nine years' existence, met under that name for the last time in Montreal. In August, 1873, a Conclave for the formation of a National Great Priory had been called to meet in Kingston, but no action was taken until 1876 in Montreal, when it was finally consummated by consent of the Supreme authorities in England.

At this meeting the Grand Sub. Prior, in order to place on record the action taken on the Memorial of Grand Priory, read the extract of the minutes of Convent General of October, 1873, and of the Great Priory of England and Wales, 10th December, 1875; the patents erecting Canada into a National Great Priory and Col. W. J. B. Macleod Moore as the first Great Prior. During the eight years' existence of the National Grand Priory, from 1876 to 1884, the following additions were made to the roll of Preceptories: "Kent" of Chatham, in 1877; "Burleigh" of St. Thomas, in 1878; "St. Elmo" of

Goderich, in 1880, this Preceptory removed to Stratford in 1896; "Ray" of Port Arthur, in 1880, name changed in 1894 to "Rhodes," and a preceptory chartered in the same year (1880) to Quebec, to be known under the old cognomen of "William de la More the Martyr." "Albert Edward" (name subsequently change to King Edward) was instituted in Winnipeg in 1880, and "Windsor," in Windsor, Ontario, in 1882.

GRAND CROSSES.

1881—In 1881 V. E. Frater A. Stavely Hill, M.P., Chancellor of the Great Priory of England, paid Canada a visit and received a Templar greeting and welcome in Richard Cœur de Lion Preceptory, Montreal. The occasion was memorable, for H.R.H., the Prince of Wales, as Grand Master, had commissioned the Eminent Knight to convey to the following fratres of Canada the decoration and patent of "Grand Cross of the Order of the Temple" to Col. Macleod Moore and W. B. Simpson, and "Knight Commanders of the Temple" to I. H. Stearns of Montreal, Hon. Robert Marshall of St. John, James Moffatt of London, C. D. Macdonald of Peterborough, and L. H. Henderson of Belleville. These were supplemented afterwards by the conferring of the "Grand Cross" upon J. A. Henderson, Q.C., D.C.L., of Kingston; James Kirkpatrick Kerr, Q.C., Toronto, and Daniel Spry, of Barrie, the Grand Chancellor, and "Knights Commander" upon G. O. Tyler, A. G. Adams, Montreal; Robert Ramsay, M.D., Orillia, and E. H. D. Hall, of Peterborough.

Convent General, the governing body of the Order, to which Canada was attached, was now practically dead. Ireland and England had disagreed over various changes, Canada had not been consulted, and much dissatisfaction had been expressed over the condition of Templar affairs. At the annual session of 1883 a resolution was passed looking to the complete independence of Great Priory.

SOVEREIGN GREAT PRIORY.

1884—On the 8th July, 1884, the Fratres of the National Great Priory met in Toronto for the ninth and last time, and having been absolved by H.R.H. the Prince of Wales from their allegiance to him as Grand Master, formally inaugurated the Sovereign Great Priory of Canada, with Col. Wm. Bury Macleod Moore, G.C.T., as Supreme Grand Master, *ad vitam*. At this session the honorary rank of "Past Supreme Grand Master of Knights Templar of Canada" was, by resolution, conferred upon H.R.H. the Prince of Wales, "as a mark of the very high esteem and affection in which he was held by the Templars of this jurisdiction."

With the change in status and nomenclature the "Order of the Temple" in Canada secured a new lease of life and energy. Harington Preceptory, dormant for some years, was resuscitated and removed to Almonte, and Gondemar Preceptory to Brockville. Many of those in existence put on more vigor, though the membership in many was somewhat small, the total roll at this time standing at twenty-six preceptories with less than 1,000 members. The Grand Encampment of the United States promptly recognized Canada's sovereignty, and an exchange of Grand Representatives between the two bodies was made. The year 1886 saw "Malta Preceptory at Truro, in Nova Scotia, instituted, and a preceptory chartered at Melbourne, in Victoria, Australia. The issuing of this Australian Warrant brought a strong protest from England, who had instituted a preceptory in that Colony some years previously, which had ceased to exist, and the territory was therefore considered practically unoccupied. With the issuing the following year of two more warrants for Victoria, trouble ensued, and the Great Priory of England severed all fraternal intercourse with the Sovereign Great Priory of Canada, which condition of affairs lasted for some years. In the year 1888 the three Australian preceptories seceded from Canada and formed the "Great Priory of Victoria," which survived for a few years, but eventually ceased to exist. In July, 1887, Sovereign Great Priory forwarded an address to "Queen Victoria," extending heartiest congratulations upon Her Majesty attaining the 50th anniversary of her reign. In the same year the City of Toronto obtained a second preceptory, which was named "Cyrene" No. 29, and which has fully justified its existence.

1890—The death of Col. W. J. B. Macleod Moore, which occurred a short time after the annual assembly, in September, 1890, removed a most enthusiastic Templar, as well as a most prominent figure in Masonic circles in Canada. He had presided over the destinies of the Knights Templar of Canada for 36 years, from 1854 to 1867 as Provincial Grand Commander, from 1868 to 1875 as Grand Prior, from 1876 to 1883 as the M.E. the Great Prior, and as Supreme Grand Master, from 1884 to 1890, and had achieved the reputation of being an able and learned historian, especially in all that pertained to the Templar Order.

A special assembly was held in Hamilton on October 21st following, and the Deputy Grand Master Frater James A. Henderson, of Kingston, unanimously elected to the vacant chair. Frater Henderson was far from well and not at the meeting, and he followed his illustrious predecessor within a few weeks of his elevation to the Grand Mastership.

At the annual assembly, July, 1891, M. E. Frater Henry Robertson, LL.B., was elected Supreme Grand Master, followed the next year, 1892, by M. E. Frater E. T. Malone, of Toronto. During the years 1893 and 1894 M. E. Frater E. E. Sheppard, also of Toronto, occupied the chair, and M. E. Frater Will. H. Whyte, of Montreal, in 1895 and 1896. Frater Whyte was the first Canadian Grand Master of Templars to officially visit the Grand Encampment of the United States. He attended the Triennial at Boston in 1895, accompanied by Most Em.

Frater Malone. M. E. Frater Daniel F. Macwatt was Grand Master in 1897 and 1898. With the death of the venerable frater who had so long presided over the destinies of the Order in Canada, the old regime passed away. New methods and new ideas had been struggling into life for some years, and with the above earnest and enthusiastic fratres in command, increasing interest was taken by the members in the Order. These years were marked by steady development, new regulations and statutes were effected for the smoother working of both the Supreme and constituent bodies and a motion brought forward providing that when the provinces were each sufficiently strong, Provincial Grand Bodies were to be formed. A by-law was adopted providing for a neat black uniform and a new edition of the Ceremonies issued, making them more attractive.

During these years nine preceptories were instituted, viz: "Western Gate" at Victoria, B.C., in 1891, followed in 1892 by "Yarmouth" at Yarmouth on the Atlantic coast. "Ottawa" Preceptory in 1893 at the Capitol was instituted by M. E. Frater Malone; and in 1894, Most Em. Frater Sheppard gave life to two Western preceptories, viz., "Cyprus" Preceptory at Calgary, and "Columbia" Preceptory at Vancouver, and Most Em. Frater Whyte was responsible in 1895 for "Prince Edward" Preceptory at Charlottetown, P.E.I., and "Ivanhoe" Preceptory at Moncton, N.B., two eastern preceptories, followed by "St. Simon of Cyrene" at Sarnia, Ont., in 1896, and by the affiliation in 1897 of the "Encampment of St. John" at St. John, N.B., holding a warrant from the Chapter General of Scotland. In 1899 Most Em. Frater Macwatt granted a Dispensation for "Rossland" Preceptory at Rossland. At the session of 1894, a communication was received from the Great Priory of England and Wales containing the information that the edict of non-intercourse against Canada had been withdrawn and friendly relations restored.

During this decade ten additions were made to the roll and an added membership of nearly 1,000. The Order received a shock at the somewhat sudden death of the oldest officer of Great Priory, Grand Chancellor Daniel Spry, G.C.T., and Hon. Past Supreme Grand Master, on August 13th, 1897, a few days before the annual assembly held at Montreal. This enthusiastic Frater had held the Grand Chancellorship of the Order in Canada for upwards of twenty years, and had also held high offices in every branch of the Masonic Fraternity. At the session in Montreal, Most Em. Frater Will H. Whyte, the retiring Grand Master, was elected to succeed Frater Spry as Grand Chancellor. 1897 being Queen Victoria's jubilee year, an address on vellum handsomely bound was transmitted, and reply received that the address had been laid before the Queen and that "Her Majesty returned her sincere thanks to the Knights Templar of Canada for the expressions of loyalty and devotion contained in the handsome volume."

1900—Great Priory met at Windsor in 1899, and Most Em. Frater J. V. Ellis was elected Grand Master, and also celebrated the Centennial of the first Knights Templar body at Kingston in 1800 by meeting in said city in 1900. Upon the death of Queen Victoria, January, 1901, profound sympathy and sincere devotion to her successor was cabled to King Edward by the Grand Master. At the City of St. John, in 1901, Most Em. Frater D. L. Carley was elected Grand Master, and during his tenure of office for two years, "Gibson" Preceptory at Sault Ste. Marie, Ont., in 1902, and "Offanto" Preceptory at Owen Sound, Ont., were instituted.

Most Em. Frater William Gibson succeeded to the chair in 1903 and 1904, and reported issuing dispensations for new preceptories at Woodstock, N.B.; Jacques de Molai at Niagara Falls, Ont.; Cape Breton, at Sydney, N.S.; Selkirk, at Cranbrook, B.C., and Mount Carmel, at Neepawa, Man., located in five of the Provinces of the Dominion and stretching from the Atlantic to the Pacific

Oceans. In September, 1904, the Earl of Euston, Grand Master of the Great Priory of England, accompanied by a suite of five of his officers, visited Montreal on his return from the Conclave of the Grand Encampment at San Francisco. They spent two very pleasant days as guests of Great Priory and Richard Coeur de Lion of Montreal, and expressed much pleasure at the attentions shown them.

Great Priory held its session the following year, 1905, in Winnipeg, Man., and M. E. Frater J. B. Tresidder, of Montreal, was elected Grand Master. At the following assembly in Montreal he reported the formation of a preceptory at Edmonton, Alta., followed the next year by dispensations for Cornwall, Ont., and Dawson City, in the Yukon. M. Em. Frater Tresidder, accompanied by a number of his Great Priory officers, paid an official visit to the Grand Encampment of the United States, at the Saratoga Triennial of 1907.

Most Em. Frater A. A. Campbell, of London, Ont., was elected Supreme Grand Master for 1907 and 1908, and at the assembly, held in Toronto in 1908, had the pleasure of welcoming Most Em. Sir Knight the Rev. Henry W. Rugg, D.D., Grand Master of the Grand Encampment of the United States. Dr. Rugg was the first Grand Master from the United States to visit the Sovereign Great Priory of Canada.

Leamington Preceptory, Ont.; Fredericton Preceptory, N.B., and Wascana Preceptory, of Regina, Sask., were instituted this year, 1908, and the following year St. George Preceptory, of Picton, Ont., was formed. At the annual session in Truro, N.S., 1909, a Concordat, which had been adopted by the Priories of England, Ireland and Scotland, was also adopted by Sovereign Great Priory, followed in 1910 by the Grand Encampment of the United States, thus uniting all the Grand Bodies of the Order in a short amicable treaty.

1910—M. Em. Frater L. B. Archibald, of Truro, was elected Supreme Grand Master and filled the office for the second year. He paid an official visit to the Triennial at Chicago, August, 1910, accompanied by a number of his leading officers, including Past Grand Masters Will H. Whyte and J. B. Tresidder, the former being made an honorary member of the Grand Encampment, the second frater so honored by this Grand Body, the Earl of Euston being the first. The death of King Edward, Honorary Past Supreme Grand Master, in May, was a momentous event, and Great Priory's deepest sympathy was cabled. Later a floral offering was forwarded upon the death of Rev. Dr. Rugg, Grand Master of the United States, and Canada's representative. Dispensations were issued for preceptories at Prince Albert, Sask., and Crusader Preceptory, at Medicine Hat, Alta. Earl Euston, the Pro-Grand Master of England, again visited Montreal with his staff on the way back from Chicago, and was entertained for several days. The new preceptories added to the roll in 1911 were Saskatoon Preceptory, Sask.; Westminster, at New Westminster, B.C., and "Beausejour," at Amherst, N.S. At the assembly in Sault Ste. Marie, Ont., 1911, the roll of preceptories stood at 57, with a membership of 6,316, doubling the membership of six years previously, and M. E. Frater Wm. P. Ryrie, of Toronto, was elected Supreme Grand Master.

Great Priory met in the City of Toronto in 1912, and Most Em. Frater Wm. B. Melish, Grand Master of the Grand Encampment U.S.A., accompanied by five of his Grand Officers, paid an official and fraternal visit. The death of the Earl of Euston, the Pro-Grand Master of the Knights Templar of England, was reported and Most Eminent I. H. Stearns, the only surviving office of the first Grand Body of the Temple in Canada, was created an Honorary Supreme Grand Master.

For the first time in its history the Great Priory met on the Pacific Coast, in the City of Vancouver, July, 1913. The death of one of the most beloved members of the Order, Past Grand Master, the Honorable John V. Ellis, was feelingly referred to, as well as the instituting of a new Preceptory—"Damascus"—at Moose Jaw, Sask., and another at Prince Rupert, B.C., named "Kincolith." The newly elected Grand Master, Philip D. Gordon, accompanied by four Past Grand Masters, returned via Denver and paid an official visit to the Grand Encampment of the U. S. A. The session of 1914, held in August, at Ottawa, was enlivened by a visit from Most Eminent Arthur MacArthur (since died), the Grand Master of the Order in the U. S. A., accompanied by five of his officers. The acceptance of the Rank of Honorary Supreme Grand Master of the Sovereign Great Priory of Canada by H. R. H. the Duke of Connaught, K.G., in succession to the late King Edward, was received with much pleasure. The instituting of two new preceptories, "Temiskawina" of Haileybury, Ont., and "Revelstoke" at Revelstoke, B.C., was reported, as well as the deaths of Past Grand Masters J. B. Tresidder and the Hon. William Gibson. The membership (August, 1915) in 62 Preceptories, was 8,052 Fratres.

ANCIENT AND ACCEPTED SCOTTISH RITE IN THE DOMINION OF CANADA.

BY ILL. BRO. W. H. BALLARD, 33°
SECRETARY-GENERAL.

THE Ancient and Accepted Scottish Rite of Freemasonry was introduced into the Dominion of Canada on the tenth day of July, 1868, by virtue of a patent held by the Illustrious Brother Col. William James Bury Macleod Moore from the Supreme Council for England and Wales and the Dependencies of the British Crown.

Under this authority the first bodies of the Rite were established as follows:

In the Province of Ontario—

Moore Sovereign Consistory S.P.R.S. 32nd at Hamilton.
Hamilton Sovereign Chapter Rose Croix at Hamilton.
London Sovereign Chapter Rose Croix at London.

In the Province of New Brunswick—

Moore Sovereign Chapter Rose Croix at Saint John (not opened, however, until April, 1870).

Other bodies under warrants from the same Supreme Council were soon after established as follows.

Keith Chapter of Rose Croix at Halifax, in the Province of Nova Scotia, in October, 1870.

Harington Consistory, at Saint John, New Brunswick, under warrant dated July, 1872; opened in September of the same year.

Macleod Moore Chapter Rose Croix at Maitland, Ontario, under warrant dated May, 1873.

Toronto Chapter Rose Croix, at Toronto, Ontario, 14th May, 1873.

Hochelaga Chapter Rose Croix, at Montreal, Province of Quebec, July, 1873.

Under a combined warrant from the Supreme Council for Scotland the following bodies were established in Saint John, Province of New Brunswick:

New Brunswick Council of Kadosh, Oct., 1871.

New Brunswick Chapter Rose Croix, Oct., 1871.

Ill. Bro. Moore, who was so active in his efforts to introduce Scottish Rite Masonry into Canada, was an enthusiastic missionary in the cause of Masonry generally. He was born in Ireland in 1810, initiated into Freemasonry at the early age of 17 years in Aberdeen, Scotland, where he also received the Royal Arch Degree. He became a Knight Templar in Ireland, received the degrees of the A. A. S. Rite in New York in 1863, and in 1868 was made an active member of the Supreme Council for England, and in the same year, as has been already shown, began the organization of the Rite in Canada. Perhaps his principal activity was manifested in Knight Templarism: in 1850 he established the first Templar Encampment in connection with Freemasonry in the Island of Malta, and soon after coming to Canada, in 1854, revived an old dormant Templar warrant. This marks the first establishment of the Templar order in this country on a constituted basis. He was rightly considered one of the greatest authorities on Knight Templarism in the world.

From the constant association and frequent interchange of visitation of members of the Rite in the Dominion with those in the United States, the heads of the order in Canada considered it necessary that the system to be followed should be assimilated as closely as possible with that which obtained in the bodies of the Rite in the Northern and Southern Jurisdictions of the United States. This was considered impossible under the regime of the Supreme Council of England and Wales which, working only the 18th, 30th, 31st and 32nd degrees, had no provision for conferring in full the degrees subordinate thereto, in many respects the most important of the system. In addition to this the scale of fees for the

Consistory degrees was so high and requiring so long an intermission of time between them, that the propagation of the Rite was so narrowly limited as to amount almost to prohibition.

Some concessions were made after considerable time had elapsed and petitions had been sent forward for modifications of these stringent rules and the Supreme Council did grant a code of regulations under which the bodies of the Rite made much more satisfactory progress. But those most deeply concerned for the welfare of the order came to the conclusion, after mature deliberation, that unless the Rite in Canada was placed under its own Sovereign Body it would never command the respect to which, through its intrinsic merit, it was entitled, and accordingly an earnest appeal was made to the Mother Body for absolution from vows of fealty and allegiance and for authority to establish a Supreme Council 33rd degree for the Dominion of Canada.

The Supreme Council in England took immediate action on this application and requested the votes of the various bodies of the Rite in Canada in order to learn whether the desire for independence proceeded from the members holding the 33rd degree only, or was the wish of the members of the Rite generally. Accordingly a vote was taken and found to be unanimous for separation.

Thereupon the Supreme Council promptly, and with the greatest kindness and courtesy, issued a Patent to the Ilustrious Brother Thomas Douglas Harington, 33rd degree (their representative at the time for the Dominion, excepting the Maritime Provinces), to open a Supreme Council 33rd degree for the Dominion, naming the said Illustrious Brother as the M. P. Sovereign Grand Commander ad vitam; whereupon by virtue thereof a convention of the members of the 33rd degree was summoned to meet at Ottawa on the 16th of October, 1874.

In obedience to the summons issued the following members of the 33rd degree assembled in convention: T. Douglas Harington, W. J. B. Macleod Moore, John W. Murton, Hugh A. Mackay, David R. Munro, together with two distinguished visitors, Ill. Bro. Albert Pike, M.P. Sovereign Grand Commander of the Supreme Council for the Southern Jurisdiction of the United States, and Ill. Bro. D. Burnham Tracy, representing Ill. Bro. Josiah H. Drummond, Sovereign Grand Commander of the Supreme Council for the Northern Jurisdiction of the United States.

By authority of the Patent, Bro. Harington appointed Robert Marshall, 33rd degree, of St. John, New Brunswick, Lieutenant Grand Commander, and they (by written consent of the latter) appointed John W. Murton, 33rd degree, the third member to hold the office of the Grand Secretary General.

Ill. Bro. Pike declared the Supreme Council to be duly and constitutionally established, and "The Supreme Council of Sovereign Grand Inspectors-General of the 33rd degree for the Dominion of Canada" had its birth.

The Supreme Council was opened in due form and the following members of the 33rd degree duly elected to active membership therein: Hugh A. Mackay; D. R. Munro; J. K. Kerr; J. Domville and H. W. Chisholm. The following members of the 32nd degree were severally elected to receive the 33rd degree, and Bro. Pike elevated them to the rank of S. G. Inspectors-General, 33rd degree, and declared them active members of the Council: John V. Ellis, of St. John, New Brunswick; William Reid, of Hamilton, Ontario; William H. Hutton, and Eugene M. Copeland, both of Montreal, Que.

The necessary elections to the various offices having been duly conducted the Supreme Council assumed its full form as follows:

T. Douglas Harington, M.P. Sovereign Grand
    Commander.
Robert Marshall, Lieut. Grand Commander.

John Walter Murton, Secretary-General.
Hugh Alexander Mackay, Treasurer-General.
John Valentine Ellis, Grand Chacellor.
David Ransom Munro, Grand Master of Ceremonies.
James Domville, Grand Mashall-General.
James Kirkpatrick Kerr, Grand Standard Bearer.
Hugh William Chisholm, Grand Captain of the Guard.
Active Members—
Col. W. J. B. Macleod Moore, Laprairie, Quebec.
William Reid, Hamilton, Ontario.
William Henry Hutton and Eugene Mortimer, both of Montreal, Quebec.

Ill. Bro. Pike, who had taken such an active interest in the formation of the new Council, loyally stood sponsor for it and immediately formulated and sent out a circular letter to the several Supreme Councils with which the Supreme Council for the Southern Jurisdiction of the United States had relations of amity and correspondence, making known that the Supreme Council for the Dominion of Canada was duly established and organized in strict accordance with the disposition of the Grand Constitution of 1786, and requesting that these Councils recognize it as a regular and lawful Supreme Council, and offer to enter into relations of amity and correspondence with it. So prompt was the response to this request that at the next annual meeting Sovereign Grand Commander Harington was able to announce that more than a dozen of these Councils had sent fraternal notices of recognition and that with the greater number of these, representatives had already been exchanged.

Of the five members of the 33rd degree who met in convention to establish the Council one still survives— Ill. Bro. Hugh A. Mackay, of Berlin, Ontario. He was elected Treasurer-General at the inaugural meeting and held the office continuously till 1913; also without intermission throughout the same period he has been the representative of the Northern Supreme Council of the United States near this Supreme Council. Bro. Mackay was at the meeting at which the Rite was inaugurated in Canada in 1868, went to London two years later to interview the English Supreme Council in the interests of greater freedom for the Canadian brethren, was raised to the 33rd degree in 1871 and has been constantly interested and active in the work of the Council ever since. There can be few living who have worn the honor longer or more worthily.

The Supreme Council having perfected its own organization undertook at once the completion of such a system of Masonry in the higher degrees as would lay down a foundation that could be hereafter built upon with confidence and success and at the same time adapt itself to the genius of the people who were to become its members.

Although the English Council had already made some concession it was thought well to depart still farther from the requirements of the British usage in devising a system to be adapted to the Dominion as a whole.

In England the 32nd and the 31st degrees were conferred by the Supreme Council and were strictly limited in number, the 31st to 99 and the 32nd to 54 members. Membership in the 30th degree was not definitely limited as to number, but no Prince Rose Croix could receive this degree unless a present or past M. W. S. and had been three years a member of the 18th degree, except by special dispensation.

In England the Lodge of Perfection as a separate body does not exist and none are named on the English register, the Rose Croix Chapter covering both the Council of Prince of Jerusalem and the Lodge of Perfection.

None of these restrictions commended themselves to the members of the Canadian Council and accordingly membership in the 30th, 31st or 32nd degree is unlimited either as to a restriction to definite numbers or to the requirement of having previously held office in a subordinate body. Lodges of Perfection exist also as a separate and distinct organizations with their own officers and system of administration, and may exist in localities where Chapters have not yet been established. Too rapid progress through the various grades of the Rite is checked, however, by statutory time limits. A candidate who has just received the symbolic degrees will require more than two years to complete those of the Scottish Rite unless under a special dispensation, which can be granted only by the Sovereign Grand Commander or by the Deputy of the Council for the province in which the candidate resides.

The degrees above that of Rose Croix are not conferred by the Supreme Council as in the United Kingdom, but by Consistories of S. P. R. S. 32nd degree, covering Tribunals of G. I. I. C. 31st degree and Councils of G. E. K. K. H. 30th degree, one, and one only, of which is allotted to each province of the Dominion.

While the number of those known as active members of the Supreme Council is limited to thirty-three the ordinary membership in the Council increases pari passu with the work done in the Lodges of Perfection, the statutes providing that "each province under the jurisdiction of the Supreme Council shall have the right to one additional Honorary Inspector-General for every additional fifty Grand Elect Perfect and Sublime Masons made in the Province without regard to Lodge or locality in which they may be members," the Council reserving to itself the right to create additional Honorary Members when, in its judgment, the interests of the Rite so require.

The Supreme Council is required to meet annually on the fourth Wednesday in October, at such place in the Dominion as it shall determine; but the meeting at which the officers shall be elected must be held at the Grand Orient, and as this occurs every third year, one annual session at least out of every three must be held in the City of Montreal. A special meeting may be called by the Sovereign Grand Commander to be held at any time or place that he may deem expedient.

Although the first Sovereign Grand Commander was appointed ad vitam and held the office till his death in January, 1882, this mode of tenure was not adopted, and all succeeding holders of the office have been elected by the active members of the Council for the statutory three years' term.

The complete list of Sovereign Grand Commanders is as follows:

  1874-1882—Thomas Douglas Harington.
  1882-1886—William Henry Hutton.
  1886-1892—John Valentine Ellis.
  1892-1898—John Walter Murton.
  1898-1904—Isaac Henry Stearns.
  1904-1913—Sir John Morison Gibson.
  1913-1916—Benjamin Allen.

The office of Secretary-General has been held as follows:

  1874-1886—John W. Murton.
  1886-1904—Hugh Murray.
  1904 —William H. Ballard.

The first Secretary-General, John W. Murton (Lieut.-Grand Commander 1886-1892, and then Sovereign Grand Commander until his death in 1898), was one of the most enthusiastic and energetic of those who interested themselves in the introduction of the Rite into Canada. He received the degrees, 4th degree to 32nd degree, in the Southern Jurisdiction U. S. in 1863 and the 33rd from the Supreme Council for England in 1868. He took a prominent part in the formation of the first bodies of the Rite and was for many years the Commander-in-Chief of the Moore Consistory, having been virtually its first presiding officer.

The Scottish Rite in Canada having thus secured its own governing Council and settled with a fair degree of definiteness by what system of statutes and regulations its bodies and members should be governed, proceeded with satisfactory rapidity to increase in numbers and influence. New bodies were rapidly formed and increased enthusiasm in the propagation of its principles soon became manifest.

The splendid and copious ritual, the high conception necessary to the proper rendering of the lessons contained in the successive degrees of the Ancient and Accepted Scottish Rite and the paraphernalia requisite to the satisfactory staging of the varying scenes demand mental capacity, a sense of devotion to Masonic duties and financial support such as smaller places can scarcely hope to furnish in sufficient abundance to insure continuity of efficient work.

The enthusiasm and zeal of a few may start a body going, but the persistent effort of the many is thereafter necessary to provide a constant force to preserve the momentum already communicated.

Thus it was that in the earlier years of the growth of the Rite flourishing bodies existed for a time in some of the smaller towns in several of the Provinces, but eventually met the inevitable fate of those who take up a burden which they cannot bear and surrendered their warrants.

Another retarding factor was found to exist in places which, though numerically large enough, had, from their situation in newly settled parts of the country, a population more or less shifting. This feature retarded the progress of the Rite to some extent in Western Canada, even so important a centre as Winnipeg moving slowly for some years; but now that fixity of residence is more pronounced in the larger centres flourishing bodies of the Rite have been instituted in Winnipeg, Vancouver, Edmonton, Regina, and Sault Ste. Marie.

The following table exhibits pretty accurately the present condition of the Rite in Canada and the growth it has made in the 40 years of its existence:

CONSISTORIES.

Name	Where Situated	No. Members	When Established
Moore	Hamilton, Ont.	771	1868
Montreal	Montreal, Que.	150	1874
New Brunswick	St. John, N.B.	73	1870
Nova Scotia	Halifax, N. S.	54	1884
Manitoba	Winnipeg, Man.	222	1886
British Columbia	Vancouver, B. C.	112	1905
P. E. Island	Charlottetown, P.E.I.	31	1909
Alberta	Edmonton, Alta.	58	1910

ROSE CROIX CHAPTERS.

Hamilton	Hamilton, Ont.	531	1868
London	London, Ont.	306	1868
Toronto	Toronto, Ont.	283	1873
Rose of Sharon	Kingston, Ont.	33	1883
Spry	Barrie, Ont.	56	1891
Murray	Ottawa, Ont.	267	1890
Hochelaga	Montreal, Que.	149	1873
Quebec	Quebec, Que.	24	1890
Harington	St. John, N.B.	91	1870
Keith	Halifax, N.S.	89	1870
Bethesda	Winnipeg, Man.	342	1880
Vancouver	Vancouver, B.C.	170	1901
Charlottetown	Charlottetown, P.E.I.	32	1898
Mizpah	Edmonton, Alta.	91	1907
Guelph	Guelph, Ont.	52	1908
Sault Ste. Marie	Sault Ste. Marie.	53	1914

LODGES OF PERFECTION.

Murton	Hamilton, Ont.	819	1874
London	London, Ont.	444	1888
Toronto	Toronto, Ont.	544	1878
Kingston	Kingston, Ont.	60	1881
Royal City	Guelph, Ont.	152	1884
Barrie	Barrie, Ont.	113	1888
Ottawa	Ottawa, Ont.	448	1889
Hochelaga	Montreal, Que.	168	1875

Name	Where Situated	No. Members	When Established
Quebec	Quebec, Que.	37	1890
St. John	St. John, N.B.	105	1878
Victoria	Halifax, N.S.	116	1887
Winnipeg	Winnipeg, Man.	518	1880
Vancouver	Vancouver, B.C.	285	1897
Albert Edward	Charlottetown, P.E.I.	54	1896
Edmonton	Edmonton, Alta	149	1904
Regina	Regina, Sask.	134	1910
Sault Ste. Marie	Sault Ste. Marie	91	1913

In the lodges in the above list whose dates are more recent than those of the corresponding Chapters, the Perfection degrees were worked under the Chapter Warrants.

SUPREME COUNCIL, 33rd DEGREE
FOR THE
DOMINION OF CANADA

GRAND ORIENT, MONTREAL, PROVINCE OF QUEBEC.

OFFICERS, 1913-16.

Benjamin Allen, M.P. Sovereign Grand Commander.
Benjamin Tooke, Lieutenant Grand Commander.
William H. Ballard, Secretary-General, H.E.
Elias T. Malone, Treasurer-General H.E.
Daniel F. Macwatt, Grand Chancellor.
Enoch B. Butterworth, Grand Master of Ceremonies.
Alexander McDougall, Grand Marshal.
Sydney A. Luke, Grand Standard Bearer.
John D. Chipman, Grand Captain of the Guard.

PAST SOVEREIGN GRAND COMMANDERS.

Sir John M. Gibson, K.C.M.G., Hamilton.
Isaac H. Stearns, Montreal.

DEPUTIES FOR THE PROVINCES.

Frederick J. Howell, Hamilton, for Ontario.
J. Alexander Cameron, Montreal, for Quebec.
Thomas Walker, M.D., St. John, for New Brunswick.

William M. Black, Wolfville, for Nova Scotia.
T. Harry Webb, Winnipeg, for Manitoba and Saskatchewan.
Donald Darrach, M.D., Kensington, for Prince Edward Islnad.
Joseph R. Seymour, Vancouver, for British Columbia.
Geo. T. Bragg, Edmonton, Special Deputy for Alberta

SOVEREIGN GRAND INSPECTORS-GENERAL, 33rd DEGREE.
ACTIVE MEMBERS.

Hugh Alexander Mackay, Berlin, Ontario.
Hon. James Kirkpatrick Kerr, K.C., Toronto, Ont.
Isaac Henry Stearns, Montreal, Quebec
Charles Napier Bell, Winnipeg, Manitoba.
Sir John Morison Gibson, K.C.M.G., Hamilton, Ont.
Hon. Wm. Henry Thorne, St. John, New Brunswick.
Enoch Bruce Butterworth, Ottawa, Ont.
William Henry Ballard, M.A., Hamilton, Ontario.
Benjamin Tooke, Montreal, Quebec.
John DeWolf Chipman, Toronto, Ontario.
Benjamin Allen, Toronto, Ontario.
Elias Talbot Malone, K.C., Toronto, Ont.
Sydney Albert Luke, Ottawa, Ontario.
Joseph Richard Seymour, Vancouver, B. C.
William Marshall Black, Wolfville, Nova Scotia.
Donald Darrach, M.D., Kensington, Prince Edward Island.
Thomas Lees, Hamilton, Ontario.
James Glanville, Toronto, Ontario.
Frederick Justus Howell, Hamilton, Ont.
Alexander McDougall, Montreal, Quebec.
T. Harry Webb, Winnipeg, Manitoba.
William Allen Young, London, Ontario.
John Alex. Cameron, Montreal, Quebec.
Thomas Walker, M.D., St. John, New Brunswick.
Daniel Fraser Macwatt, Sarnia, Ontario.

Alexander Stephen, Halifax, Nova Scotia.
John McKechnie, Winnipeg, Manitoba.
Roderick McNeill, M.D., Charlottetown, P.E.I.
Alfred Frederick Webster, Toronto, Ont.
Augustus Toplady Freed, Hamilton, Ont.

PAST ACTIVE MEMBERS, 33rd DEGREE.

Hon. James Domville, Rothesay, New Brunswick.
Herbert Swinford, Vancouver, British Columbia.

HONORARY INSPECTORS-GENERAL, 33rd DEGREE.

Gavin Stewart, Hamilton, Ontario.
Daniel Hunter McMillan, K.C.M.G., Winnipeg, Man.
William Robert White, K.C., Pembroke, Ontario.
John Ross Robertson, Toronto, Ontario.
Donald McPhie, Hamilton, Ontario.
Charles Raynes, Montreal, Quebec.
William Henry Wetherby, Halifax, Nova Scotia.
Albert E. Cooper, London, Ontario.
John McKnight, Toronto, Ontario.
Joseph Elwood Miller, Victoria, British Columbia.
Harry Holgate Watson, Vancouver, British Columbia.
Robert Allen Thompson, LL.D., Hamilton, Ontario.
John Thomas Blundell Persse, Winnipeg, Manitoba.
Frank Goodell Wait, M.A., Ottawa, Ontario.
John Crawford Scott, Ottawa, Ontario.
George Moore, Hamilton, Ontario.
Peter William Dumas Brodrick, Toronto, Ontario.
William Piggot Ryrie, Toronto, Ontario.
James Alexander Ovas, Winnipeg, Manitoba.
Robert Hobson, Hamilton, Ontario.
Lewis Frederick Riggs, D.D.S., Toronto, Ont.
Edward Ainslie Braithwaite, M.D. Edmonton, Alberta
George Thomas Bragg, Edmonton, Alberta.
Frank McDonald Morgan, Edmonton, Alberta.
George Black Hegan, St. John, New Brunswick.
George Blake, St. John, New Brunswick.
Rev. Frank Charters, D.C.L., Montreal, Quebec.

Harry Herbert Campkin, Regina, Saskatchewan.
James Scroggie, Winnipeg, Manitoba.
George Samuel May, Ottawa, Ontario.
Herbert Spohn Griffin, M.D., Hamilton, Ontario.
Walter Hammill Davis, Hamilton, Ontario.
Robert William Clewlo, Toronto, Ontario.
William Clement Eddis, Toronto, Ontario.
Francis James Burd, Vancouver, British Columbia.
William Carey Ditmars, Vancouver, British Columbia.
James Henry Winfield, Halifax, Nova Scotia.
Joseph Orr Rose, Guelph, Ontario.
Thomas George Davis, London, Ontario.
Thomas Rowe, London, Ontario.
Absalom Shade Allan, Guelph, Ontario.
Edward Thomas Davies Chambers, Quebec, Quebec.
George Frederick Carruthers, Winnipeg, Manitoba.
Walter Mackie Ross, Ottawa, Ontario.
Samuel Sproule Davidson, Ottawa, Ontario.
William McGregor Logan, Hamilton, Ontario.

THE ROYAL ORDER OF SCOTLAND.

Compiled by OSBORNE SHEPPARD from the writings of ALBERT G. MACKEY, M.D., 33°, and Other Masonic Historians.

THE Royal Order of Scotland consists of two degrees, namely, Heredom and Rosy Cross. The first may be briefly described as a Christianized form of the Third Degree, purified from the dross of Paganism, and even of Judaism, by the Culdees, who introduced Christianity into Scotland in the early centuries of the Church. The second degree is an Order of civil knighthood, supposed to have been founded by Robert Bruce after the battle of Bannockburn, and conferred by him upon certain Masons who had assisted him on that memorable occasion. He, so the tradition goes, gave power to the Grand Master of the Order for the time being to confer this honor, which is not inherent in the general body itself, but is specially given by the Grand Master and his Deputy, and can be conferred only by them, or Provincial Grand Masters appointed by them. The number of knights is limited, and formerly only sixty-three could be appointed, and they Scotchmen; now, however, the number has been much increased, and distinguished Masons of all countries are admitted to its ranks. In 1747 Prince Charles Edward Stuart, in his celebrated Charter to Arras, claimed to be the Sovereign Grand Master of the Royal Order, "Nous Charles Edouard Stewart, Roi d'Angleterre, de France, de l'Ecosse, et d'Irlande, et en cette qualité, S. G. M. du Chapitre de H." Prince Charles goes on to say that H. O. or H. R. M. is known as the "Pelican and Eagle." "Connu sous le titre de Chevalier de l'Aigle et de Pelican, et depuis nos malheurs et nos infortunes, sous celui de Rose Croix." Now, there is not the shadow of a proof that the Rose Croix, says Bro. Reitam, was ever known in England till twenty years after 1747; and in Ireland it was introduced by a French

Chevalier, M. L'Aurent, about 1782 or 1783. The Chapter at Arras was the first constituted in France—:"Chapitre primordial de Rose Croix"; and from other circumstances (the very name Rose Croix being a translation of Rosy Cross) some writers have been led to the conclusion that the degree chartered by Prince Charles Edward Stuart was, if not the actual Royal Order in both points, a Masonic ceremony founded on and pirated from that most ancient and venerable Order.

This, however, is an error; because, except in name, there does not appear to be the slightest connection between the Rose Croix and the Royal Order of Scotland. In the first place, the whole ceremonial is different, and different in essentials. Most of the language used in the Royal Order is couched in quaint old rhyme, modernized, no doubt, to make it "understanded of the vulgar," but still retaining sufficient about it to stamp its genuine antiquity.

Clavel says that the Royal Order of Heredom of Kilwinning is a Rosicrucian degree, having many different gradations in the ceremony of consecration. The kings of England are *de jure*, if not *de facto*, Grand Masters; each member has a name given him, denoting some moral attribute. In the initiation the sacrifice of the Messiah is had in remembrance, who shed his blood for the sins of the world, and the neophyte is in a figure sent forth to seek the lost word. The ritual states that the Order was first established at Icomkill, and afterwards at Kilwinning, where the King of Scotland, Robert Bruce, took the chair in person; and oral tradition affirms that, in 1314, this monarch again reinstated the Order, admitting into it the Knights Templar who were still left. The Royal Order, according to this ritual, which is written in Anglo-Saxon verse, boasts of great antiquity.

Findel disbelieved in the Royal Order, as he did in all the Christian degrees. He remarks that the Grand

Lodge of Scotland formerly knew nothing at all about the existence of this Order of Heredom, as a proof of which he adduces the fact that Laurie, in the first edition of his "History of the Grand Lodge of Scotland," has not mentioned it. Oliver, however, as it will be seen, had a high opinion of the Order, and expressed no doubt of its antiquity.

As to the origin of the Order, we have abundant authority.

Thory thus traces its establishment:

"On the 24th of June, 1314, Robert Bruce, king of Scotland, instituted, after the battle of Bannockburn, the Order of St. Andrew of the Thistle, to which was afterwards united that of Heredom, for the sake of the Scottish Masons who had composed a part of the thirty thousand men with whom he had fought the English army, consisting of one hundred thousand. He formed the Royal Grand Lodge of the Order of Heredom at Kilwinning, reserving to himself and his successors forever the title of Grand Masters."

Oliver, in his "Historical Landmarks," defines the Order more precisely, thus:

"The Royal Order of Heredom had formerly its chief seat at Kilwinning, and there is every reason to think that it and St. John's Masonry were then governed by the same Grand Lodge. But during the sixteenth and seventeenth centuries Masonry was at a very low ebb in Scotland, and it was with the greatest difficulty that St. John's Masonry was preserved. The Grand Chapter of Heredom resumed its functions about the middle of the last century at Edinburgh; and, in order to preserve a marked distinction between the Royal Order and Craft Masonry,— which had formed a Grand Lodge there in 1736, the former confined itself solely to the two degrees of Heredom and Rosy Cross."

Again, in the history of the Royal Order, officially printed in Scotland, the following details are found:

"It is composed of two parts, Heredom and Rosy Cross. The former took its rise in the reign of David I., king of Scotland, and the latter in that of King Robert the Bruce. The last is believed to have been originally the same as the most ancient Order of the Thistle, and to contain the ceremonial of admission formerly practised in it.

"The Order of Heredom had formerly its seat at Kilwinning, and there is reason to suppose that it and the Grand Lodge of St. John's Masonry were governed by the same Grand Master. The introduction of this Order into Kilwinning appears to have taken place about the same time, or nearly the same period, as the introduction of Freemasonry into Scotland. The Chaldees, as is well known, introduced Christianity into Scotland; and, from their known habits, there are good grounds for believing that they preserved among them a knowledge of the ceremonies and precautions adopted for their protection in Judea. In establishing the degree in Scotland, it is more than probable that it was done with the view to explain, in a correct Christian manner, the symbols and rites employed by the Christian architects and builders; and this will also explain how the Royal Order is purely catholic,—not Roman Catholic,—but adapted to all who acknowledge the great truths of Christianity, in the same way that Craft or Symbolic Masonry is intended for all, whether Jew or Gentile, who acknowledge a supreme God. The second part, or Rosy Cross, is an Order of Knighthood, and, perhaps, the only genuine one in connection with Masonry, there being in it an intimate connection between the trowel and the sword, which others try to show. The lecture consists of a figurative description of the ceremonial, both of Heredom and Rosy Cross, in simple rhyme, modernized, of course, by oral tradition, and breathing the purest spirit of Christianity. Those two degrees constitute, as has already been said, the Royal Order of Scotland. The Grand Lodge of Scotland, Lodges or Chapters cannot legally meet elsewhere, unless possessed of a Charter from it or the Grand Master, or his deputy. The office of the Grand Master is vested in the person of the king of Scotland, (now of Great Britain), and one seat is invariably kept vacant for him in whatever country a Chapter is opened, and cannot be occupied by any other member. Those who are in possession of this degree, and the so-called higher degrees, cannot fail to perceive that the greater part of them have been concocted from the Royal Order, to satisfy the morbid craving for distinction which was so characteristic of the continent during the latter half of the last century.

"There is a tradition among the Masons of Scotland that, after the dissolution of the Templars, many of the Knights repaired to Scotland and placed themselves under the protection of Robert Bruce, and that, after the battle of Bannockburn, which took place on St. John the Baptist's day, 1314, this monarch instituted the Royal Order of Heredom and Knights of the Rosy Cross, and established the chief seat at Kilwinning. From that Order it seems by no means improbable that the present degree of Rose Croix de Heredom may have taken its origin. In two respects, at least, there seems to be a very close connection between the two systems. They both claim the kingdom of Scotland and the Abbey of Kilwinning as having been at one time the chief seat of government, and they both seem to have been instituted to give a Christian explanation to Ancient Craft Masonry. There is, besides, a similarity in the name of the degrees of Rose Croix de Heredom and Heredom and Rosy Cross amounting almost to an identity, which appears to indicate a very intimate relation of one to the other."

Bro. Randolph Hay, in the London "Freemason," gives us this legend, "the real history of the Royal Order," and which he, at least, religiously believed to be true:

"Among the many precious things which were carefully preserved in a sacred vault of King Solomon's Temple was a portrait of the monarch, painted by Adoniram, the son of Elkanah, priest of the second court. This vault remained undiscovered till the time of Herod, although the secret of its existence and a description of its locality were retained by the descendants of Elkanah. During the war of the Maccabees, certain Jews, fleeing from their native country, took refuge, first in Spain and afterwards in Britain, and amongst them was one Aholiab, the then possessor of the documents necessary to find the hidden treasure. As is well known, buildings were then in progress in Edinburgh, or Dun Edwin, as the city was then called, and thither Aholiab wended his way to find employment. His skill in architecture speedily raised him to a prominent position in the Craft, but his premature death prevented his realizing the dream of his life, which was to fetch the portrait from Jerusalem and bestow it in the custody of the Craft. However, prior to his dissolution, he confided the secret to certain of the Fraternity under the bond of secrecy, and these formed a class known as 'The Order of the King,' or 'The Royal Order.' Time sped on; the Romans invaded Britain; and, previous to the crucifixion, certain members of the old town guard of Edinburgh, among whom were several of the Royal Order, proceeded to Rome to enter into negotiations with the sovereign. From thence they proceeded to Jerusalem, and were present at the dreadful scene of the crucifixion. They succeeded in obtaining the portrait, and also the blue veil of the Temple rent upon the terrible occasion. I may dismiss these two venerable relics in a few words. Wilson in his 'Memorials of Edinburgh,' (2 vols., published by Hugh Patton), in a note to Masonic Lodges, writes that this portrait was then in the possession of the brethren of the Lodge St. David. This is an error, and arose from the fact of the Royal Order then meeting in the Lodge St. David's room in Hindford's Close. The blue veil was converted into a standard for the trades of Edinburgh, and became celebrated on many a battle-field, notably in the First Crusade as 'The Blue Blanket.' From the presence of certain of their number in Jerusalem on the occasion in question, the Edinburgh City Guard were often called Pontius Pilate's Prætorians. Now, these are facts well known to many Edinburghers still alive. Let 'X. Y. Z.' go to Edinburgh and inquire for himself.''

"The brethren, in addition, brought with them the teachings of the Christians, and in their meetings they celebrated the death of the Captain and Builder of our Salvation. The oath of the Order seals my lips further as to the peculiar mysteries of the brethren. I may, however, state that the Ritual, in verse, as in present use, was composed by the venerable Abbot of Inchaffray, the same who, with a crucifix in his hand, passed along the Scots' line, blessing the soldiers and the cause in which they were engaged, previous to the battle of Bannockburn. Thus the Order states justly that it was revived, that is a profounder spirit of devotion infused into it, by King Robert, by whose directions the Abbot reorganized it.''

In this account, it is scarcely necessary to say that there is far more myth than of legitimate history.

In olden times when there was a King of Scotland, he was hereditary Grand Master of the Order, and at all assemblies a chair was kept vacant for him.

Provincial Grand Lodges are held in Glasgow, Rouen in France, in Sardinia, Spain, the Netherlands, Calcutta, Bombay, China, and Canada. The Provincial Grand Lodge of London was established in July, 1872, and there the membership is confined to those who have previously taken the Rose Croix, or eighteenth degree of the Ancient and Accepted Scottish Rite.

THE MYSTIC SHRINE.

Compiled by Osborne Sheppard from the writings of Noble W. Ross and Noble Alex. B. J. Moore.

MORE than six thousand years ago Egypt burst upon the world and history a full-grown nation, with a full-blown civilization in the flower of its matchless perfection, with no evidence of so-called patriarchal life, rude beginning or infancy. It is unquestionably the father of the civilized peoples and nations of the world—yes, the civilized world for more than two thousand years. Hence, the inexorable logic of this fact is, that there is where the memorial name of God, forever among all generations, was of record and renown.

Here, also, were discovered the tablets and papyrus writings which settled forever the true and only legitimate origin of the Order of the Mystic Shrine thousands of years before its introduction into the United States.

Dr. Fleming is entitled to all the glory of its importation into this country through his old friend, Noble William J. Florence, and those who immediately translated its ritual and secret teachings, and whose names will be handed down to posterity as the prime movers in its adoption and practice within the jurisdiction of North America, will also have a niche adorned with their names in the great hall of Fame, and Nobles, yet unborn will stand there with uncovered sconce and memorize the names of Fleming, Florence, Rawson and Patterson. They early assumed "The Arab's Vow" and were the most enthusiastic disciples and the most demonstrative appreciators of the esoteric ceremonials among the few who showed their strength of purpose when the Order first saw the light of day in New York. From helpless infancy it emerged into strengthening youth and thence into a sturdy manhood, and from that time the Order has been progressive, popular and honored for its Charity, Hospitality, Sincerity, and Brotherly Attachment to each member thereof. In this meed of praise there are others who gave of their wisdom and experience a goodly quantity, among whom should be mentioned Noble Charles T. McClenachan, who was long identified with the Order in the Western Hemisphere, and with his wise counsel and advice held its best interests at heart. He officiated upon the most important Committees, especially those of the Ritual, the Statutes and Regulations, Jurisprudence and Laws, and being an expert parliamentarian and a profound ritualist insured the future success and longevity of this beautiful Oriental institution.

Although the Order was introduced into America in 1871, the "Imperial Grand Council" was not proclaimed until June 6, 1876, since which time it has held annual sessions regularly. The beginning was a struggle, but this was harmonized into a union of all factions for the general good of the Order and the Crescent was soon in the ascendant. The Nobles who sacrificed their time and money to establish it upon a firm and lasting basis started with the hope that the day would not be far distant when the "Crescent," the "Templar Cross" and the "Consistory Eagle" would stand intermingled through the length and breadth of the Old and New Worlds, and that the tripod of Foundation, Stability and Longevity would rest indestructible, one each in the insignia of these three great Institutions that shall defy Battle, Age and Decay. "The adverse faction" has been overcome. Success has been achieved by patient study of the principles of manhood and good common sense, and with a membership of 212,517 faithful and enthusiastic Nobles in 137 Temples, (January 1st, 1915), the door is opened for all eligible men of honor and ability to associate with an institution that brings pleasure to all in its ritualistic work and social happiness and rest to the man of business. It is an institution at once grand in the hearts of its disciples, who esteem Justice, Truth and Mercy, and abhor oppression, fanaticism and intolerance. May its sanctuaries be populated with the good, the upright, and the just. May they honor the worthy, select men of honor and of rank, character and worth, for the all-powerful mass of memberhood, and being faithful, zealous and steadfast in the purpose, Allah will bestow his blessings upon them on earth and set apart for them a haven in Paradise hereafter. Carry not the Unwritten Law too far decipherable in the esoteric issues. Verbal and oral confidences supersede, in safety and retention, all manuscriptal or published treasures, however code-bound. These wise words are translated by Abd-El-Kader Ben Makhi-Ed-Deen.

Looking backward towards the home of the Order, we find the Brotherhood in Egypt flourishing and fruitful in good works, as beautiful as are the queenly palms which wave their feathery arms in the soft airs that crinkle the surface of the lordly Nile into rippling lines of loveliest corrugations, or cast their cooling shadows upon the star-eyed daughters of Egypt. The ritual there is exemplified within the secret walls, and is superb and full of harmonious proportions, both to the eye and ear. All the senses are stirred to their deepest by the elaborate and luxuriant beauty of detail and fulfilment. It is the perfection of high art. It works, by grand and elegant threads, up to a gorgeous consummation as easily and as brilliantly as Aurora's dawn, finally, but without crisis, sinks into the sea of glory with which Egypt's Sun God floods the green delta and the golden sands.

It is to see the living, pulseful, throbbing sunrise in the land of Egypt to appreciate the metaphor, for nowhere else on earth is that scene so magnificent. It glorifies all it touches, and makes even the scarred and monstrous Pyramid of Cheops a tangible dream of eternal beauty.

THE FEZ AND ITS SIGNIFICANCE.

The Nobles wear rich costumes of Eastern character, made of silk and brocaded velvet of oriental intensity of color. The ordinary costume for street parade is conventional black with the regulation fez.

When pilgrimages to Mecca were interrupted by the Crusades about A.D. 980, the Mohammedans west of the Nile journeyed to Fez (or Fas), in Morocco, as to a holy city. Among the flourishing manufactures of the city was a head covering called tarboosh, now known as a fez, which was dyed scarlet for the students in a great school at that city. In that way it became a mark of learning, and gradually displaced other forms and colors of hats. It was carried in all directions by caravans, and thus became the distinguishing head-dress of Moslems in every part of the empire.

The Jewel of the Order is a Crescent, formed of any substance. The most valued materials are the claws of the Royal Bengal tiger, united at their bases in a gold setting which includes their tips, and bears on one side of the centre the head of a sphinx, and on the other a pyramid, urn, and star, with the date of the wearer's reception of the Order, and the motto,

Arabic—Kuwat wa Ghadab."
Latin—"Robur et Furor."
English—"Strength and Fury."

The crescent has been a favorite religious emblem in all ages in the Orient, and also a political ensign in some countries, such as in modern Turkey and Persia. The ancient Greeks used the crescent as an emblem of the universal Mother of all living things, the Virgin Mother of all souls, who was known as Diana, Artemis, Phœbe, Cynthia, and other names, varying with the character of her attributes in different localities. The chief seat of the Diana cult and worship was at Ephesus, and the great temple built in her honor at that city was the pride and glory of the Greeks.

The secret knowledge symbolized by the crescent has always had its devotees, in every age, in all civilized countries, and it is yet the master-key to all wisdom. The Greek philosopher Plato, when asked the source of his knowledge, referred to Pythagoras. If we consult the writings of Pythagoras, we shall find that he points to the far East, whence he derived his instruction. In imitation of the humility of the wisest of mankind, we look to the East for light, and find placed there the beautiful emblem of newborn light, the Crescent.

This is yet only a symbol, and refers to a higher and purer source, the great fountain of light, the Sun, which is also an emblem of the Great First Cause, of Light and Intelligence. Thus do we lead the mind of the initiate step by step from the sterile and shifting sand of the desert, which typifies ignorance and darkness, into the halls of science, the chambers of culture, until he stands in the presence of the emblem of Light and Intelligence, in possession of the key that will open to the diligent inquirer every truth in nature's wide domain.

For esoteric reasons we hang the horns pointing downward, representing the setting moon of the old faith at the moment of the rising sun of the new faith in the brotherhood of all mankind—the essential unity of humanity as of one blood, the children of one fatherhood.

The salutation of distinction among the Faithful is, "Es Salamu Aleikum!"—"Peace be with you!" to which is returned the gracious wish, "Aleiku mes Salaam!"—"With you be Peace!"

The prerequisite for membership in America is the 32° in the Ancient Accepted Scottish Rite, or a Knight Templar in good standing. An English 18° Ancient Accepted Scottish Rite, however, is eligible for admission, as the membership in the Higher Bodies in England is limited to 99 members of the 31° and 54 in the 32°.

The generous proposition to make the Order of Nobles an organization for the exercise of charity, the improvement of the mind, and an ally of the Fraternity of Freemasonry in the United States, was primarily adopted by the Imperial Council.

Subordinate Temples have been chartered in nearly every State in the Union and Canada by dispensation or in other constitutional manner, under the authority of the Imperial Council.

RANK OF TEMPLES ACCORDING TO DATE OF CHARTERS.

	Temple	Location	Date of Charter
1	Mecca	New York	Sept. 26, 1872
2	Damascus	Rochester, N.Y.	June 7, 1876
3	Mt. Sinai	Montpelier, Vt.	Oct. 31, 1876
4	Al Koran	Cleveland, O.	Nov. 16, 1876
5	Cyprus	Albany, N.Y.	Feb. 2, 1877
6	Oriental	Troy, N.Y.	Feb. 7, 1877
7	Syrian	Cincinnati, O.	Feb. 8, 1877
8	Pyramid	Bridgeport, Conn.	April 18, 1877
9	Syria	Pittsburgh, Pa.	May 27, 1877
10	Ziyara	Utica, N.Y.	Oct. 30, 1877
11	Kaaba	Davenport, Ia.	July 1, 1878
12	Moslem	Detroit, Mich.	April 27, 1880
13	Aleppo	Boston, Mass.	June 23, 1882
14	Medinah	Chicago, Ill.	Oct. 30, 1882
15	Islam	San Francisco, Cal.	Mar. 6, 1883
16	Lu Lu	Philadelphia, Pa.	Dec. 31, 1883
17	Murat	Indianapolis, Ind.	Mar. 13, 1884
18	Boumi	Baltimore, Md.	April 1, 1884
19	Kosair	Louisville, Ky.	Dec. 5, 1884
20	Tripoli	Milwaukee, Wis.	Mar 8, 1885
21	Jerusalem	New Orleans, La.	Mar. 30, 1885
22	Osman	St. Paul, Minn.	July 13, 1885
23	Zuhrah	Minneapolis, Minn.	July 22, 1885
24	Almas	Washington, D.C.	Jan. 17, 1886
25	Palestine	Providence, R.I.	Feb. 6, 1886
26	El Kahir	Cedar Rapids, Ia.	Feb. 9, 1886
27	Saladin	Grand Rapids, Mich	April 22, 1886
28	Moolah	St. Louis, Mo.	April 26, 1886
29	Acca	Richmond, Va.	June 9, 1886
30	Osiris	Wheeling, W. Va.	July 22, 1886
31	Abdallah	Leavenworth, Kan.	Mar. 28, 1887
32	Isis	Salina, Kan.	Mar. 29, 1887
33	**Rameses**	**Toronto, Ont.**	**April 21, 1887**
34	Hella	Dallas, Tex.	May 31, 1887
35	Ballut Abyad	Albuquerque, N.M.	June 11, 1887

Temple	Location	Date of Charter
36 Sesostris	Lincoln, Neb.	June 22, 1887
37 Kismet	Brooklyn, N.Y.	July 2, 1887
38 Ismailia	Buffalo, N.Y.	Nov. 5, 1887
39 El Jebel	Denver, Colo.	Dec. 11, 1887
40 Moila	St. Joseph, Mo.	Dec. 11, 1887
41 Ararat	Kansas City, Mo.	Dec. 11, 1887
42 Al Kader	Portland, Ore.	Jan. 3, 1888
43 Al Malaikah	Los Angeles, Cal.	Feb. 28, 1888
44 Algeria	Helena, Mont.	Mar. 23, 1888
45 Morocco	Jacksonville, Fla.	Mar. 28, 1888
46 El Riad	Sioux Falls, S.D.	May 25, 1888
47 Afifi	Tacoma, Wash.	Aug. 1, 1888
48 Sahara	Pine Bluff, Ark.	April 16, 1889
49 Tangier	Omaha, Neb.	April 24, 1889
50 Alhambra	Chattanooga, Tenn.	Sept. 17, 1889
51 Yaarab	Atlanta, Ga.	Dec. 8, 1889
52 El Zagal	Fargo, N.D.	Dec. 14, 1889
53 El Kalah	Salt Lake City, Utah	June 8, 1890
54 El Katif	Spokane, Wash.	June 10, 1890
55 Zem Zem	Erie, Pa.	Nov. 10, 1890
56 Zamora	Birmingham, Ala.	Nov. 10, 1890
58 Media	Watertown, N.Y.	Mar. 19, 1891
58 Al Chymia	Memphis, Tenn.	May 10, 1891
59 Ben Hur	Austin, Tex.	June 2, 1891
60 Kora	Lewiston, Me.	Dec. 6, 1891
61 Hamasa	Meridian, Miss.	May 22, 1892
62 Rajah	Reading, Pa.	Aug. 20, 1892
63 Naja	Deadwood, S.D.	Sept. 19, 1892
64 India	Oklahoma City, Okla.	May 3, 1893
65 Mohammed	Peoria, Ill.	June 12, 1893
66 Aladdin	Columbus, O.	June 14, 1893
67 Ahmed	Marquette, Mich.	June 14, 1893
68 Tebala	Rockford, Ill.	May 10, 1894
69 Korein	Rawlins, Wyo.	Oct. 8, 1894
70 Oasis	Charlotte, N.C.	Oct. 10, 1894
71 Irem	Wilkes Barre, Pa.	Oct. 18, 1895
72 El Zaribah	Phœnix, Ariz.	Jan. 20, 1896
73 Sphinx	Hartford, Conn.	April 13, 1896

Temple	Location	Date of Charter
74 Alee	Savannah, Ga.	June 23, 1896
75 Al Korah	Boise City, Idaho	June 23, 1896
76 Beni Kedem	Charleston, W. Va.	June 26, 1896
77 Melha	Springfield, Mass.	June 9, 1897
78 Antioch	Dayton, O.	June 9, 1898
79 Zenobia	Toledo, O.	June 14, 1898
80 Kalurah	Binghampton, N.Y.	June 14, 1898
81 **Karnak**	**Montreal, Que.**	**Oct. 9, 1899**
82 Za-Ga-Zig	Des Moines, Ia.	May 23, 1900
83 Aloha	Honolulu, H.I.	May 23, 1900
84 El Mina	Galveston, Tex.	June 11, 1902
85 Gizeh	Victoria, B.C.	Aug. 1, 1902
86 Salaam	Newark, N.J.	May 4, 1903
87 Abba	Mobile, Ala.	June 18, 1903
88 **Luxor**	**St. John, N.B.**	**June 26, 1903**
89 AbouBenAdhem	Springfield, Mo.	July 9, 1903
90 Jaffa	Altoona, Pa.	July 9, 1903
91 Cairo	Rutland, Vt.	July 9, 1903
92 Zembo	Harrisburg, Pa.	July 14, 1904
93 Yelduz	Aberdeen, S.D.	July 14, 1904
94 Crescent	Trenton, N.J.	July 14, 1904
95 **Khartum**	**Winnipeg, Man.**	**Nov. 19, 1904**
96 Al Amin	Little Rock, Ark.	Dec. 19, 1904
97 Bektash	Concord, N.H.	Jan. 25, 1905
98 Aad	Duluth, Minn.	Sept. 5, 1905
99 El Hasa	Ashland, Ky.	Mar. 3, 1906
100 Elf Khurafeh	Saginaw, Mich.	June 13, 1906
101 Kalif	Sheridan, Wyo.	June 13, 1906
102 Anezeh	Mexico City	Dec. 1, 1906
103 Kerak	Reno, Nev.	Dec. 10, 1906
104 Omar	Charleston, S.C.	Dec. 25, 1906
105 El Maida	El Paso, Tex.	May 8, 1907
106 Abu Bekr	Sioux City, Ia.	May 8, 1907
107 Calam	Lewiston, Idaho	May 8, 1907
108 **Al Azhar**	**Calgary, Alta.**	**Sept. 27, 1907**
109 **Mocha**	**London, Ont.**	**Jan. 1, 1908**
110 Oleika	Lexington, Ky.	Jan. 1, 1908
111 Nile	Seattle, Wash.	July 15, 1908

Temple	Location	Date of Charter
112 Rizpah	Madisonville, Ky.	July 15, 1908
113 Hilla'h	Ashland, Ore.	July 15, 1908
114 Orak	Hammond, Ind.	April 27, 1909
115 Hadi	Evanston, Ind.	April 21, 1909
116 Mizpah	Fort Wayne, Ind.	April 27, 1909
117 Kem	Grand Forks, N.D.	June 9, 1909
118 Khedive	Norfolk, Va.	June 9, 1909
119 Mirza	Pittsburgh, Kan.	June 9, 1909
120 Zorah	Terre Haute, Ind.	June 9, 1909
121 Midian	Wichita, Kan.	June 9, 1909
122 Aahmes	Oakland, Cal.	April 13, 1910
123 Al Sihah	Macon, Ga.	April 13, 1910
124 Wa-Wa	**Regina, Sask.**	**Dec. 1, 1911**
125 Bagdad	Butte, Mont.	Jan. 20, 1911
126 Akdar	Tulsa, Okla.	July 12, 1911
127 Philæ	**Halifax, N.S.**	**July 12, 1911**
128 Bedouin	Muskogee, Okla.	July 12, 1911
129 Wahabi	Jackson, Miss.	July 12, 1911
130 Al Bahr	San Diego, Cal.	May 4, 1912
131 Ainad	East St. Louis, Ill.	May 8, 1912
132 Al Menah	Nashville, Tenn.	May 8, 1912
133 Nemesis	Parkersburg, W. Va.	May 8, 1912
134 El Karubah	Shreveport, La.	May 14, 1913
135 Alcazar	Montgomery, Ala.	May 14, 1913
136 Ansar	Springfield, Ill.	
137 Hoslah	Fort Worth, Texas	

ST. PAUL'S LODGE, MONTREAL, P.Q., No. 374 UNDER THE GRAND LODGE OF ENGLAND.

By a Committee appointed by Hugh M. Lambert, P.M.

THE history of St. Paul's Lodge takes one back to the commencement of British Rule in Canada.

Shortly after the capitulation of Montreal in September, 1760, a brief reference to its founding is noted in an old book which belonged to one of the Past Masters, but which is now in the possession of the Lodge; and in 1770 a Warrant issued to St. Paul's Lodge by the then Provincial Grand Master, Honorable John Collins, gives authenticity to its early establishment in Canada; but the fire which, on the 24th April, 1833, destroyed the Masonic Hall, where St. Paul's Lodge had held meetings for several years, destroyed at the same time almost all the old books, records and papers belonging to the Lodge. This was a very serious loss, as much information, valuable in antiquity as well as in material, for compiling any history of the Lodge, and extending no doubt a long way back, was irretrievably lost.

The earliest mention of St. Paul's Lodge has reached us in a curious manner. Some time ago, in December, 1869, through the courtesy of the Mechanics' Institute of this city, an old book from the Library of that Institution, called "Looking unto Jesus," came into the possession of the Lodge. This book appears to have been printed in Edinburgh, in 1723, and it bears on its title-page the name of its owner, in his sign manual—Gywn Owen Radford,—who was Master of St. Paul's from December, 1803, to June, 1804. On the inside cover of this book is pasted part of a summons of St. Paul's Lodge, No. 12, dated Montreal, 8th June, 1818, and on which was written, apparently in Bro. Radford's handwriting, "Founded by Lord Aberdour's Warrant 1760." Now Lord Aberdour was Grand Master of England from 18th May, 1757, to 3rd May, 1762, and, during his term of office, a Provincial Grand Master was appointed to Canada (see Preston's Masonry, sec. 10). This points to the actual existence of St. Paul's Lodge ten years earlier than shown in any other record, and, though unsupported by any other testimony available, it is not likely, seeing that a Provincial Grand Master was appointed to Canada, at some period between 1757 and 1762, that this statement would have been put forth, unless it way known to have been the fact and could have been established at that time.

While, of course, it cannot therefore actually substantiate the existence of the Lodge at this early date, incidental circumstances point to its extreme probability. It was a period of great activity in Masonry, which was very flourishing, both in England and abroad, under the English Constitution; so much so, as to be called the "Golden Era of Free-Masonry." This being so, with a Provincial Grand Master appointed to Canada, there is every reasonable ground for belief that a regularly constituted Lodge, under a Warrant derived from the Grand Lodge of England, was working in Montreal, then a place of some importance, as far back as 1760, but, whether before, or after, its capitulation to the British Forces, on the 8th September of that year, we have no means of ascertaining. It is quite possible, however, that at this period a "St. Paul's Lodge" may have been attached to one of the regiments under command of General Amherst, at the capitulation, as some ten or eleven thousand men were here at that time, and encamped in and about the neighborhood of what is now the Beaver Hall portion of the city, and if this were so, it would, of course, move with the regiment, and so explain the later date of a warrant issued to a "St. Paul's Lodge," with a fixed domicile in the city, the name of which may have been suggested by recollections of the other.

But, that St. Paul's Lodge was established in Montreal, as early as the year 1770, by warrant dated 8th November, 1770, granted by the R. W. and Hon. John Collins, Provincial Grand Master for Canada, by virtue of a Patent from His Grace the Duke of Beaufort, who was Grand Master of England from 27th April, 1767, until 4th May, 1772, and which Patent bore the date of London, 2nd September, 1767, admits of no doubt whatever. This Patent or Warrant was in existence in 1831, and was destroyed by fire in April, 1833, and though it has been impracticable to ascertain the names of the Masters who presided over the Lodge from that year until 1778, the names of those who filled the Chair from that date onwards, and in regular succession, down to the present day, are known and given in the various editions of the By-Laws and History of the Lodge. The list, up to December, 1830, inclusive, was compiled from official documents existing in 1831, by the R. W. Bro. D.P.G.M. Frederick Griffin, Q.C., an old Master of St. Paul's, and, from that date down to the present time, the list is completed from existing and regular records of the Lodge.

Among the documents in existence connected with the Lodge, and which carry it back to 1797, is a copy of the By-Laws printed in 1814, the preamble to which, dated Montreal, 18th August, 1797, sets forth that they are the "Rules, Order and Regulations which are to be punctually observed and kept by the Free and Accepted Ancient York Masons of St. Paul's Lodge No. 12, held in the City of Montreal, in the Province of Lower Canada." The Lodge derived its Charter of 1760, and that of 1770, from the Grand Lodge of England, whose central authority was in London; and though the Provincial Grand Lodge, which issued the Warrant to St. Paul's Lodge, in 1770, appears to have lapsed from some cause now involved in obscurity, yet another Provincial Grand Lodge was established at some period antecedent to 1791, with the R. W. Brother Sir John Johnson, Bart., as Provincial Grand Master, under authority of a Warrant from the Right Hon.

Thomas Earl of Effingham, acting G. M. under His Royal Highness Henry Frederick, Duke of Cumberland, elected Grand Master of England in 1781. And while it is natural to suppose that St. Paul's Lodge then hailed from that Grand Lodge, it is found working in 1797, under the Grand Lodge of all England, deemed the Mother Lodge of England, and whose central authority was in the City of York. These bodies were quite distinct in their jurisdiction, and wholly independent of each other; but we have no means now of arriving at the causes which led to the lapsing of the old Warrants, to the change of jurisdiction, or to the period when it took place.

Considering that authentic records did exist to show that St. Paul's Lodge was regularly established in 1770, it may seem somewhat strange that it does not hold a higher position at present on the Registry of England; but no record can be found that it ever had a status on it, prior to 1824, when the Lodge was No. 782 E.R. From the subsequent renumbering of the Lodges, it became No. 514 E.R., in 1832, and so continued until 1863, when it ranked No. 374 E.R., at which it now stands. A copy of a Circular Letter, dated Quebec, 27th Dec., 1820, addressed to Masonic bodies, by the Chevalier Brother Robert d'Estemauville, Grand Secretary of the Provincial Grand Lodge of Lower Canada, held at Quebec, gives a list of Grand Officers for the year 1821, with a list of the Lodges under its jurisdiction; of these, three only, and all meeting in Quebec are on the Registry of England; the others twenty-six in number, are on the Registry of Lower Canada; and St. Paul's Lodge appears as No. 12. In the early days of the Lodge, up to 1785 inclusive, it was No. 10. From 1786, to 1st May, 1797, it was No. 4; no mention being made of any rank on the Registry of England. In all the old documents available, it is called No. 12, and so continued until 1823, when the masonic territory, under the jurisdiction of the Provincial Grand Lodge of Quebec, was divided into two districts, that of Quebec and Three Rivers, with the R.W. Bro. Claude Denechau as Provincial

Grand Master; and that of Montreal and the Borough of William Henry, with the R. W. Bro. William McGillivray as Provincial Grand Master. His installation took place at the Masonic Hall, on the 8th October, 1823, by virtue of a Warrant from the M. W. the Grand Master of England, His Royal Highness the Duke of Sussex. At this time, St. Paul's Lodge became No. 3; and, more recently, when, after being dormant for many years, the P.G. Lodge for Montreal and William Henry was reorganized in the Spring of 1846, with the R. W. Bro. the late Hon. Peter McGill as Provincial Grand Master, it became No. 1 on the Provincial Registry.

Moreover, it appears on reference to a letter written in December, 1845, by the late R. W. Bro. P. D. P. G. M. McCord, giving a short sketch of the masonic state of this section of the Province, that, immediately on the installation of the R. W. Bro. William McGillivray, the Lodges then recorded as working, or in existence, were ordered to send in their Warrants, and received dispensations to work from the Provincial Grand Master, until new Warrants should be forwarded to them from England. Of the twelve Lodges then known, nine complied with the order, and among them, St. Paul's Lodge; and there can be no doubt that it was the issue of these new Warrants with a number on the Registry of England (in St. Paul's case, No. 782 E.R.), that first gave them a status on the Roll of the Grand Lodge of England, and which were evidently intended to supersede the others, the old Provincial Warrants—which carried no status outside of the jurisdiction of Lower Canada. Had St. Paul's Lodge possessed it before, no local cause, such as the division of an old masonic district, or the creation of a new one here, could affect its status in England, or call for new Warrants thence. Such a contingency could only arise from, or follow, circumstances within the exclusive preogative and initiative of the Grand Lodge of England.

There can be no question of the Lodge being fairly entitled to precedence, much above its present number,

(No. 374), on the Registry of England; for though, before the union in 1813, the Lodge may have been working under its number on the Registry of Canada only, and been known only by it, it will not be disputed that it did exist under a genuine Warrant emanating from rightful and legal authority derived immediately from one of the two Grand Lodges of England, holding in the Cities of London or York, and from whichever of the two it hailed, at the time of the union, there can be no doubt whatever that St. Paul's Lodge was legally working, and in active existence, for a very long period anterior to the Union, since the names of all those who filled the office of Master from 1778 to the present time, in regular succession, are known from official records.

While, therefore, the failure to register in England, from whatever cause it may have arisen, may, perhaps, in a strictly legal sense, bar the claim to be placed higher on the roll, yet the Lodge is entitled to it in equity; and, at any rate, to lay claim to every other privilege which so long and unbroken a record as St. Paul's Lodge unquestionably possesses and carries with it; among others, the right to possess and wear the Centenary Jewel. Registering regulations first commenced in England, 28th October, 1768. This is eight years subsequent to the alleged date of St. Paul's existence, during Lord Aberdour's Grand Mastership, and two years prior to that during the Duke of Beaufort's tenure of office. In the first case, the Lodge could have no number in England, because the registering regulations did not exist; in the other, with the then tardy means of intercommunication, and the limited intercourse that probably existed between Masonic bodies here and in England, the existence of these regulations may have remained unknown for an indefinite period, or may not have been compulsory on Lodges out of England.

No Lodge could now find itself in so anomalous a position; for the Constitution makes it imperative that all applications for Lodge Warrants shall be made to the Grand Master of England; and while, pending the issuing of them, provisional Warrants may be granted by District or Provincial Grand Master, any authority they carry ceases at once, on the receipt of the Warrant from England.

An interesting fact became known to the Lodge in the Spring of 1875, and which helped to bridge the gap, created by the loss of its old records, between St. Paul's Lodge of more modern days and the early part of the present century. This was the accidental discovery, in the old Dorchester Street Protestant Burying Ground, in May 1875, of the grave of one of the old worthies of the Lodge, Worshipful Brother John Greatwood, who was elected Master in June, 1803, and died in the month of October following, during his actual tenure of office. The existence of the grave was made known to the Lodge through Brother James Vaughan Morgan, and the remains were removed on 25th May, and reinterred on the 15th June, 1875, in a lot purchased by the Lodge, No. 503, Section G, on the S. W. side of Mount Royal Cemetery, and a new tombstone was placed over it with this much of the old inscription on it:—

ERECTED

By the Members of

ST. PAUL'S LODGE No. 12,

(Ancient York Masons)

To the Memory of their late

WORSHIPFUL MASTER

JOHN GREATWOOD,

Who Died 13th October, 1803.

AGED 23 YEARS.

In taking out the old tombstone, it fell to pieces, and could not be put in sufficient repair again to withstand the elements, an it was unfortunately broken up and the fragments scattered.

Of the antecedents or standing of the members of St. Paul's Lodge, in its early days, or of its mode of working, no accurate data is obtainable. For more than half a century it has occupied a foremost place among Masonic bodies, and has had a name, not only throughout Canada, but elsewhere, as well for the excellence of its working, as for the social standing and prominent position of its members generally,—and, as "in England, our order has been thought worthy of the attention of many of the best and most able men, and has secured to itself the sympathy of well-cultivated minds of all ranks and conditions; the flower of the nobility, the greatest excellence and genius among the Commoners of the three kingdoms having belonged to it and played a conspicuous part in its pages," so can the roll of St. Paul's Lodge show many well-known and distinguished names, not only as Freemasons, but as members of society, eminent in their public and private capacities and avocations.

The Lodge had a large military membership from the various regiments that were quartered here, during a long succession of years, and the names of many able and distinguished officers will be found who hailed St. Paul's as their mother Lodge, or who have affiliated with it from other Lodges. Among these, may be mentioned the Duke of Atholl, who received his M. M. degree in this Lodge, when Marquis of Tullibardine, the Earl of Dunmore, Colonel Lord Abinger, Major Lord Edward W. P. Clinton, General Piper, Lieut.-General the Hon. George Cadogan, C.B., Lieut.-General C. A. Lewis, Maj.-General Brownrigg, C.B., Major-General Claremont, C.B., Major-General Sir Charles Stavely, K.C.B., Major-General Stephenson, C.B., Major-General Sir Garnet Wolseley, K.C.B., K.C.M.G., Surgeon-General Longmore, C.B., Colonel the Honorable John Elphinstone, Colonel W. B. Ainslie, C.B., Colonel Edward W. D. Bell, V.C., C.B., Colonel Hampden Moody, C.B., Colonel Talbot, Colonel Currie, Lieut.-Colonel Reddie, Colonel Pasley, Lieut.-Colonel G. H. Moncrieff, Lieut.-Colonel Penn, C.B., Brigade-Major Maquay, School of

Military Engineering, Surgeon-Major Smith, D.I.G., Surgeon-Major Prescott, Colonel Kenneth M. Moffatt, Captain John S. D. McGill, &c.

In her allegiance to the Grand Old Mother Lodge of England, St. Paul's Lodge has been true and steadfast. Amid the changes which have taken place in the Masonic Jurisdictions of Canada, though a good deal of pressure has been brought to bear upon her to affiliate with the Canada Grand Lodges now in existence, she has steadily resisted it, and announced her firm determination to remain on the Registry of that Grand Old Lodge, to which over 3,000 subordinate Lodges in all parts of the world, owe masonic allegiance and obedience; to hand down to those who may come hereafter, that goodly heritage which is to be found in the prestige which attaches to our connection with England, the "cradle of masonic history, where freemasonry has developed itself into a union embracing all mankind"; and to bequeath to future members of St. Paul's Lodge, as a legacy, the earnest hope that she will always continue to cherish the associations that have gathered round a connection of more than a century, and the ties that have formed and strengthened with it during that long period, as too highly prized, too close and intimate in their nature, to admit of their being sundered or severed.

In December, 1830, the date of the oldest minute book at present extant, St. Paul's Lodge held its meetings in the "Masonic Hall," situated on the corner of St. Paul and Bonsecours Street. This "Masonic Hall" was erected by the W. Bro. the Hon. John Molson, an old Past Master of the Lodge, and who afterwards became Provincial Grand Master for Montreal and William Henry. An entire story was set aside for the purposes of the craft, and it was at the especial request of St. Paul's Lodge No. 3, that that portion of the building, was solemnly dedicated to the purposes of masonry, with the usual masonic rites and ceremonies, by the Provincial Grand Lodge of the District, on the 13th May, 1825.

The Lodge room was most chastely and classically fitted up, with double rows of columns, of the Tuscan, Doric, Ionic and Corinthian Orders, in pairs, and terminating, on the Eastern side, by a magnificent throne of the Composite order.

In this Hall, the Lodge continued to meet until the destruction of the building by fire, on the 24th April, 1833. After that, it met at Mack's Hotel, afterwards the Central Police Station, whence it removed, on the 12th May, 1835, to Rasco's Hotel, St. Paul Street. Here it remained until the 13th December, 1836. On the 27th of that month, the Lodge assembled at Privat's Hotel and so continued until the 2nd of June, 1837. On the 15th November of that year it was found at Mussen's, Notre Dame Street, where it was held, (with the exception of two meetings that took place, on the 21st March and 18th April, 1838, at the late Brother Campbell Sweeney's rooms, which were in a large building, long known as the Natural History Society Building, but, for the holding of which meetings there, no reason is given), until the 13th November, 1838. On the 10th December, 1838, and until the 10th December, 1839, the "Globe Inn" was its place of meeting. Thence it removed to "Sword's Hotel," on the East side of St. Vincent Street, where it is found on the 27th December, 1839, and until the 14th December, 1841, when it again met at Rasco's Hotel, on St. Paul Street, and so continued until the 16th May, 1844. On the 24th June, 1844, it was domiciled at Tetu's Hotel, Great St. James Street and St. Peter Street, where it remained until the 9th April, 1850. After that date, it removed to Freemason's Hall, Notre Dame Street and Dalhousie Square. The total destruction of this building by fire, in the tremendous conflagration of 8th July, 1852, when some 1,200 houses were burnt, again left St. Paul's Lodge without a lodge room. On the 27th October, 1852, its sittings were resumed in the "Zetland" lodge room, No. 731, E.R., held in Murphy's Hotel, Notre Dame and Gosford Streets, and we find it there until the

10th May, 1853. In the interval between that date and the 8th November, 1853, a removal to the "Saint Lawrence Hall" took place, and there it met for a continuous period of seventeen years. On the 8th November, 1870, the brethren assembled in a new lodge room, No. 910 St. Catherine Street, and continued to meet there until the 13th April, 1875. After that date, the Brethren met, on the 11th May and 9th November, at the "Royal Albert" Lodge Room, No. 6, Philip's Square, and, on the 14th and 27th December, 1875, at the Asylum of the Ancient and Accepted Scottish Rite, No. 1052, St. Catherine Street, where, on the latter date, the Installation of Officers for 1876 took place.

On the 11th January, 1876, the Lodge held its first regular Communication in the New Lodge Room, Academy of Music Victoria Street, the banquet on St. John's day, 27th Dec., 1875, having been previously held in the Lodge Room.

On the 10th February, 1885, the Lodge met for the first time in the new Lodge Rooms in Hall & Scott's building, McGill College Avenue and St. Catherine Street, and since that date has continued to meet at that place.

Within its portals, St. Paul's Lodge has always inculcated harmony among its members, and the great principles of brotherly love, relief and truth. They have come together as "faithful friends in a Society modelled according to the perfection of good fellowship"; and while always given to a generous hospitality after work, the Lodge meetings have always been most pleasant gatherings where, aloof from the toil and trouble and turmoil of the outer world, many happy hours have been spent, and the associations connected with them long remembered and treasured.

LIST OF MASTERS OF ST. PAUL'S LODGE, MONTREAL, C. E.

No. 10—Register of Canada.

Robert Gordon	(Not known)
Christopher Carson (Died March, 1779)	December, 1778
Robert Gordon	April, 1779
Thomas Busby	June, 1779
Thomas McMurray	December, 1779
John Daly	June, 1780
Thomas Oakes	December, 1780
Henry Rowley	June, 1781
James Noel	June, 1782
Levi Willard	December, 1782
Henry Lœdel	June, 1783
James Noel	December, 1783
Thomas Busby	December, 1784
Conrad Marsteller	December, 1785

No. 4—Register of Canada.

James Noel	June, 1786
Conrad Marsteller	June, 1788
Thomas Sullivan	December, 1788
John Platt	December, 1789
James Noel	December, 1790
John Molson	June, 1791
Samuel David	December, 1791
John Devereux	June, 1793
John McArthur	June, 1794
Thomas Busby	December, 1794
John Molson	June, 1795
Thomas J. Sullivan	June, 1796

No. 12—Register of Canada.
(By Warrant Dated 1st May, 1797).
Ancient York Masons.

Thomas J. Sullivan	June, 1797
William Martin	June, 1798

Louis Charles Foucher	June, 1801
John Greatwood	June, 1803
Gwyn Owen Radford	December, 1803
Arthur Gilmour	June, 1804
Jacob Hall	June, 1805
William Martin	December, 1805
Arthur Gilmour	June, 1807
James Dow	December, 1807
Thomas McLaren	December, 1808
Jabez D. De Witt	June, 1810
George Platt	December, 1810
Jabez D. De Witt	June, 1811
Austin Cuvillier	June, 1812
Jabez D. De Witt	June, 1813
Abner Rice	June, 1814
Charles Gore Lester	June, 1815
Jabez D. De Witt	June, 1817
Michael Scott	December, 1817
Jabez D. De Witt	December, 1819
Turton Penn	December, 1820
Michael Scott	December, 1822

No. 3—Register of Montreal and William Henry.

Turton Penn	December, 1823

No. 782—Register of United Grand Lodge of England.

Rev. John Bethune	December, 1824
John Samuel McCord	December, 1825
	December, 1826
Turton Penn	December, 1827
William Badgley	December, 1828
	December, 1829
Frederick Griffin	December, 1830
Turton Penn	December, 1831

No. 514—On Registry of England.

Alexander Buchanan	1832
James Guthrie Scott	1833 and 1834
William Badgley	1835 and 1836

William Forsyth _____1837
William Badgley _____1838 and 1839
Isaac Valentine _____1840
John Samuel McCord _____1841
William Badgley _____1842 and 1843
John Samuel McCord _____1844
Moses Samuel David _____1845

No. 1—Register of Montreal and William Henry.

David Lewis MacPherson _____1846 and 1847
James Sutton Elliott _____1848 and 1849
Strachan Bethune _____1850 and 1851
John Ogilvy Moffatt _____1852 and 1853
Archibald Hamilton Campbell _____1854 and 1855
Robert Denny Collis _____1856 and 1857
Strachan Bethune _____1858
Archibald H. McCalman _____1859 and 1860
John Shuter D. McGill _____1861
Richard Arnaud Brooke _____1862

No. 374—Register of United Grand Lodge of England.

Richard Arnaud Brooke _____1863
Walter Scott _____1864
William Osborne Smith _____1865
James Godschall Johnson _____1866
William Henry Hutton _____1867, 1868, 1869
Dr. Gilbert Prout Girdwood (* 10th Jan.) _____1871
John Taylor _____1872 and 1873
Frank Bond _____1874 and 1875
David R. McCord _____1876 and 1877
William Henry Hutton _____1878 and 1879
Charles G. Geddes _____1880 and 1881
Francis R. F. Brown _____1882
Louis Sutherland _____1883 and 1884

*The Election of Master, on this day, arose from the inability of Brother Richard B. Angus to accept the office to which he had been elected on 13th December, 1870. The installation took place 24th January, 1871.

William Henry Hutton _____1885
Angus W. Hooper _____1886, 1887 and 1888
J. C. N. Badgley _____1889 and 1890
H. Markland Molson _____1891 and 1892
Campbell Lane _____1893, 1894 and 1895
Charles Raynes _____1896 and 1897
John Hamilton Dunlop _____1898 and 1899
W. T. H. Spragge _____1900 and 1901
J. L. M. Marler _____1902 and 1903
H. D. Hamilton, M.D. _____1904 and 1905
D. Donald MacTaggart, M.D. _____1906 and 1907
Arthur Browning _____1908 and 1909
Hugh M. Lambert _____1910, 1911 and 1912
R. A. Kerry, M.D. _____1913
A. R. Doble _____1914
H. J. Stuart Nichol _____1915

MASONIC TRADITION.

Compiled by OSBORNE SHEPPARD from Old Records, &c.

THE City of York is celebrated for its traditional connection with Masonry. No topic in the history of Freemasonry has engaged the attention of Masonic scholars, or given occasion to more discussion, than the alleged facts of the existence of Masonry in the tenth century at the city of York as a prominent point, of the calling of a congregation of the Craft there in the year 926, of the organization of a General Assembly and the adoption of a Constitution. During the last century, the Fraternity in general have accepted all of these statements as genuine portions of authentic history; and the adversaries of the Order have, with the same want of discrimination, rejected them all as myths; while a few earnest seekers for truth have been at a loss to determine what part was historical and what part legendary. The discovery of many old manuscripts directed the labors of such great scholars as Hughan, Woodford, Lyon, and others, to the critical examination of the early history of Masonry, and that of York particularly engaged their attention.

For a thorough comprehension of the true merits of this question, it will be necessary that the student should first acquaint himself with what was, until recently, the recognized theory as to the origin of Masonry at York, and then that he should examine the newer hypotheses advanced by modern writers. In other words, he must read both the tradition and the history.

In pursuance of this plan, I propose to commence with the legends of York Masonry, as found in the old manuscript Constitutions, and then proceed to a review of what has been the result of recent investigations. Of all those who have subjected these legends to historical criticism, the late William James Hughan must unhesitatingly be acknowledged as the ablest and most trustworthy investigator. He was the first and the most successful remover of the cloud of tradition which so long had obscured the sunlight of history.

The legend which connects the origin of English Masonry at York in 926 is sometimes called the "York Legend," sometimes the "Athelstane Legend," because the General Assembly, said to have been held there, occurred during the reign of that king; and sometimes the "Edwin Legend," because that prince is supposed to have been at the head of the Craft, and to have convoked them together to form a Constitution.

The earliest extant of the old manuscript Constitutions is the ancient poem commonly known as the Halliwell MS., and the date of which is conjectured (on good grounds) to be about the year 1390. In that work we find the following version of the legend:

"Thys craft com ynto Englond as y yow say,
Yn tyme of good kynge Adelstonus' day;
He made tho bothe halle and eke bowre,
And hye templus of gret honowre,
To sportyn him yn bothe day and nygth,
An to worschepe hys God with alle hys mygth.
Thys goode lorde loved thys craft ful wel,
And purposud to strenthyn hyt every del,
For dyvers defautys that yn the craft he fonde;
He sende about ynto the londe
After alle the masonus of the crafte,
To come to hym ful evene strayfte,
For to amende these dafautys alle
By good consel gef hyt mygth falle.
A semblé thenne he cowthe let make
Of dyvers lordis yn here state
Dukys, erlys, and barnes also,
Knygthys, sqwyers and mony mo,
And the grete burges of that syté,
They were ther alle yn here degré;
These were there uchon algate,
To ordeyne for these masonus astate,
Ther they sowgton by here wytte
How they mygthyn governe hytte:
Fyftene artyculus they there sowgton,
And fyftene poyntys ther they wrogton."

For the benefit of those who are not familiar with this archaic style, the passage is translated into modern English.

"This craft came into England, as I tell you, in the time of good king Athelstan's reign; he made then both hall, and also bower and lofty temples of great honor, to take his recreation in both day and night, and to worship his God with all his might. This good lord loved this craft full well, and purposed to strengthen it in every part on account of various defects that he discovered in the craft. He sent about into all the land, after the masons of the craft, to come straight to him, to amend all these defects by good counsel, if it might so happen. He then permitted an assembly to be made of divers lords in their rank, dukes, earls, and barons, also knights, squires, and many more, and the great burgesses of that city, they were all there in their degree; these were there, each one in every way to make laws for the estate of these masons. There they sought by their wisdom how they might govern it; there they found out fifteen articles, and there they made fifteen points."

The next old document in which we find this legend recited is that known as the "Cooke MS.," whose date is placed at 1490. The details are here much more full than those contained in the Halliwell MS. The passage referring to the legend is as follows:

"And after that was a worthy kynge in Englond, that was callyd Athelstone, and his yongest son lovyd well the sciens of Gemetry, and he wyst well that hand craft had the practyke of the sciens of Gemetry so well as masons; wherefore he drew him to consell and lerynd [the] practyke of that sciens to his speculatyfe. For of speculatyfe he was a master, and he lovyd well masonry and masons. And he bicome a mason hymselfe. And he gaf hem [gave them] charges and names as it is now usyd in Englond and in other countries. And he ordeyned that they schulde has resonabull pay. And purchesed [obtained] a fre patent of the kyng that they schulde make a sembly when thei sawe resonably tyme a [to] cum togedir to her [their] consell of the whiche charges, manors & semble as is write and taught in the boke of our charges wherefor I leve hit at this tyme."

This much is contained in the MS. from lines 611 to 642. Subsequently, in lines 688-719, which appear to have been taken from what is above called the "Boke of Charges," the legend is repeated in these words:

"In this manner was the forsayde art begunne in the lond of Egypt bi the forsayd maister Euglat [Euclid], & so hit went fro londe to londe and fro kyngdome to kyngdome. After that, may yeris, in the tyme of Kyng Adhelstone, wiche was sum tyme kyng of Englonde, bi his counsell and other gret lordys of the lond bi comin [common] assent for grete defaut y-fennde [found] among masons thei ordeyned a certayne reule amongys hem [them]. On [one] tyme of the yere or in iii yere, as nede were to the kyng and gret lordys of the londe and all the comente [community], from provynce to provynce and fro countre to countre congregacions sholde be made by maisters, of all maisters masons and felaus in the forsayd art. And so at such congregacions they that be made masters schold be examined of the articuls after written, & be rensacked [thoroughly examined] whether thei be abull and kunnyng [able and skilful] to the profyte of the lordys hem to serve [to serve them], and to the honor of the forsayd art."

Seventy years later, in 1560, the Lansdowne MS. was written, and in it we find the legend still further developed, and Prince Edwin for the first time introduced by name. That manuscript reads thus:

"Soone after the Decease of St. Albones, there came Diverse Warrs into England out of Diverse Nations, so that the good rule of Masons was dishired [disturbed] and put down until the tyme of King Adilston. In his tyme there was a worthy King in England, that brought this Land into good rest, and he builded many great workes and buildings, therefore he loved well Masons, for he had a sone called Edwin, the which Love'd Masons much more than his Father did, and he was soe practized in Geometry, that he delighted much to come and talke with Masons and to learne of them the Craft. And after, for the love he had to Masons and to the Craft, he was made Mason at Windsor, and he gott of the King, his Father, a Charter and commission once every yeare to have Assembley, within the Realme where they would within England, and to correct within themselves Faults & Trespasses that were done as touching the Craft, and he held them an Assembly, and there he made Masons and gave them Charges, and taught them the Manners and Comands the same to be kept ever afterwards. And tooke them the Charter and commission to keep their Assembly, and Ordained that it should be renewed from King to King, and when the Assembly were gathered together he made a Cry, that all old Masons or young, that had any Writeings or Vnderstanding of the Charges and manners that weere made before their Lands, wheresoever they were made Masons, that they should shew them forth, there were found some in French, some in Greek, some in Hebrew, and some in English, and some in other Languages, and when they were read and over seen well the intent of them was vnderstood to be all one, and then he caused a Book to be made thereof how his worthy Craft of Masonrie was first founded ,and he himself commanded, and also then caused, that it should be read at any tyme when it should happen any Mason or Masons to be made to give him or them their Charges, and from that, until this Day, Manners of Masons have been kept in this Manner and forme, as well as Men might Governe it, and Furthermore at diverse Assemblyes have been put and Ordained diverse Charges by the best advice of Masters and Fellows.''

All the subsequent manuscripts contain the legend substantially as it is in the Lansdowne; and most of them appear to be mere copies of it, or, most probably, of some original one of which both they and it are copies.

In 1723 Dr. Anderson published the first edition of the Book of Constitutions, in which the history of the fraternity of Freemasons is, he says, "collected from their general records and their faithful traditions of many ages." He gives the legend taken, as he says, from "a certain record of Freemasons written in the reign of King Edward IV." As the old manuscripts were generally inaccessible to the Fraternity, it is to the publication of the legend by Anderson that we are to attribute its general adoption by the Craft. The form of the legend, as given by Anderson in his first edition, varies slightly from that in his second. In the former he places the date of the occurrence at 930; in his second, at 926; in the former, he styles the congregation at York a General Lodge; in his second, a Grand Lodge. Now, as the modern and universally accepted form of the legend agrees in both respects with the latter statement, and not with the former, it must be concluded that the second edition, and the subsequent ones by Entick and Noorthouck, who only repeat Anderson, furnished the form of the legend as now popular.

In the second edition of the Constitutions (p. 63), published in 1738, Anderson gives the legend in the following words:

"In all the Old Constitutions it is written to this purpose, viz.:

"That though the antient records of the Brotherhood in England were most of them destroyd or lost in the war with the Danes, who burnt the Monasteries where the Records were kept; yet King Athelstan, (the Grandson of King Alfred), the first annointed King of England, who translated the Holy Bible into the Saxon language, when he had brought the land into rest and peace, built many great works, and encouraged many Masons from France and elsewhere, whom he appointed overseers thereof: they brought with them the Charges and Regulations of the foreign Lodges, and prevail'd with the King to increase the wages.

"That Prince Edwin, the King's Brother, being taught Geometry and Masonry, for the love he had to the said Craft, and to the honorable principles whereon it is grounded, purchased a Free Charter of King Athelstan his Brother, for the Free Masons having among themselves a Connection, or a power and freedom to regulate themselves, to amend what might happen amiss, and to hold an yearly Communication in a General Assembly.

"That accordingly Prince Edwin summon'd all the Free and Accepted Masons in the Realm, to meet him in the Congregation at York, who came and form'd the Grand Lodge under him as their Grand Master, A.D. 926.

"That they brought with them many old Writings and Records of the Craft, some in Greek, some in Latin, some in French, and other languages; and from the contents thereof, they framed the Constitution of the English Lodges, and made a Law for themselves, to preserve and observe the same in all Time coming, etc., etc., etc."

Preston accepted the legend, and gave it in his second edition (p. 198), in the following words:

"Edward died in 924, and was succeeded by Athelstane, his son, who appointed his brother Edwin patron of the Masons. This prince procured a Charter from Athelstane, empowering them to meet annually in communication at York. In this city, the first Grand Lodge of England was formed in 926, at which Edwin presided as Grand Master. Here many old writings were produced in Greek, Latin, and other languages, from which it is said the Constitutions of the English Lodge have been extracted."

Such is the "York legend," as it has been accepted by the Craft, contained in all the old manuscripts from at least the end of the fourteenth century to the present day; officially sanctioned by Anderson, the historiographer of the Grand Lodge in 1723, and repeated by Preston, by Oliver, and by almost all succeeding Masonic writers. Only recently has any one thought of doubting its authenticity; and now the important question in Masonic literature is whether it is a myth or a history—whether it is all or in any part fiction or truth—and if so, what portion belongs to the former and what to the latter category?

Made in the USA
San Bernardino, CA
28 January 2014